27.99

In this volume a group of distinguished moral and social thinkers address the urgent problem of terrorism. The essays attempt to define terrorism, discuss whether the assessment of terrorist violence should be based on its consequences (beneficial or otherwise), and explore what means may be used to combat those who use violence without justification.

Among other questions raised by the volume are: What does it mean for a people to be innocent of the acts of its government? May there not be some justification in terrorists' targeting certain victims but not others? May terrorist acts be attributed to groups or to states?

The collection will be of particular interest to moral and political philosophers, political scientists, legal theorists, and students of international studies and conflict resolution.

Violence, terrorism, and justice

Cambridge Studies in Philosophy and Public Policy

GENERAL EDITOR: Douglas MacLean

The purpose of this series is to publish the most innovative and up-to-date research into the values and concepts that underlie major aspects of public policy. Hitherto most research in this field has been empirical. This series is primarily conceptual and normative; that is, it investigates the structure of arguments and the nature of values relevant to the formation, justification, and criticism of public policy. At the same time it is informed by empirical considerations, addressing specific issues, general policy concerns, and the methods of policy analysis and their applications.

The books in the series are inherently interdisciplinary and include anthologies as well as monographs. They are of particular interest to philosophers, political and social scientists, economists, policy analysts, and those involved in public administration and environmental policy.

Violence, terrorism, and justice

edited by

R. G. FREY & CHRISTOPHER W. MORRIS
BOWLING GREEN STATE UNIVERSITY

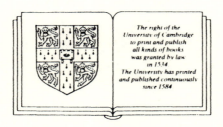

The right of the
University of Cambridge
to print and publish
all kinds of books
was granted by law
in 1534.
The University has printed
and published continuously
since 1584.

CAMBRIDGE UNIVERSITY PRESS

CAMBRIDGE

NEW YORK   PORT CHESTER   MELBOURNE   SYDNEY

Published by the Press Syndicate of the University of Cambridge
The Pitt Building, Trumpington Street, Cambridge CB2 1RP
40 West 20th Street, New York, NY 10011, USA
10 Stamford Road, Oakleigh, Melbourne 3166, Australia

First Published 1991

Library of Congress Cataloging-in-Publication Data
Violence, terrorism, and justice / edited by R. G. Frey & Christopher
W. Morris.
p.   cm. – (Cambridge studies in philosophy and public policy)
Papers from a conference held at Bowling Green State University in
the fall of 1988.
ISBN 0-521-40125-9. – ISBN 0-521-40950-0 (pbk.)
1. Terrorism – Moral and ethical aspects – Congresses. 2. National
liberation movements – Congresses.   I. Frey, R. G. (Raymond
Gillespie)   II. Morris, Christopher W.   III. Series.
HV6431.V56   1991
363.3'2 – dc20   91-7848
                                                       CIP

British Library Cataloguing in Publication Data
Violence, terrorism, and justice. – (Cambridge studies in
philosophy and public policy)
1. Terrorism
I. Frey, R. G. (Raymond G.)   II. Morris, Christopher W.
363.32

ISBN 0-521-40125-9 hardback
ISBN 0-521-40950-0 paperback

Transferred to digital printing 2001

Contents

Contributors

Annette C. Baier, Professor of Philosophy, University of Pittsburgh

Claudia Card, Professor of Philosophy, University of Wisconsin, Madison

Jonathan Glover, Fellow and Tutor in Philosophy, New College, Oxford University

Virginia Held, Professor of Philosophy, City University of New York, Graduate School and Hunter College

Thomas E. Hill, Jr., Professor of Philosophy, University of North Carolina, Chapel Hill

Gregory S. Kavka, Professor of Philosophy, University of California, Irvine

Loren E. Lomasky, Professor of Philosophy, Bowling Green State University

Jan Narveson, Professor of Philosophy, University of Waterloo

Onora O'Neill, Professor of Philosophy, University of Essex

Alan Ryan, Professor of Politics, Princeton University

Thomas C. Schelling, Professor of Economics and Public Affairs, University of Maryland

Contributors

R. G. Frey, Professor of Philosophy, Bowling Green State University

Christopher W. Morris, Associate Professor of Philosophy, Bowling Green State University

Preface

The use of violence for social/political ends, whether by individuals, organized groups, or the state, is a troubling feature of contemporary life. On the one hand, we denounce it, even as we increasingly encounter it on all sides; on the other, we often find ourselves wanting to pick and choose rather more carefully the objects of our denunciation. Is the view we take of Middle Eastern kidnappings and bombings or the many killings perpetrated by the Irish Republican Army in Britain and Western Europe to be the same as that we take of Nelson Mandela and the African National Congress? What is to be our view when a group within a state, such as the Tamil Tigers in Sri Lanka, resorts to violence against the majority Sinhalese population, in the names of religious and political freedom? And what are we to make of Indian and Sinhalese attempts to crush the Tigers? More locally, how exactly are we to regard those who blow up abortion clinics? Are we to see them in the same light as those who break into animal laboratories? And what of those people who experience – and resist – rather violent police methods, including, after arrest, those employed in interrogation? The overwhelming temptation for many of us is to favor some causes as opposed to others and to do so on the ground that we think these causes just.

Yet violence and terrorism in support of what we regard as a just cause appear to represent the very antithesis of the democratic pursuit of social/political ends, which we try to adhere to ourselves and advocate that others adhere to also. Terrorism is often held to be wrong not only because it deliberately inflicts harm upon the innocent and violates the rights of persons but also because it represents the adoption of nondemocratic means to social/political ends. Rather curiously, given the degree of coercion present in, for example, Anglo-American society, we hold to a picture of ourselves as nations of laws, in which respect for law and the rights of others is held in tandem with the claim that social, political, and legal change is always possible through democratic means. Of course, where such means do not exist, we still condemn terrorism on grounds of harming the innocent and violating rights; but the question how else to bring about change except through violence can seem to weigh against this condemnation, especially as we cast our eyes on other peoples, in other lands.

In the fall of 1988, we held a conference at Bowling Green State University on some of these issues connected with violence and terrorism on the one hand and justice on the other. This volume is based on the conference papers, supplemented with several invited essays. Our aim has been to bring together different approaches to the issues but at no loss in philosophical depth; we have tried to be careful as well, however, to achieve breadth, in order to be faithful to our understanding of how ubiquitous a feature of modern life violence and threats of violence have become.

Numerous people have helped us with both the conference and this volume, especially among the graduate students, staff, and faculty of the philosophy department at Bowling Green, and we are grateful to them all. We are also indebted to our series editor, Douglas MacLean, and our Cambridge editor, Terence Moore, for their advice and encouragement. The referees for Cambridge proved helpful as well.

Bowling Green, Ohio   R.G.F.
                                                          C.W.M.

Chapter 1

Violence, terrorism, and justice

R. G. FREY and CHRISTOPHER W. MORRIS

Unless one is a pacifist, one is likely to find it relatively easy to think of scenarios in which the use of force and violence against others is justified. Killing other people in self-defense, for example, seems widely condoned, but so, too, does defending our citizens abroad against attack from violent regimes. Violence in these cases appears reactive, employed to defeat aggression against or violence toward vital interests. Where violence comes to be seen as much more problematic, if not simply prohibited, is in its direct use for social/political ends. It then degenerates into terrorism, many people seem to think, and terrorism, they hold, is quite wrong. But what exactly is terrorism? And why is it wrong?

Most of us today believe terrorism to be a serious problem, one that raises difficult and challenging questions. The urgency of the problem, especially to North Americans and Western Europeans, may appear to be that terrorism is an issue that we confront from outside – that, as it were, it is an issue for us, not because violence for political ends is something approved of in our societies, but because we are the objects of such violence. The difficulty of the questions raised by contemporary terrorism has to do, we may suppose, with the complexity of issues having to do with the use of violence generally for political ends.

The first question, that of the proper characterization of terrorism, is difficult, in part because it is hard to separate from the second, evaluative question, that of the wrongness of terrorism. We may think of terrorism as a type of violence,

1

that is, a kind of force that inflicts damage or harm on people and property. Terrorism thus broadly understood raises the same issues raised generally by the use of violence by individuals or groups. If we think of violence as being a kind of force, then the more general issues concern the evaluation of the use of force, coercion, and the like: When may we restrict people's options so that they have little or no choice but to do what we wish them to do? Violence may be used as one would use force, in order to obtain some end. But violence inflicts harm or damage and consequently adds a new element to the nonviolent use of force. When, then, if ever, may we inflict harm or damage on someone in the pursuit of some end? This question and the sets of issues it raises are familiar topics of moral and political philosophy.

Without preempting the varying characterizations of terrorism developed by the authors in this volume, however, we can think of it more narrowly; that is, we can think of it as a particular use of violence, typically for social/political ends, with several frequently conjoined characteristics. On this view, terrorism, as one would expect from the use of the term, usually involves creating terror or fear, even, perhaps, a sense of panic in a population. This common feature of terrorism is related to another characteristic, namely, the seemingly random or arbitrary use of violence. This in turn is related to a third feature, the targeting of the innocent or of "noncombatants." This last, of course, is a more controversial feature than the others, since many terrorists attempt to justify their acts by arguing that their victims are not (wholly) innocent.

Thus characterized, terrorism raises specific questions that are at the center of contemporary philosophical debate. When, if ever, may one intentionally harm the innocent? Is the justification of terrorist violence to be based entirely on consequences, beneficial or other? Or are terrorist acts among those that are wrong independently of their consequences? What means may one use in combating people who use violence without justification? Other questions, perhaps less familiar, also arise. What does it mean for people to be innocent, that is, not responsible for the acts, say, of their governments? May there not be some justification in terrorists' targeting some victims but not others? May terrorist acts be attributed to groups or to states? What sense, if any, does it make to think of a social system as terrorist?

Additionally, there are a variety of issues that specifically pertain to terrorists and their practices. What is the moral standing generally of terrorists? That is, what, if any, duties do we have to them? How do their acts, and intentions, affect their standing? How does that standing affect our possible responses to them? May we, for instance, execute terrorists or inflict forms of punishment that would, in the words of the American Constitution, otherwise be "cruel and unusual"? What obligations might we, or officials of state, have in our dealings with terrorists? Is bargaining, of the sort practiced by virtually all Western governments, a justified response to terrorism? How, if at all, should our responses to terrorists be altered in the event that we admit or come to admit, to some degree, the justice of their cause?

Considered broadly, as a type of violence, or, even more generally, as a type of force, terrorism is difficult to condemn out of hand. Force is a common feature of political life. We secure compliance with law by the use and threat of force. For many, this may be the sole reason for compliance. Force is used, for instance, to ensure that people pay their taxes, and force, even violence, is commonplace in the control of crime. In many such instances, there is not much controversy about the general justification of the use of force. The matter, say, of military conscription, though endorsed by many, is more controversial. In international contexts, however, the uses of force, and of violence, raise issues about which there is less agreement. Examples will come readily to mind.

More narrowly understood, involving some or all of the three elements mentioned earlier (the creation of terror, the seemingly random use of violence, and the targeting of the innocent or of noncombatants), the justification of terrorism is more problematic, as a brief glance at several competing moral theories will reveal.

3

Act-consequentialists, those who would have us evaluate actions solely in terms of their consequences, would presumably condone some terrorist acts. Were some such act to achieve a desirable goal, with minimal costs, the consequentialist might approve. Care, however, must be taken in characterizing the terrorists' goals and means. For contemporary consequentialists invariably are universalists; the welfare or ends of all people (and, on some accounts, all sentient beings) are to be included. Thus, terrorists cannot avail themselves of such theories to justify furthering the ends of some small group at the cost of greater damage to the interests of others. Merely to argue that the ends justify the means, without regard to the nature of the former, does not avail to one the resources of consequentialist moral theory.

Two factors will be further emphasized. First, consequentialist moral theory will focus upon effectiveness and efficiency, upon whether terrorist acts are an effective, efficient means to achieving desirable goals. The question naturally arises, then, whether there is an alternative means available, with equal or better likelihood of success in achieving the goal at a reduced cost. If resort to terrorism is a tactic, is there another tactic, just as likely to achieve the goal, at a cost more easy for us to bear? It is here, of course, that alternatives such as passive resistance and nonviolent civil disobedience will arise and need to be considered. It is here also that account must be taken of the obvious fact that terrorist acts seem often to harden the resistance of those the terrorists oppose. Indeed, the alleged justice of the terrorists' cause can easily slip into the background, as the killing and maiming come to preoccupy and outrage the target population. Second, consequentialist moral theory will focus upon the goal to be achieved: Is the goal that a specific use of terrorism is in aid of desirable enough for us to want to see it realized in society, at the terrible costs it exacts? It is no accident that terrorists usually portray their cause as concerned with the rectification and elimination of injustice; for *this* goal seems to be one the achievement of which we might just agree was desirable enough for us to tolerate significant

4

cost. And it is here, of course, that doubts plague us, because we are often unsure where justice with respect to some issue falls. In the battle over Ireland, and the demand of the Irish Republican Army for justice, is there nothing to be said on the English side? Is the entire matter black and white? Here, too, a kind of proportionality rule may intrude itself. Is the reunification of Ireland worth all the suffering and loss the IRA inflicts? Is this a goal worth, not only members of the IRA's dying for, but also their making other people die for? For consequentialists, it typically will not be enough that members of the IRA think so; those affected by the acts of the IRA cannot be ignored.

Finally, consequentialist moral theory will stress how unsure we sometimes are about what counts as doing justice. On the one hand, we sometimes are genuinely unsure about what counts as rectifying an injustice. For instance, is allowing the Catholics of Northern Ireland greater and greater control over their lives part of the rectification process? For the fact remains that there are many more Protestants than Catholics in the North, so that *democratic* votes may well not materially change the condition of the latter, whatever their degree of participation in the process. On the other hand, we sometimes are genuinely unsure whether we can rectify or eliminate one injustice without perpetrating another. In the Arab–Israeli conflict, for example, can we remove one side's grievances without thereby causing additional grievances on the other side? Is there *any* way of rectifying an injustice in that conflict without producing another?

Thus, while consequentialist moral theory *can* produce a justification of terrorist acts, it typically will do so here, as in other areas, only under conditions that terrorists in the flesh will find it difficult to satisfy.

It is the seeming randomness of the violence emphasized by terrorism, understood in the narrower sense, that leads many moral theorists to question its legitimacy. Many moral traditions, especially nonconsequentialist ones, impose strict limits on the harm that may be done to the innocent. Indeed, some theories, such as those associated with natural law and

5

Kantian traditions, will impose an indefeasible prohibition on the intentional killing of the innocent, which "may not be overridden, whatever the consequences." Sometimes this prohibition is formulated in terms of the rights of the innocent not to be killed (e.g., the right to life), other times in terms merely of our duties not to take their lives. Either way the prohibition is often understood to be indefeasible.

If intentionally killing the innocent is indefeasibly wrong, that is, if it may never be done whatever the consequences, then many, if not most, contemporary terrorists stand condemned. Killing individuals who happen to find themselves in a targeted store, café, or train station may not be done, according to these traditions. Contemporary terrorists, who intend to bring about the deaths of innocent people by their acts, commit one of the most serious acts of injustice, unless, of course, they can show that these people are not innocent. Much turns on their attempts, therefore, to attack the innocence claim.

Just as natural law and Kantian moral theories constrain our behavior and limit the means we may use in the pursuit of political ends, so they constrain our responses to terrorists. We may not, for instance, intentionally kill innocent people (e.g., bystanders, hostages) while combating those who attack us. Our hands may thus be tied in responding to terrorism. Many commentators have argued that a morally motivated reluctance to use the nondiscriminating means of terrorists makes us especially vulnerable to them.

Some natural law or Kantian thinkers invoke the notions of natural or of human rights to understand moral standing, where these are rights which we possess simply by virtue of our natures or of our humanity. Now if our nature or our humanity is interpreted, as it commonly is in these traditions, as something we retain throughout our lives, at least to the extent that we retain those attributes and capacities that are characteristic of humans, then even those who violate the strictest prohibitions of justice will retain their moral standing. According to this view, a killer acts wrongly without thereby ceasing to be the sort of being that possesses moral standing. Terrorists, then, retain their moral standing, and consequently, there are limits to what we may do to them, by way either of resistance or of punishment. Conversely, though there is reason to think consequentialists, including those who reject theories of rights to understand moral standing, would not deny terrorists such standing, what may be done to terrorists may not be so easily constrained. For harming those who harm the innocent seems less likely to provoke outrage and opposition and so negative consequences.

Certainly, not every member of these nonconsequentialist traditions will agree with this analysis. John Locke, for instance, believed that a murderer has "by the unjust Violence and Slaughter he hath committed upon one, declared War against all Mankind, and therefore may be destroyed as a *Lyon* or a *Tyger*, one of those wild Savage Beasts, with whom Men can have no Society nor Security."[1] It may, however, be argued that the analysis accords with many parts of these traditions, as well as with much of ordinary, commonsense morality.

Whether we follow these theories in understanding the prohibition on the intentional killing of the innocent to be indefeasible or not, this principle figures importantly in most moral traditions. Care, however, must be taken in its interpretation and application. Even if we understand terrorism narrowly, as involving attacks on the innocent, it may not be clear here as elsewhere exactly who is innocent. As made clear in the just war and abortion literature, the term "innocent" is ambiguous. The usual sense is to designate some individual who is not guilty of moral or legal wrongdoing, a sense usually called the moral or juridical sense of the term. By contrast, in discussing what are often called "innocent threats" – for instance, an approaching infant who unwittingly is boobytrapped with explosives, a fetus whose continued growth threatens the life of the woman – it is common to distinguish a "technical" or "causal" sense of "innocence." People lack innocence in this second sense insofar as they threaten, whatever their culpability.

Determining which sense of "innocence" is relevant (and

7

this is not to prejudge the issue of still further, different senses) is controversial. In discussions of the ethics of war, it is often thought that "noncombatants" are not legitimate targets, because of their innocence. Noncombatants, however, may share some of the responsibility for the injustice of a war or the injustice of the means used to prosecute the war, or they may threaten the adversary in certain ways. In the first case, they would not be fully innocent in the moral or juridical sense; in the second, they would lack, to some degree, causal innocence.

This distinction is relevant to the moral evaluation of terrorist acts aimed at noncombatants. Sometimes attempts are made at justification by pointing to the victims' lack of innocence, in the first sense. Perhaps this is what Emile Henry meant when he famously said, in 1894, after exploding a bomb in a Paris café, "There are no innocents." Presumably in such cases, where the relevant notion of innocence is that of nonculpability, terrorists would strike only at members of certain national or political groups. Other times it might be argued that the victims in some way (for instance, by their financial, electoral, or tacit support for a repressive regime) posed a threat. In these cases, terrorists would view themselves as justified in striking at anyone who, say, was present in a certain location. The distinction may also be of importance in discussions of the permissibility of various means that might be used in response to terrorist acts. If the relevant sense of innocence is causal, then certain means, those endangering the lives of victims, might be permissible.

Of course it is hard to understand how the victims of the Japanese Red Army attack at Israel's Lod airport in 1972 or of a bomb in a Paris department store in 1986 could be thought to lack innocence in either sense. In the first case, the victims were travelers (e.g., Puerto Rican Christians); in the second case, the store in question was frequented by indigent immigrants and, at that time of year, by mothers and children shopping for school supplies. It is this feature of some contemporary terrorism that has lead many commentators to distinguish it from earlier forms and from other political uses of violence.

The analogies here with another issue that has preoccupied moral theorists recently, that of the ethics of nuclear deterrence and conflict, are significant. The United States, of course, dropped atomic weapons on two Japanese cities at the end of the last world war. For several decades now, American policy has been to threaten the Soviet Union with a variety of kinds of nuclear strikes in the event that the latter attacked the United States or its Western allies with nuclear or, in the case of an invasion of Western Europe, merely with conventional weapons. These acts or practices involve killing or threatening to kill noncombatants in order to achieve certain ends: unconditional surrender in the case of Japan, deterrence of aggression in that of the Soviet Union. The possible analogies with terrorism have not gone unnoticed. Furthermore, just as some defenders of the atomic strikes against the Japanese have argued, those we attack, or threaten to attack, with nuclear weapons are themselves sufficiently similar to terrorists to justify our response.

A still different perspective on these issues may be obtained by turning from the usual consequentialist and natural law or Kantian theories to forms of contractarianism in ethics. Although this tradition has affinities with natural law and Kantian theories, especially with regard to the demands of justice or the content of moral principles, there are differences that are especially noteworthy in connection with the issues that are raised by terrorist violence.

According to this tradition, justice may be thought of as a set of principles and dispositions that bind people insofar as those to whom they are obligated reciprocate. In the absence of constraint by others, one has little or no duty to refrain from acting toward them in ways that normally would be unjust. Justice may be thus thought, to borrow a phrase from John Rawls, to be a sort of "cooperative venture for mutual advantage." According to this view, justice is not binding in the absence of certain conditions, one of which would be others' cooperative behavior and dispositions.

9

Adherents to this tradition might argue that we would be in a "state of nature," that is, a situation where few if any constraints of justice would bind us, with regard to terrorists who attack those who are innocent (in the relevant sense). As Hume argues in the *Second Enquiry*, when in "the society of ruffians, remote from the protection of laws and government," or during the "rage and violence of public war," the conventions of justice are suspended:

> The laws of war, which then succeed to those of equity and justice, are rules calculated for the *advantage* and *utility* of that particular state, in which men are now placed. And were a civilized nation engaged with barbarians, who observed no rules even of war, the former must also suspend their observance of them, where they no longer serve to any purpose; and must render every action or rencounter as bloody and pernicious as possible to the first aggressors.[2]

Unlike the earlier views, then, this view holds that terrorists who, by act or by intent, forswear the rules of justice may thereby lose the protection of those rules, and so a major part of their moral standing.

Similarly, partisans of terrorism might argue that it is the acts of their victims or of their governments that make impossible cooperative relations of fair dealing between themselves and those they attack. The acts, or intentions, of the latter remove them from the protection of the rules of justice.

In either case, the acts of terrorists and our response to them take place in a world beyond, or prior to, justice. Students of international affairs and diplomacy will recognize here certain of the implications of a family of skeptical positions called "realism."

Consequentialists, it should be noted, are likely to find this exclusive focus on the virtue of justice to be misguided, and they are likely to be less enamored of certain distinctions involving kinds of innocence or types of violence that are incorporated into contractarianism. In general, they will argue, as noted earlier, that terrorism *can* be justified by its consequences, where these must include the effects not merely on the terrorists but also on their victims (and others). As terrorist acts appear often not to produce sufficient benefits to outweigh the considerable costs they inevitably exact, there will most likely be a moral presumption, albeit defeasible, against them. But wrongful terrorism will be condemned, not because of the existence of mutually advantageous conventions of justice, but because of the overall harm or suffering caused. Consequentialists, then, will doubtless stand out as much against contractarian views here as they do against natural law or Kantian ones.

The foregoing, then, is a sketch of different ways terrorism may be understood and of different types of moral theories in which its justification may be addressed. There is serious controversy on both counts, and this fact alone, whatever other differences may exist, makes the works of philosophers and political and social scientists on terrorism contentious even among themselves. Though the essays that follow exhibit this contentiousness, their different arguments, their different attempts to impress an approach or point of view upon us, and their engagement from different perspectives with these twin issues (and others) confer a depth upon the discussion that no mere recitation of possible analyses and theoretical encounters with terrorism can provide.

The focus of the first essays is the political terrorism that attracts so much of the attention of people and of the media. Later essays explore other forms of terrorism, especially those perpetrated by states or by one class or group upon another. As indicated, virtually all of the essays raise direct questions about how we should think of and evaluate the different forms of terrorism.

Thomas Schelling notes that "internationalism terrorism," the sort that newspapers and television bring into our homes today, is not very successful, at least as measured by the perpetrators' goals or aims. The interesting question, he thinks, is why this is the case. He ponders why acts of extortion, backed by threats of violence, are not generally more common, given how easy they seem to be, and his general

11

answer is that, although the acts themselves may be simply accomplished, benefiting from them is not. Curiously, though the behavior of people and of states may be affected by acts of terrorism, the aims of terrorists rarely seem to be furthered by them. Terrorism of a certain sort is an unwieldy weapon, Schelling suggests; for it is difficult to identify the ends that it has achieved or could achieve, and so difficult, at least sometimes, not to see it as self-defeating.

Annette Baier focuses on revolutionary terrorists, whom she understands as "violent demonstrators"; these are people who typically use violence openly, with an eye to publicity, and identify the cause on whose behalf they kill and maim. Her interest is in how these features affect our evaluation of their behavior. The terrorists upon whom she focuses are protestors of sort; they aim to attract attention. Baier urges that we deplore the inhumanity of the terrorists' methods; but she stresses that "until our own humanity is a bit more exemplary, and our intolerance of inhumanity closer to home a bit more active, we will not be in a very good position to feel a special righteous indignation at the terrorist's methods." Terrorists, of the sort under consideration, characteristically have (deep) grievances, and we should not ignore these in our condemnations. "If we are to respond to terrorism not just with trite moral comparisons of what is better, what worse, but in a way that we could reasonably believe might eventually end terrorism," Baier suggests, "then we have to hope for a new Grotius-cum-Hobbes, who will codify neither the old honor code of the generals, soldiers, and diplomats of established powers, nor maxims of enlightened self-interest for single persons, but rather the arts of successful peacemaking, of forming workable plans for lasting peace, ways of removing the group grievances that threaten peace."

In her essay, "Terrorism, Rights, and Political Goals," Virginia Held considers various characterizations of terrorism and returns to one she developed in an earlier essay: Terrorism is a form of violence, which aims to achieve political goals, often through the creation of fear. She now suggests that the intention to create fear may not be a necessary feature and explores various problems with common characterizations of terrorism. While trying to determine whether it is always impermissible to kill noncombatants, as is so often claimed in discussions of terrorism and just war theory, Held and others question the moral distinction between combatant and noncombatant and focus upon possible rights violations. Thus, when she considers the issues from a perspective that places special emphasis upon the moral rights of individuals, she argues that in situations where there must be violations of rights, it is morally preferable that these be equitably distributed among all parties. Terrorism, she concludes, cannot be condemned in all situations by appeals to the sort of rights principles that she favors: "Depending on the severity and extent of the rights violations in an existing situation, a transition involving a sharing of rights violations, if this and only this can be expected to lead to a situation in which rights are more adequately respected, may well be less morally unjustifiable than continued acceptance of ongoing rights violations."

Loren Lomasky, on the other hand, finds the distinctiveness of terrorism in the perpetrators' rejection of standard constraints regarding the choice of victims. It is the terrorists' *attitudes* that are distinctive and the key to an appreciation of the political significance of terrorism; it is to be understood, not in terms of the ends it allegedly aims to achieve, but in the attitudes that it *expresses*. It is a form of nihilism: It "is to shuck off in particularly violent and blatant fashion the restraints that divide civil society from the state of nature." The terrorist differs from the criminal or gangster, who seeks wealth, power, status, through illicit means; for the latter's activity in some sense depends on civil society. By contrast, terrorists, through their relatively indiscriminate targeting of civilians, explicitly reject familiar political categories and the limitations on violence they embody. If the expressive analysis is correct, then there is truth to the claim that terrorism is a deadly threat to civil order.

Jan Narveson thinks of terrorism as, in part, the view that

13

terror may be used for political ends, typically by instilling fear in members of a population by means of random acts of violence, acts that may be visited, without warning, upon anyone. What makes terrorism so dreadful is precisely what makes ordinary crime so dreadful, namely, its destructive violence, a violence compounded by the perpetrators' intent to harm and by the fact that its victims have little control over its occurrence. By means of a contractarian account of morality, according to which morality consists of internalized rules, general adherence to which brings about mutually beneficial consequences, Narveson argues that violators of such rules, which have as a part strong prohibitions against the use of violence, put themselves back into a Hobbesian "state of nature" and consequently outside the protection of (many) such rules. His general conclusion is that terrorism is wrong in virtually all circumstances, though in the present world perhaps sometimes forgivable.

Terrorism is commonly thought to involve, or to be a type of, violence or coercion. But what exactly is coercion? Frustrated by the analyses of theorists, Onora O'Neill proposes to ask the experts, those who have little trouble distinguishing coercive acts from others, namely, the coercers. They look for "offers" that *you* cannot refuse, and they have a practical end in mind. They aim to have the victim do, or desist from doing, something; the means is to influence the latter's will so as to bring this about. Coercion is thus particular in purpose; it seeks to obtain something from a specific person or group. It imposes a certain choice, as it were, upon its victim, and accordingly, O'Neill argues, fails to respect the latter's agency and integrity. The key to understanding coercion is grasping the manner in which the "offer" is placed "beyond refusal" by being connected to consequences that, if accepted, would affront the victim's dignity and would impair, if not destroy, the victim's integrity or sense of self. Coercers prey on people's vulnerabilities.

How is one to respond to terrorists, especially if one rejects a consequentialist moral theory and seeks to adhere to certain strict principles governing responses to threats? In this regard, Thomas Hill tries to determine whether a basically Kantian ethic has any reasonable and coherent way to approach troublesome cases regarding permissible and impermissible responses to terrorism. The problem essentially is that making exceptions to the rule, as it were, seems to involve abandoning what is central to Kantian morality and embracing some form of consequentialism. He argues that the Kantian concern to treat humanity as an end in itself does not entail that it is always wrong to kill humans or to risk killing innocent humans in response to terrorism. Further, and rather surprisingly for a Kantian, he defends a Kantian way of thinking about hard choices that would allow one to take into account, at some level, the relative numbers of individuals whose lives can be prolonged by different policies. Most emphatically, he rejects the view, commonly attributed to Kantian ethics, that there is an absolute "clean hands" principle requiring one to refrain from killing the innocent, whatever others threaten to do.

In "State and Private; Red and White," Alan Ryan considers whether we must, while invoking a generally utilitarian standpoint, distinguish state from individual violence, as well as Red terror, that committed in the cause of justice, from White terror, that committed in the name of order. Terrorist activities, he thinks, are marked by two distinguishing characteristics: They use methods that deprive their victims of the power of a graduated, rational response, and they express, through their nature, the unwillingness to abide by any restraint. Though governments may typically eschew these means, they do not always do so; thus the distinction, made by Hannah Arendt, between (state) power and (individual) violence, is forced. The distinction between Red and White terror fares no better.

Jonathan Glover also focuses upon state terrorism, whose features and prevalence can escape notice with so much attention given to individual terrorist acts. He discusses what he considers to be some important characteristics of state terrorism, in the context of actual examples, and compares and contrasts these with some prevalent features of individual terrorism. He claims that state terrorism, in both quantity and cruelty, dwarfs the individual variety, and, indeed, is a morally worse affair. Additionally, Glover looks at some of what he takes to be the psychological roots of state terrorism, and he concludes that these are too widespread and deepseated for comfort. For the psychological profile they make up not only enables us in part to understand state officials' reliance upon terrorism, but also enables us to understand why stopping their practice of it is going to be difficult.

It has often been said that nuclear strikes and the threat of such a strike are forms of terrorism. Is threatening another society with nuclear destruction a form of hostage taking, as Thomas Schelling has elsewhere claimed? Is it thus to be condemned, as such? Gregory Kavka argues that this analogy does not apply to and morally infect nuclear deterrence. "Nuclear hostages," unlike the hostages of terrorists, do not suffer loss of liberty, and the risk of death imposed on them is arguably less harmful. Also, invoking a variety of considerations from just war theory, he argues that the moral case against nuclear hostage taking is less strong than that against the other sort. If self-defense allows people to impose risks on others, as Kavka contends, then the practice of holding others as nuclear hostages may be justifiable.

When we think of terrorism we typically, as do most of the authors in this volume, think of a variety of acts, committed by individuals or groups in the name of some cause or committed by states for repressive purposes. Claudia Card urges us to think of rape as a terrorist practice. It is, she suggests, a practice, in that it is a form of social activity structured by rules, though not one supervised or controlled by any single person or group. The concern of rape as a practice is sexual politics: Rape as a terrorist practice supports a protection racket that benefits men. That it is a practice is disguised or hidden from us, or we hide it from ourselves, and the benefits males derive from it may be, to some limited degree, unnoticed. The rules of the practice are varied; for example, a man cannot "rape" his wife, prostitutes are fair game, and women can "ask for it" by dressing provocatively.

Seeing rape as a form of terrorism is important, Card argues, because it enables us both to understand the institution as such and to guide more effectively the selection of means for opposing it.

Our aim, certainly our hope, with these essays is to further understanding of the myriad practical and theoretical issues that surround terrorism today and to show the interplay among these different sets of issues. But there is nothing detached, nothing of the ivory tower, about them; in every case, they seek to come to grips with the violence in our midst and our attempts, sometimes in a mood of despair and with a palpable sense of futility, to sort the sinners from the pure.

NOTES

1   John Locke, *Second Treatise of Government*, in *Two Treatises of Government*, ed. Peter Laslett (Cambridge: Cambridge University Press, 1988), p. 274 (chap. 2, sec. 11).
2   David Hume, *An Enquiry concerning the Principles of Morals*, in *Enquiries concerning Human Understanding and the Principles of Morals*, ed. L. A. Selby-Bigge, 3d ed., ed. P. H. Nidditch (Oxford: Clarendon, 1975), pp. 187–8 (sec. 3, pt. 1).

Chapter 2

What purposes can "international terrorism" serve?

THOMAS C. SCHELLING

I confine my discussion to what is often called "international terrorism," terrorism committed by nationals of one country, or by members of nationalist groups or organizations, against governments, institutions, or people in another country. I exclude the terrorism used by one or both sides in civil wars in Algeria, Vietnam, and Nicaragua. I exclude the terrorism exercised by despotic governments in Iran, Argentina, or South Africa, or the regimes of Stalin, Hitler, or Mao Tse Tung. I include most of the terrorism attributed to leftist movements, Arab nationalists, and groups like the Serbian separatists acting outside Yugoslavia. Some of what I shall say applies to terrorism directed against the terrorists' own government, but on a scale drastically short of attempted revolution.

What I have in mind is epitomized by the capture of Israeli athletes in Munich, the machine gunning of people at a TWA ticket counter, the hijacking of aircraft by leftist or nationalist groups, the kidnapping of an American general assigned to NATO. I exclude hijacking for fun, for profit, or for free transportation. I am thinking of terrorist acts that have at least ostensibly some political purpose.

I probably have in mind the kinds of terrorist activity that most viewers of television and readers of newspapers remember most vividly. The publicity this kind of terrorist activity receives is hugely disproportionate to the actual violence, compared with the outrages and occasional heroics committed by terrorist governments, occupying authorities, and insurgent or revolutionary movements. Part of what I am going to say is that it really does not amount to much, but an interesting question is why it does not.

At first glance there is something very cheap and exceedingly potent about what terrorists can do. I once began the preface to a book on nuclear strategy with the observation that "one of the lamentable principles of human productivity is that it is easier to destroy than to create. A house that takes several man-years to build can be burned in an hour by any young delinquent who has the price of a box of matches. Poisoning dogs is easier than raising them."[1] And in discussing coercion and extortion with my undergraduate students I point out that there must be a million people who live within the public transportation radius of my home who could burn down my house with impunity with a dollar's worth of gasoline or could have run over my children as they played in the street on a winter's evening, when I used to have small children living at home. What I would pay to forestall such easily accomplished damage is at least the life-time earnings of a twenty-year-old at the federal minimum wage discounted at today's interest rate, and probably several times that much. I invite my class to speculate on why I have never been targeted by an extortionist.

And I am myself led to speculate on why international political terrorism is such an infinitesimal activity on the world scene when measured not in audience appeal but in damage actually accomplished or even attempted. Even in Israel the fatalities and injuries to Israeli civilians from terrorist attacks since, say, the 1967 War would barely deserve a separate line in the national mortality and morbidity statistics if their significance were purely quantitative. In media coverage terrorist activity, though it comes in short intensive bursts, exceeds earthquakes, floods, and until recently famine. But we need some explanation of why there is so little of it and so little damage from it.

It isn't even clear that terrorist activity is very significant in the fear and anxiety that it produces. Anger and frustration, yes; drama and entertainment, certainly; but seldom panic and little observable behavior motivated by fear, anxiety, or prudential considerations. Individually targeted persons will indeed take protective measures, driving to work along randomly selected routes or having their mail X-rayed before they open it; but there are probably more foreign business executives in Argentina and Italy who take protective measures against ordinary for-profit kidnapping than government officials who take such measures against international terrorist threats. (Domestic assassination may be the greater worry for many of them.)

In seeking plausible answers to why there is so little evident terrorist activity – I admit the possibility of secret terrorist activity of which we do not become aware – I think a good place to begin is with the observation that acts of terrorism almost never appear to accomplish anything politically significant. True, an intermediate means toward political objectives could be attracting attention and publicizing a grievance, and terrorism surely attracts attention and publicizes grievances. But with a few exceptions it is hard to see that the attention and the publicity have been of much value except as ends in themselves. Maybe the Serbian separatists are closer to national autonomy because of the communiqué for which they secured publication in major newspapers while negotiating from a hijacked aircraft, but I doubt whether would-be terrorists take encouragement from that example. One can argue that the most recent civil violence in Israel, the response of the Israeli electorate, and the action of the Palestinian National Council are significantly due to twenty years of terrorist infiltration into Israel and assassination of Israeli officals abroad and the hijacking of Israeli-related aircraft, but I wouldn't know how to document that storming a school in Kiriat Shmona and killing a score of schoolchildren played any role in recent events. And it is far from clear that the residents of Gaza and the West Bank are better off or will be than if there had been no terrorism against Israeli citizens since the occupation of the territories in 1967.

In a moment I will mention a few apparent terrorist successes, but at this point I want to draw an inference oriented toward that question why there is so little international political terrorism. And one answer that I propose is that, despite the high ratio of damage and grief to the resources required for a terrorist act, terrorism has proved to be a remarkably ineffectual means to accomplishing anything. I do not mean that terrorism couldn't be terribly effective; there may be potential terrorist organizations and strategies of terrorism that could be exceedingly effective. But most of the international terrorism that we have witnessed has been pitifully crude and clumsy and ineffectual, with little follow-up, no sustained drive, hardly any evident purpose except the performance of an expressive act. Most of the considerations I can think of in wondering why nobody has made a good living by threatening to burn down my house come down to the fact that whereas burning my house is cheap and easy, making money out of it is not. Bombing a disco or a consulate or an air terminal may be easy; turning the act to any use may be beyond the wits not only of the terrorist perpetrators but of any minds, if any, that provide their guidance and motivation.

I shall mention a few successes, at least to try to show that I am not altogether blind to them. The most dramatically successful terrorist campaign I can think of is, somewhat ironically, the campaign of militant Palestinians against moderate Palestinian leaders in the West Bank. The sequence of bombings that killed or dismembered mayors and other leaders accused of collaborating with Israel appears to have made it exceedingly difficult during the past several years for any moderate public leadership to survive.

A special case, not quite meeting my definition of international political terrorism but closely analogous, was the trading of several hundred captured "terrorists," many or most of whom could as well be characterized as prisoners of war, for several Israeli soldiers captured in Lebanon. We do not know, but it seems likely, that as in olden times Israeli soldiers who might have been promptly killed were kept intact as trading assets. The Israeli government was greatly

21

embarrassed in explaining how this "wartime prisoner exchange" differed from "negotiating with terrorists," something it was publicly resolved never to do.

Terrorist activity has occasionally forced the release of convicted and imprisoned terrorists. One of the acute vulnerabilities of any antiterrorist campaign is the danger that captured terrorists can be sprung by the capture, by terrorists still at large, of "assets" that can be traded, either kidnapped individuals or hijacked aircraft or possibly occupied structures. (An interesting question, which I cannot pursue here, is whether convicted terrorists might constitutionally be transferred to some international holding institution that had no authority to release any of its prisoners against even the highest-level demand or plea by the government that originally captured and convicted them.)

Another "success" that probably falls outside my definition, which may have begun as something rather like international terrorism, was the influence on U.S. activity of the holding of the embassy prisoners in Teheran. Rarely are terrorist victims so susceptible to being held in "steady state," the captors themselves in no danger, and no time pressure on the captors as when fuel runs out in a hijacked aircraft or supplies run out in an occupied embassy in another country. Except for the final financial negotiation, there is no visible indication that the government of Iran compelled any U.S. activity by the threat of continued incarceration or bodily harm, but there may have been acts from which the U.S. government was disuaded for fear of reprisals against the imprisoned embassy personnel.

Hijacked aircraft have been traded for money, but not by international terrorists as far as I know; they have been traded for release of prisoners, but not on a significant scale.

Finally, the machine gunning at Leonardo da Vinci Airport of passengers at the TWA counter did cause air passengers, for a brief period, to prefer other airlines, and was reported, for a brief period, to have affected cross-Atlantic tourism. The principle that terrorism could influence the behavior of large numbers of people was demonstrated. Whether that was the purpose is unclear. There was surely no follow-up, and there is no sign that people who changed their reservations to British Airways or Air France were doing the terrorist cause, whatever that may have been, any good.

A purpose that may be successfully served by terrorism is to build morale among the supporters of the movement that the terrorists represent. Maybe some lost causes are kept alive by the demonstration that the political enemy is at least being hurt. Conceivably an otherwise lost cause is kept alive long enough for the cause to become genuinely promising. At this point I am only guessing, but it may be that Irish Republican terrorism kept alive, but only barely, a political movement that after decades of futility reached something like critical mass and became a genuine political force, the ultimate outcome still unknown but a possible outcome favorable to the IRA cause not out of the question.

In a moment I want to begin an analysis of what it is that terrorists might hope to accomplish politically and why it may be so difficult, even if they are brave and resourceful. But I want to offer another conjecture on why international political terrorism is so rare. That is that whereas individual acts of terrorism may be easily within the capabilities of quite ordinary individuals, a sustained campaign on any scale may require more people and more organization than could be viable in most target countries. And there may be some negative feedback from the low success rate to the low attempt rate: Resourceful individuals, people with brains or people with money, may find terrorism so unpromising that they do not choose to contribute effort or money. And any organization that is secret and dangerous risks both defection and infiltration; a group of people large enough to carry on a sustained campaign, perhaps simultaneously in different target areas, may simply be too vulnerable to defection and infiltration. Even seeking financial help risks being informed on.

I mention this because a colleague whom I trust has been in touch with some of the European antiterrorist police organizations and tells me that the number of people believed

23

to be actively engaged in political terrorism in Germany, France, and Italy is likely in the dozens, not the hundreds. Twenty years ago when radical student uprisings claimed so much attention the situation may have been drastically different; terrorist or potentially terrorist cells may have wasted away with time, till only a few remain, and initiating a new cell except in times of radical enthusiasm and activity may be dangerous, difficult, and frustrating.

Let me begin a discussion of terrorist strategy and tactics by looking at the concept of negotiation with terrorists. "Never negotiate with terrorists" is pretty standard advice and the announced policy of the U.S. and Israeli governments and somewhat less vociferously of European governments. The policy is not easy to define. But "never negotiate" at least has the quality that it is a rule that in principle one could follow. Intercept them, apprehend them, infiltrate them, capture them, deny them entry, deny them weapons – these things may or may not be possible; but "never negotiate" is a rule imposed on oneself, and ought at least to be enforceable.

The first thing to notice about most of the terrorism of the kind that falls within my definition is that usually there is nothing to negotiate. A soldier is killed in a disco in Germany. A bomb explodes in front of an Israeli consulate. Japanese Black Septembrists unpack automatic weapons in the Lod airport and start shooting. The perpetrators don't ask anything, demand anything, or make themselves available for any kind of communication except possibly if they are captured alive.

This is not to say that there wouldn't be "negotiation" of some sort if there were sustained terrorist activity known to be conditioned on failure of some authority to comply with some implicit or explicit demand. If an American Embassy employee somewhere in the world is assassinated every week and it is understood that the sequence will come to an end only if and when the U.S. government discontinues some activity of its own, the terrorism could be thought of as an essential part of a "negotiation," just as strikes, sabotage, and labor violence are part of the process of industrial negotiation. But it is hard to find examples.

There could be secret examples. Smart terrorists might appreciate that if they keep their demands from the public a government that has pledged never to negotiate, never to give in, may more willingly give in because its doing so will remain secret. If the terrorist acts could be carried out in such a way that they would not be generally recognized as a systematic campaign of terrorism, the entire "negotiation" might remain secret. And not only would a complying government avoid public embarrassment at having yielded; it might rationalize its secretly yielding with the argument that it provides no incentive to other terrorists because to them the government continues to look unyielding.

The only sustained campaign I can think of was two decades of Arab Nationalist bombs and shootings in Israel and of Israeli citizens elsewhere, but compared with what the PLO or the Arab countries wanted of Israel, nobody could have imagined that those terrorist acts added any detectable pressure on Israel's resolution.

There is one kind of "negotiation" that is hard to avoid. One can refuse to meet with or take a phone call from a "terrorist negotiator," but one cannot ignore terrorist demands that are publicly associated with terrorist acts. One cannot avoid being available to hear what is demanded, even when one might prefer not to listen. When hijackers and kidnappers can talk directly to the media, public negotiation is in process. Public statements by a target government in response to publicized terrorists' demands are, in turn, negotiation. If a government publicly rationalizes legalistically why it will not extradite a terrorist in its custody wanted elsewhere for capital crimes, it may be both negotiating and giving in, while pretending to be doing no such thing.

Probably the kind of "negotiation" most likely to succeed is what I call "deterrence" in contrast to "compellance." I use "deterrence" in the dictionary sense of inducing the second party not to take an action, and "compellance" to mean inducing the other party to take an action. There are a number of strategically important differences between these two classes of coercive efforts, an important one being that to comply with a compellant threat is much more likely to involve visible compliance, whereas merely continuing not to do something that one might have been about to do is not so visibly an act of yielding. Quietly letting it be known that every time a terrorist is captured by American agents some number of American officials will be shot or some significant American installation, like a hotel or business firm, will be bombed or burned with people inside, could dishearten American efforts to capture terrorists without this looking like compliance. Demanding release of prisoners, or the abrupt cessation of some visible activity – quartering marines in Lebanon – would require a more visible act of compliance.

The easiest way to exercise terrorist influence may be to intimidate populations. Bomb threats, especially if bombs are occasionally found, and most especially if some occasionally go off, probably could significantly affect tourism and even business travel if the targets were aircraft and hotels. Terrorism of the cheap and easy kind on a large scale, if the large scale were compatible with its being cheap and easy, might induce embassy employees and overseas business-people to send their families home. But again it is hard to see what purpose would be served.

What sorts of things might terrorists seek to negotiate? The answer will partly depend on what it is they threaten in return. One possibility is to threaten some future act of destruction, with or without identifying the particular target, with or without identifying themselves or their location. But most scenarios in which negotiation is envisioned involve capturing something or somebody. Aircraft, trains, buses, and ships have been hijacked. People have been kidnapped. Buildings have been occupied with captives inside. Domestic terrorists took over the legislature in Spain and the supreme court in Colombia; foreign terrorists occupied embassies in London, Khartoum, and other cities. People have imagined terrorists occupying nuclear power plants, airport control towers, electric facilities where the safeguards against black-out are exercised.

An important limitation on what may be negotiated is how long the occupation or the kidnapping may last. Exhaustion and the need for sleep may determine the time schedule if the terrorists are too few for some to keep adequate guard while others sleep. The approach of night may limit nego-tiations if the electricity can be turned off and antiterrorist squads can use the cover of darkness. Food and drink may be a limitation. The timing is important because the threat will be futile if what is demanded cannot be accomplished within the limited time. (A related point is that ultimata is-sued by the terrorists may not impose deadlines too early to make compliance feasible; during a joint hijacking of three aircraft taken to the Jordan desert, meeting the demands required the concurrence of some five different governments, a patent impossibility within the time limit imposed, and the terrorists had to extend the deadline of the ultimatum, weak-ening their negotiating position.)

What are some of the things, then, that terrorists may ask in a negotiation? Most urgently, if they are themselves at risk, they demand safe departure. Guarantees of safe de-parture may require the taking or provision of hostages, even the volunteer provision of hostages whose lives are pledged against the guarantee of safe departure. But except when some act of capture has itself accomplished all that was in-tended, as may have been the case at the Munich Olympic Games, safe departure is only ancillary; occupying a hospital and demanding safe departure is merely an adventure.

Money may be demanded. Domestic American aircraft hi-jackers succeeded in collecting ransom, but terrorist demands for money are likely to be against rich individuals or busi-nesses rather than governments. As we know from books and movies, receiving money in exchange for a kidnap victim without giving away one's location or identity can require great ingenuity. Safe return of the victim must be guaranteed and safe receipt of the ransom must be arranged. An ingenious solution may be to demand that money be paid to an innocent third party. The captors of Patty Hearst demanded $4 million but did not have to give their mailing address or pick up a brown envelope because they demanded that the $4 million be in food distributed free to poor people in San Francisco.

Weapons may be demanded. We learned from Irangate that even a government pledged never to negotiate with terrorists might yield to weapons extortion. As far as I can tell, the prisoners for whom the weapons were to be exchanged were kidnapped originally by people whom we would describe as international terrorists. Had they held the prisoners and offered to return them only when Iran received the military equipment, it would indeed have been international terrorism within my definition, with a third-party beneficiary of the ransom. But the negotiating was apparently with government officials in Iran, which makes it an interesting species of terrorism that probably should be excluded from the definition I am working with.

I earlier mentioned the possibility that terrorism may take forms in which both the perpetrators and the respondent governments share an interest in secrecy. The Iranian arms deal dramatically suggests that the negotiation with terrorists that takes place underground can be hugely important compared with anything we get to observe.

Release of terrorists or other prisoners by the governments that incarcerated them is and has been an important possibility. Publication of a communiqué or a list of grievances has often been the apparent object of hijackings. (Interestingly, inmates in American prisons who capture guards and occupy buildings typically demand the equivalent of safe departure – amnesty – and appropriate publication of grievances.)

An ambitious demand would be withdrawal of some authority or military presence from some territory. The withdrawal of American marines from Lebanon was not, as far as we know, a demand attached to a terrorist threat. It could have been. And if the marines had been more vulnerable to piecemeal slaughter than they were, rather than blowing up the entire barracks terrorists might have picked them off one by one until continued occupation became meaningless and unbearable. Essentially, killing some with the evident threat of continued killing until withdrawal took place would have been negotiation of the kind we are interested in. Separatist movements frequently demand, in effect, withdrawal of the authority and the instruments of power of either the occupying government or the national government from which independence is desired. Northern Ireland may be an example.

Negotiation could be political and diplomatic. That would clearly have been the case with the terrorism against Israeli civilians if we interpreted that terrorism as having been significant enough to count as part of the pressure on Israel to negotiate. Perhaps the intent, at least of the individual perpetrators if not of those who backed them, was to bring Israel to its knees diplomatically and politically. The apparent fact that it did no such thing merely means that as a bargaining weapon terrorism simply was not up to the job.

I cannot think of an instance in which terrorists demanded the resignation or removal of some official. That would be a likely objective of domestic terrorists and undoubtedly has been in Central and South America. And resignation could easily be the objective of terrorists trying to bring about political change under an occupying power, when the goal was not independence but amelioration.

Finally, hostages, in the original literal sense of the term, could be demanded as security against a pledge. If terrorists have captured or occupied something that they cannot hold long enough to come to terms in a negotiation, they may extend their extortionate power by trading a short-lived asset for something longer-lived. If they have occupied the control tower at rush hour in bad weather and planes are stacking up and there is no way that a president or a governor can respond to their demands before disaster happens, they may ask for people they can take with them as they evacuate the control tower, so that they retain their bargaining advantage in a more stable form. And it is possible that the response demanded of the target government is some protracted activity, or some permanent cessation or abstinence from an activity, and once the terrorists lose their bargaining power they have no leverage over the government's behavior. In that case doing as Julius Caesar did, taking a permanent supply of hostages to assure good behavior, might appeal to them. That may be essentially what was being done in Teheran during the last year of the Carter administration.

There is always the possibility that my estimate of the inconsequential nature of the accomplishments of international political terrorism could be abruptly reversed by some dramatic terrorist seizure of control over some catastrophic happening. In an earlier article I looked at the possibility of terrorist use of a nuclear weapon, and although I could not then and do not now rule out the possibility, I do not find it credible that the kinds of groups that we have thought of as terrorist during the past quarter century are the kinds that would likely get their hands on a usable nuclear weapon. We might, however, imagine an assault on a nuclear power reactor somewhere, and occupation of it with the potential to cause a meltdown. Considering that Three Mile Island and Chernobyl were brought about by people who were trying *not* to let any such thing happen, it must take no great skill and sophistication to engage in the kind of sabotage that would threaten local nuclear disaster. Attempts to rescue the reactor from terrorists who had captured it might be deterred just as attempts to rescue passengers from hijacked aircraft are deterred, namely, by the threat to do something irreversible that would lead to meltdown.

This is probably not something that terrorists would threaten to initiate; threatening in advance would undoubtedly lead to enhanced security measures that would make the capture impossible. So the threat would take the form of overcoming any security guards and other resistant employees and gaining possession of the facility. One can imagine that this might be done in secret so that only high government officials knew what was going on and negotiations remained secret, with no public alarm and outcry, but the likelihood of that possibility must be small. So let's assume that the news is out instantly; civil defense and national guard are invoked, possibly with evacuation plans ordered into effect. If evacuation is not officially ordered, there will nevertheless be prudential departure of people downwind for whom immediate travel to safer parts is possible, such evacuation probably being observed and commented on and leading to alarming feedback, possibly panic. Following the fiftieth anniversary of Orson Welles's *War of the Worlds*, a few years years after Chernobyl, this scenario is fairly plausible.

So if the terrorists want to cause confusion and panic, disruption, economic loss, and a demonstration of civilian vulnerability to catastrophic harm at the hands of a comparatively small terrorist squad, success does not seem out of reach.

There are a number of countries that might be vulnerable to this kind of terrorist threat. I shall assume that the object would be not merely to cause meltdown but to achieve something by exercising the threat, with safe exit one of the terms of the bargain, and probably with operating control of the reactor left in the hands of the original employees or, if the original employees had to be immobilized in the takeover, with new operators admitted to keep the reactor safe.

If the reactor were shut down it would continue to be vulnerable to meltdown for a few days; if it continued operating, nothing but the food supply would limit how long the terrorists might maintain possession and control.

What could they demand? They would have to demand some irreversible act. Once the crisis was over and they had been safely escorted out of the country, no government would feel bound by anything it yielded under that kind of duress, and probably no legal obligation or even a treaty signed under such duress would stand up for a moment. Demand diplomatic recognition of the PLO, and relations will be broken immediately afterward. Demand continuous supply of weapons and materials to some favorite nation or

31

organization, and the commitment will be instantly broken once the reactor is evacuated. Perhaps if the terrorists could set up housekeeping permanently in the reactor they could hold a continuing threat, but given enough time the CIA or the FBI should find tactics or technologies by which to recapture the plant before the terrorists could produce irreversible damage.

I shall keep thinking about it, because there may be terrorists somewhere who are thinking about it, and wondering what they could accomplish by acquiring such a threat. And it may be an advantage to anticipate what they might think they could accomplish.

But at this point it strikes me as an exceedingly unwieldy weapon, one that perhaps terrorizes too much to be useful.

NOTES

This essay was written for the Conference on Violence, Terrorism, and Justice, Bowling Green State University, November 18–20, 1988.

1   Thomas C. Schelling, Preface to *Arm and Influence* (New Haven, Conn.: Yale University Press, 1966), p. v.

Chapter 3

Violent demonstrations

Annette C. Baier

When is life-endangering violence to be morally excused, or at least forgiven? Does the fact that what endangers human life is someone's violent or coercive action (hijacking a plane, shooting a hostage, planting a bomb in a store) rather than more insidious death dealing (laying down slow-acting poisonous wastes, using life-endangering chemicals in marketed meat and wine, selling human blood that one knows is infected with a fatal disease) make the death dealing more unforgivable? Does the fact that the killing is done openly, with an eye to publicity, make it better or worse than killings done quietly and with attempted secrecy? Does the fact that the terrorist typically identifies, to her victim and the world, the group on whose behalf she claims to act, that she, as member of that group, claims responsibility for what is done, make her better or worse than the intelligence agent who tries to kill anonymously or pseudonymously? The person we call a terrorist typically does her violence in the public eye, and lets the public know whose cause she believes to justify her violence. She is a violent demonstrator.

Like most demonstrators, she need not expect the demonstration itself to bring about the changes she demands. A successful demonstration gets attention. In one way or another it will be hoped that this attention will prepare the ground for other methods, either violent ones like assassination of leaders and armed uprising, or nonviolent ones like negotiation, legislation, or elections. Even when the hope of eventual success is faint, when the demonstrator acts more

33

in despair than in hope, it will still seem important that attention be given to the cause. That it may be a losing cause, even that the demonstration itself may reasonably be thought to hasten its defeat, need not affect the perceived need to get attention, to proclaim one's cause. The terrorist's heroes can be not just the Stern Gang, who graduated into statesmen, leading "just wars," but also Samson, who brought down the temple on himself, as well as on some of his enemies and on some innocent victims. The terrorist puts on a spectacular show of self-righteous violence, which may or may not be believed to be helping her toward her group's victory. It is no new phenomenon that people grow more reckless of the lives of others as their own lives become more wretched, insecure, and intolerable. People who have been dispossessed, degraded, humiliated, but whose spirit has not been broken, understandably want to proclaim their grievances, whether or not they expect the proclamation to advance their cause. They expect the demonstration to get their cause noticed, to put it in the limelight. The ones we call terrorists are ones who have succeeded in that goal, and used violence to succeed in it.

Not all of those who resort to the self-righteous violence we call terrorism have been driven to it by the extreme mistreatment of the group for whom they claim to act. Some simply choose terrorism to advance a political goal, such as the collapse of capitalism, although they have suffered no significant maltreatment by capitalists. Some are driven to terrorism by extreme mistreatment in the home rather than in the *polis*. Terrorists typically are angry or resentful about something, but it is very easy to deceive oneself about what it is that angers one. Some self-appointed demonstrators for groups with real grievances are avocational terrorists, who are looking for dramatic and violent outlets for what are essentially private angers. We could call them terrorists for emotional hire. Doris Lessing, in *The Good Terrorist*, gives a convincing portrayal of such angry, pathetic, and dangerous people, flailing about for a social cause to which to attach their variously caused private rage. "Women are angry," she has them, both men and women, proclaim as they court violent confrontation with authorities, "angry about Ireland, sexism, Trident...."[1] As long as the display of outrage is thrilling, attention-getting and fulfilling, their "cause" will have served its purpose for them. But other terrorists, Palestinians for example, do have in the cause they proclaim the genuine cause of their anger. (This is not to say that they may not also have private angers that get expression in their terrorist activities.) We need to distinguish, then, between what we could call the self-deceived and the honest terrorist. In what follows I shall be speaking of the honest terrorist.

We do, and we should, give the terrorist our attention. To attempt to frustrate the terrorist's "demonstration" by denying it media coverage, as once proposed by John O'Sullivan of the London *Times*, would be to censor information that surely the public has a right to get. We should get all the information we can about the incidence of violence, wherever it occurs (in the home, in the school, in airports) so that we can know what we are risking in all these places. We have a right to available information about the incidence of deaths from drunken driving and other causes of highway fatalities, to figures about the safety record of different airlines, about the likelihood of disease in different parts of the world we might travel to, or settle in, and so on. As we should make public what information there is about AIDS, so we should make public the available information about the incidence, in different parts of the world, of any political violence that affects civilians, and so of terrorism, whether self-deceived or honest. The terrorist wants our attention and, in fairness to us, should get it.

It is not plausible to suppose that the terrorist aims to deter people from congregating in or traveling to the parts of the world where she has acted, or from traveling on the airlines whose planes have been hijacked. We do not aid and abet her if, like the University of Maryland Institute for Philosophy and Public Policy, we publish figures about where the terrorist attacks have occurred, and about the occupations of the main victims.[2] (These figures would encourage supercautious persons to take their vacations in the USSR and Eastern bloc, the safest places.) The terrorist, at least if the politically motivated hijacker is a typical terrorist, may be ill named. She need not want to terrorize us from traveling, or from crossing paths with her. For what good would that do her? Nor surely does the politically motivated hijacker expect to produce such generalized gibbering terror in the hearts of either her audience or her target population[3] that their normal activities grind to a halt. The terrorist wants the shocked attention of her audience population, but scarcely expects by occasional bombing to bring about the internal collapse of even the target population's economy or morale. Those who, like the Red Army Faction in Germany, did however unrealistically aim at such an internal collapse were as much assassins and guerrilla fighters as they were terrorists. Internal terrorism, terrorism by nationals against the regime of their own nation, is often indistinguishable from guerrilla war, and often involves carefully targeted rather than randomly chosen victims. I am distinguishing terrorism from assassination, taking terrorism to involve the random murder of members of the target population. Such randomness, however, is compatible with some selectivity – the IRA will try to give its own supporters some assurance that they will not be among its victims. Random selection of victims within a group taken to exclude the terrorist's own supporters is the terrorist's chosen method. Terrorism can be state terrorism, or revolutionary terrorism. The forms it takes when it is state terrorism are particularly evil, since then the murder of randomly chosen victims can be on a grand scale, and can serve its purpose of stilling active opposition to the regime even when the policy is secret and unannounced, but widely known, like the disappearances in Argentina. I shall not address the special features and special evils of state terrorism,[4] but shall restrict myself to protest or revolutionary terrorism.

Assassins, by their carefully targeted killing, may expect to discourage persons from assuming public leadership of certain parties, corporations, and regimes, or to avert the granting of diplomatic status to certain regimes, but the ter-

rorist can scarcely expect to deter tourism or even membership in the military forces of the target or audience
populations. The average tourist's or military person's
chances of being a victim of terrorism are not high enough
for that, and if the terrorist wanted to raise them, she would
shoot most people on a hijacked plane or ship, not one or
two. In the past I myself suggested that the terrorist is an
expert at discerning trust relationships that the rest of us so
take for granted that we can in good times ignore them, trust
in fellow passengers, in fellow shoppers, and so on.[5] Michael
Walzer says of terrorism that "its purpose is to destroy the
morale of a nation or class, or under cut its solidarity; its
method is the random murder of innocent people."[6] As already indicated, I am following Walzer's usage in using the
label "terrorist" for those whose method is the random murder of people in some sense "innocent." But if the terrorist's
purpose really were to destroy the morale of a nation or class,
by terror, then the efficient terrorist would increase her killings as much as is compatible with randomness. She would
shoot all except a random one or two of the passengers on
the hijacked plane or ship. If terrorists do have both the
purpose and the method Walzer ascribes to them, then there
have been pathetically few efficient (nonstate) terrorists. Our
usual principle of charity requires that we look for purposes
that allow us to make actual politically motivated random
killings come out a little more "rational" than most would
be on Walzer's construal of them, even if we agree with
Thomas Schelling that, given the limits of what a rational
terrorist can expect to achieve, the actual dangers posed or
likely to be posed to human life by nonstate terrorism are
relatively insignificant.[7] The terrorist, unlike the assassin,
kills fairly randomly. Unlike the subversive or the revolutionary guerrilla fighter, she does not kill in the expectation
of thereby destroying the enemy or its regime. If the terrorist,
like the subversive, aimed at the total collapse of the target
community, then the more "enemy" deaths the better, even
at a cost in their randomness, and such killing could be done
anonymously, without proclamations. The subversive can

destroy efficiently and anonymously, postponing self-identification and bids for recognition until she takes over in the graveyard and ruins she has wrought. But the one we label the terrorist typically does make proclamations as she kills – indeed, she often seems to include her target population within her audience population. She typically does identify her group to her victims, and to the rest of us. Like the soldier she has standard-bearers, at least in the rear. Indeed, she is a sort of standard-bearer, using her victims as a sort of living flare.

The terrorist who is a violent demonstrator risks her own life to raise her standard in the chosen place. Like standard-bearers in old-fashioned armies, she risks her life as well as that of others to make her symbolic and declaratory point. The military standard-bearer wears a uniform, and hopes not to kill those not wearing enemy uniforms, whereas the terrorist's victims can be in mufti. Nor does the terrorist's own clothing, like the soldier's, proclaim a bloody profession. She may don some identificatory scarf once she has taken over the plane, and she may pick as her first victim any who *are* wearing the military uniform of the target community, but even her military victims will be used as scapegoats, as sacrificial victims. Their deaths will not, by their killers, be seen as an intended increase in "enemy dead," a boost to the "body count." The killing is not incipient genocide, nor done to diminish the number of the opposing forces, to remove living obstacles to the terrorist's cause. Hijackers have been very sparing in their use of lethal force. Terrorist bomb throwers are restrained, not saturation bombers.

What perceived point is there to the killing that violent demonstrators do? I have already given the answer – it is a sure way to get attention. As a child may kick or bite whoever is handy, when its more civil demands go unheeded or ignored, so desperate peoples may seize and sometimes kill the easiest suitable "others" to attack, when they see no hope of recognition by less lethal means. Their action is not irrational, or rather it is irrational only if they have reason to believe that they will get our serious attention more readily by other means. They may also be regarded as irrational if there is reason for them to think that their cause is not necessarily doomed, but that terrorist activity will doom it. Have they reason to think that terrorist activity can defeat an otherwise live cause?

"No deals with terrorists" is not a policy that has been, or is likely to be, consistently carried out. History gives us evidence of plenty of deals with those once regarded as guilty of terrorism. In Palestine, and in Ireland, the British made deals. The Home Rule eventually granted to the Irish was admittedly not a deal with the leaders of the unsuccessful 1916 Easter uprising, all of whom had been executed as criminals, but was made with the new leaders who took over as their successors, working in the same way for the same cause. Shows of bloody force, in which there were nonparticipant victims, and displays of the determination to get, bear, and use arms without the permission of the ruling power, did not disqualify the Irish from eventual recognition and success, any more than it disqualified those earlier rebels against British rule, the American colonies. The prospects for the success of a cause do not seem in the past to have been reduced by resort to unauthorized force, by violent demonstrations that cost some innocents their lives. Or are we to reserve the term "terrorism" for the violent tactics of only the ultimately unsuccessful defiers of powers that claimed authority over them?

The terrorist who is a violent demonstrator need not be acting irrationally. Is she acting immorally? Do we, and should we, condemn all violent demonstrations? Should we excuse violence when it is a last resort to draw attention to a claimed serious wrong? Should we require that the excusable violent demonstrator have some sort of mandate from the aggrieved group for whom she claims to act, some sort of license to kill on its behalf? How like must that be to the sort of license that soldiers and other state-licensed killers have for their lethal activities? Do states ever license violent demonstrations, as distinct from more "utilitarian" killings?

Our attitudes to killing and to violent assault seem, in their

39

baroque complexities, more amenable to historical and psychological explanation than to rational systematization and justification. Like the criminal law on assault and murder, our moral attitudes to violence and killing are bearers of the vestiges of attitudes acquired during our long history as a species who has lived by its lethal skills, and sometimes propagated by rape and sexual violence. As meat eaters we had to be able to take life, and some of us had to be very good at killing. As patriarchs, half of us became very good at throwing our weight around, violently if we felt like it, to get our way. The important moral questions have always been "Whom or what may I assault and kill and when and how may I kill it?" not "May I assault and kill?" Boundaries between human and nonhuman, between fetus and infant, between one's own domestics and someone else's, between ingroup and outgroup, ally and enemy, military and civilian, attackers and defenders, guilty and innocent, authorities and protesters against authority, or aspirants to authority, have to be learned, and learning them, rather than just learning the Sixth Commandment (out of context), constitutes our education in the morality of violence.

Most of us have had the luxury of learning these lessons as members of fairly well recognized groups with recognized territories and authority structures, groups whose rights to defend their official values from perceived attack, or to express their expansionist colonial values, have been taken for granted. As a New Zealander I, for example, learned early that it had been all right for the British troops protecting my colonialist ancestors to kill Maoris who resisted British rule, that their killing was in a different moral category from the "barbaric" assaults of Maori tribesmen on white settlements, let alone their occasional ritual eating of an uninvited missionary or intruding British official. I later learned that it was all right for my uncles and older schoolfellows to set sail around the world to Europe, in order to kill Germans and Italians; or to kill their Japanese Pacific neighbors, since we were at war with these peoples and God was on our side. Still later, once peace was made, I learned that it was retrospectively all right for at least some of those Germans, Italians, and Japanese to have killed my fellow countrymen, since they were soldiers whose job was to kill, and they may have been nonculpably ignorant of the fact that God was not on their side. As I went on to study history, it became clear that the answer to the question who it is who makes someone a soldier, or other member of a military force, rather than a mere murderer or barbaric warrior, the question who gives out the licenses to kill, could not simply be "authorities of a nation-state." For I learned that that was a relatively recent and for a long time a largely European phenomenon. Many who with some sort of blessing took up arms against fellow persons got their licenses and their blessings from different authorities, Crusaders from popes and Holy Roman Emperors, or like Joan of Arc from their own visions. (As I write this in Vienna, a current production of Schiller's *Virgin of Orleans* portrays her as a saintly terrorist.) And once there *were* nation-states, there were those like Cromwell who conscientiously rejected their anointed sovereigns and tried armed takeovers; there were Washingtons who raised armies against the colonial powers that were. Both the wars before the emergence of the nation-state and all the civil and religious wars within and across such states show the moral learner that the authority to raise an army, to issue licenses to kill, is highly contested, jealously competed for, and fiercely fought for. Indeed, much of the organized and deliberate killing of human persons by human persons has occurred in contests for the monopoly of the right to raise armies and authorize that and other uses of deadly force.

Wars of religion, between Jews and Egyptians, Jews and Babylonians, Jews and Romans, Christians and Muslims, Catholics and Protestants, also remind the moral learner of the fact that we are not merely a contentious and violence-prone species, but also a religion-prone one, and that in the center of several of our religions we have enshrined the idea of sacrificial killing. Not merely are we willing to kill heretics and heathen to defend the true religion, but the god we worship is a god who requires sacrificial killing. The idea of scapegoats, and of spotless human sacrifices, is all too familiar. We have been taught that higher beings can not merely allow but require that innocent life be taken. We learned about sacrificial violence when we learned that the god in whose image we are made would attend better to us and our prayers if living things were sacrificed on his altars, that he could demand the sacrifice of Isaac by his father, and would later sacrifice his own son. We in these traditions cannot pretend to be unfamiliar with expressive and demonstrative killing. We and our gods deliberately kill not just our competitors and our threatening enemies, but selected innocents. As long as our gods are bloodthirsty gods, the sacrifice of selected innocents in bloody spectaculars can be counted on to get our respectful attention.

As Christianity limits the sacrificial killing to one actual death, safely in the past, and merely symbolically or sacramentally rebreaks (and eats) that one body all down the *annos Domini*, and so civilizes the human sacrifice, simultaneously restricting and ramifying it, so to a lesser degree does the terrorist violent demonstrator both ration and broadcast her violence. Like the Christian god, the terrorist is willing to include self-sacrifice along with the sacrifice of suitable others (the crucified has to be both a person of the god to whom the sacrifice is made, and a man, one of those needing redemption). This offensive parallel should not be pushed too far. (Like the terrorist, I intend to offend.) Just far enough to remind us that, while learning about domestic expressive violence in the patriarchal home, many of us also simultaneously learned of solemn ritual violence in our various patriarchal Sabbath and Sunday schools. We should not have incomprehension of how the terrorist can do what he or she does (and now is the time to switch from "she" to "he").

The violent demonstrator's tactic is to command the attention of the more powerful, to display the seriousness of his purpose and the ruthlessness of his will to those who he has good reason to think respect strength of will, and so are unlikely to ignore the particular violent show he is putting on, his sacrifice of the more or less innocent. He counts on his show of deadly force to command our fearful respect, if also our revulsion. He wants not love but recognition for his will, for his right and his group's right to join the other violent assertors of will in the world.

Demonstrations of force that at least risk death to non-demonstrators are something that established powers are addicted to. In the summer of 1988 I happened to witness on July 14 the low fly over the Seine in Paris (its banks and bridges crowded), a flypast by antiquated bombers and fighters as well as by the latest of death machines. And I watched on television the deaths of the spectators at the Ramstein U.S. air show, an inadvertently fiery demonstration of killing power, that did not prevent the Farnborough air show shortly after Ramstein. Violent demonstrations of lethal force are an accepted part of normal life. The fact that so many attend these shows itself bears witness to the truth of the assumption that a show of deadly force commands awed attention.

The pilots at Ramstein did not deliberately kill themselves or their innocent victims (guilty only of wanting to gawk at the death machines doing their stuff, so only averagely guilty). The terrorist deliberately pulls the trigger or throws his bomb. He not merely risks killing innocent people, but like the performer of a ritual human sacrifice he aims at just that. This puts his category of violent demonstration into a special class, different from the Ramstein killings. It is, we might say, high-minded demonstrative murder rather than high-minded demonstration-caused manslaughter. The morality of violence we have learned puts great weight on the distinction between intended and merely foreseen killing, or calculated risk of killing, or rather puts great weight on it outside battlefields. (Are military airfields permanent battlefields?) For the gunner on the battlefield, let alone the bayonet wielder, is not just foreseeing the enemy's death as a side effect of the main intended effect (victory); he is intending to kill. The doctrine of double effect, even from its devotees, gets a battlefield supplement in the doctrine of the just war. Only as long as we can draw clear lines round some fields, marked "fields for battles between duly licensed and uniformed intentional killers," and other areas marked "enemy cities, suitable for strategic but not saturation bombing, for foreseen but not intended killing of civilians," or "hospitals, suitable for knowing but unintended lettings die, or acts of choosing whom to save," or "our own cities, suitable for knowing pollution," or "seas, great for dumping wastes, since who knows where that poisoned bread on the waters will turn, or when it will return?" can we continue to polish and treasure the distinction between deliberate targeted killing and knowing but deplored (and sometimes less focused) killing. The bomber and the dumper are usually spared the sight of their victims, the knowledge of who exactly they have killed and how they died. The reproaches of such faceless victims will be easier to ignore than those of face-to-face killings, especially when the killers are themselves not barefaced, but mere masks for higher authorities who gave the orders.

These fine moral distinctions learned off the battlefield will not and should not make much sense to those who can discern no lines between battle- and other fields, whose right to raise armies is contested, whose license to authorize violence is not recognized by the club of licensors, whose flags do not get treated as national flags, nor given the respect granted to papal banners or Red Cross or United Nations banners. The terrorist's group is an outlaw group, since refused inlaw status, and for outlaws all fields are battlefields.

Does that mean that the doctrine of the just war should extend beyond the fields where recognized armies clash, should be generalized into a doctrine of just violence? As most armies have claimed their war to be a just war, so assassins and terrorists will reliably see their violence as just or righteous violence. The rules of fair violent play will not be much use if they and their interpretation are as highly contested as the prizes for which the violent fights go on. We need, I suppose, a new Grotius, or a new Hobbes, or both, to work out the rights of violence and nonviolence for all groups at odds with other groups, both groups who are not yet nations and ones who are recognized nations, rights for the dispossessed and wretched of the earth as well as its successful proprietors, for minorities as well as majorities, for the refugees, the desperate and homeless, as well as the conspicuous consumers of tourism and pleasure cruises. The first step toward getting articles of peace for our condition is to eschew righteous indignation, to put ourselves into the shoes of those driven to terrorism, to entertain the thought that there but for the lottery of history (and perhaps but for saving cowardice) go we.

There indeed, or very close, went our revered rebel ancestors and many of our heroes and heroines. Do we on reflection prefer that people meekly tolerate oppression, dispossession, nonrecognition, indignity; that they sit quietly in the shadows watching others flaunt their status, exercise their privileges, put on their shows of lethal force, give each other medals for their violent killing? Do we sincerely admire the gentleness that the less powerful have in the past shown the more violent powerful? Do we, for example, admire the docility with which women for so long put up not just with domination, but with male violence in and out of the home? Or do we agree with Nietzsche that only stupidity or smallness of soul can explain why women did not use their allowed rule of the kitchen to poison more of the masters? Do we admire good, faithful, obedient slaves more than rebellious slaves? Do we encourage protest of perceived wrong?

Protest, demonstration, rebellion, always involve some dangers to human life, and these endangering protests regularly seem unjustified to many of those who have not suffered the injustices or inhumanities that are protested, and to those with limited imaginations or limited sympathy. The real risks entailed by demonstrations against perceived wrongs must be tolerated, if we think self-respect a primary good, and if we respect each other's sense of justice and injustice, right and wrong. Nonviolent demonstration is not easily prevented from escalating into violent demonstration, and that can lead to rebellion. In accepting nonviolent protest, we accept at least the risk of violent protest.

We will of course deplore violent demonstrations, prefer nonviolent to violent protest, hope for nonbloody revolutions. We will try to teach our children that strength and violence are not the same; we will hope that their protests, when they must strongly protest, will not involve human sacrifice. But if we fail, we should not be very surprised. Nonviolence is not easy, and our own practice has not been so exemplary. (Nor does violent self-denunciation necessarily reduce the amount of violence.)

The terrorist presents us with a distorted mirror of ourselves, so makes us exceedingly uncomfortable. He provokes extreme reactions in us – shrill outrage even from the descendants and heirs of successfully violent rebels, or vicarious thrills at such dramatic self-assertion, or self-punitive guilt, a masochistic welcoming of the small shiver of apprehension that the terrorist's next victim could be oneself.

Were one actually to become such a victim, should moral indignation then mix with the terror one would undoubtedly feel? That, surely, depends entirely on the particular terrorists, the predicament of the group for which they claim to act, and the basis of that claim. It seems to me in principle no harder, no less appropriate, to forgive the terrorist who sincerely believes that he has no other effective way to make his seriously aggrieved group's case, that he and they have nothing to lose, than to forgive the glory-seeking or super-security-seeking national leader in whose war one dies as a conscript, or as a civilian victim. And it should be easier to forgive one's terrorist killer, with his high-minded motives, his drive to right wrongs, than to forgive the profit seeker from whose poisonous wastes one dies. When what the terrorist strikes for is basic recognition, rather than glory, for redress of perceived injustice, rather than for profit or special privileges, his motives at least will not be unforgivable.

Can and should one forgive him his methods? He "uses" his victim to draw attention to his cause. Is this deplorable method harder to forgive than the methods of generals using human cannon fodder to ensure that they win their battles and get their medals or memorial statues, or scientists who withhold their discoveries of AIDS blood tests or remedies until they secure their best chances of a Nobel Prize? All these people sacrifice the life ("use" the death) of those who die because of their decisions. The terrorist is just more open than most about his willingness to use his fellows, when he judges that his goal justifies it. None of these methods are humane ones; all of them are ruthless ones. The terrorist's methods (if he is, say, a Palestinian) are not clearly more inhumane than the treatment he and his people have suffered. We can and should deplore the inhumanity of his methods, but until our own humanity is a bit more exemplary, and our intolerance of inhumanity closer to home a bit more active, we will not be in a very good position to feel a special righteous indignation at the terrorist's methods.

The fact that the terrorist and his people have suffered inhumane treatment does not justify, but might excuse, his inhumanity. If he, a representative of the victims of exclusion, wrong, or inhumanity, acts inhumanely toward members of groups who he thinks could have prevented, or ended or lessened, the wrongs his people have suffered, then he acts as a sort of blunt instrument of retributive justice, a blind avenger meting out the sort of inhumane and violent punishment that punitive authorities regularly administer.[8] Parents who strike children who are disrespectful, church authorities who burned witches (disrespect indeed, to set up as rival magicians), schoolmasters beating insolent pupils, all respond to perceived wrongs with violence. For them to claim plausibly to be punishing, they must have made some effort to separate the innocent from the guilty, but the effort need not have been very successful. We are quite familiar with the custom of penalizing a whole school class for misdemeanors of unidentified individuals within it, punishing all one's children for the mess or noise or other nuisance made by some of them, one knows not whom. Nor do all punishers have official licenses to punish. Parents' licenses to use violence seem to be as self-issued as the terrorists' – official authorities may step in to limit parents' rights to treat their offending children with violence, and so officially concede some limited punitive rights, but the prima facie right of parents to punish, to be prosecutor, judge, jury, and executioner, is often taken as a natural one. Should we grant each other the right to anger-blinded vigilante justice against our own relatively powerless children, or pupils, but not against strangers who are citizens of offending alien powers? And if so, why?

The terrorist's violence is not a straightforward case of punitive reactive violence (albeit inaccurately aimed), any more than it is ritual human sacrifice (of the not quite spotless), or a small ruthless war, or a case of a dangerous display of deadly force that ends in accidental death. I have likened aspects of the terrorist's violence to these violent acts closer to home (and more amenable to our control) to help us understand it, not to classify and judge it. The categories of the "innocent," of "deserved punishment," "soldier," "declared war," "permitted display," all presuppose a mutually accepted authority structure, and that is precisely what the terrorist and his victims and critics lack. Michael Walzer accuses those who produce apologies for terrorism, and in so doing point to parallels with tolerated violence, of "erasing all moral distinctions along with the men and women who painfully worked them out."[9] He accuses them (us) of a "malign forgetfulness" of the historical past. I do not think that we need be guilty of those dreadful impieties to question whether our hard-won deontological moral categories do help us much in trying to understand terrorism, and respond appropriately to it. We can stick to our old authoritarian moral notions, which work well enough within an established authority structure of the sort within which they were forged, but when we extend them into the no-man's-land beyond it, they will not get agreed application; they will at best half fit. I have tried to place the terrorist's violence in our familiar violent landscape without fully assimilating it to the forms to which I have likened it. I have done this multiple likening as a preventive against too hasty or too self-righteous judgment, but I have not done much to guide any judgment, or to describe helpful and appropriate reaction. It is fairly easy and trite to say that the clearer it is that the terrorist group's case is *not* being listened to in decision making affecting it, and that less violent ways to get attention have been tried in vain, the more excuse has the terrorist got; that his case is the better the more plausible his claim to represent his group's sense of injustice or wrong, not just his own; that the more limited, the less indiscriminate, his violence, the less outrage will we feel for his inhumanity. Those are not exciting conclusions.

If we are to respond to terrorism not just with trite moral comparisons of what is better, what worse, but in a way that we could reasonably believe might eventually end terrorism, then we have to hope for a new Grotius-cum-Hobbes, who will codify neither the old honor code of the generals, soldiers, and diplomats of established powers, nor maxims of enlightened self-interest for single persons, but rather the arts of successful peacemaking, of forming workable plans for lasting peace, ways of removing the group grievances that threaten peace. Such a theorist would need to have a benign memory for any small periods of peace and incidents of successful peacemaking, or satisfactory settling of grievances, that our historical past and recent past contain. From these we might get some useful potions against continued violence, some recipes for stable and contagious nonviolence. Impressive efforts at peacemaking, and success at truce making, went on in the summer of 1988 when the general secretary of the United Nations, Javier Perez de Cuellar, showed exemplary willingness to talk with aggrieved troublemakers, and to do so with exemplary patience, indefatigability, and a gentle, nonmoralizing dignity. Grotius wrote: "The person who has authority to begin a war is the only one to whom the right of making peace can properly belong, according to the general maxim that everyone is best judge in the management of his own affairs."[10] This general maxim needs to be balanced with the equally plausible "No man is a fit arbitrator in his own cause," Hobbes's seventeenth law of nature. Grotius thought that it followed from his maxim that only kings and sovereign powers can make war and peace.

But when wars or at least fighting and violence are conducted because of disagreement or contest over sovereignty and authority, then less definite conclusions follow even from the dubious maxim that everyone is best judge in her own affairs. When there no longer are restricted battlefields, when violence spreads to and threatens all of us, then the "making of peace" (in both senses) becomes our affair, and we will do best to treat as war any organized violence that it becomes our affair to try to end. We should not be too picky about which violence is "war," and who has a right to start or end it. Successful peacemakers will not reserve their ear for the duly appointed representatives of recognized nation-states, with previously agreed rights to declare war and make peace. The first thing we must do to deter terrorism is to provide aggrieved groups a better way than violence to get our serious attention. Successful peacemakers will realize that the contentious and touchy groups for whom a civilized plan of coexistence needs to be found have not merely different degrees of power, but also different degrees of past recognition, shifting boundaries, varying customs of appointing representatives, of giving and transferring authority, of raising armies, conducting wars, selecting scapegoats.

The evil of terrorism is the more general evil of violence, when this is resorted to by representatives of disaffected groups and used on randomly selected representatives of resented other groups. To mitigate this evil we would need both to provide a less deadly and equally effective or more effective way for resentful groups to express their grievances, and also to find a way to reduce the general human tendency to choose violent methods over less violent ones, even when violence does not increase effectiveness. Only when we have nonviolent people, and people who have effective nonviolent ways open to them to express their grievances, can we expect to be rid of terrorists. Denouncing terrorism not only is pointless, but can be counted on to increase the anger and resentment that terrorism expresses.

When, to get guidance on the morality of killing, of violence and nonviolence, we turn to the great moral philosophers, we find some striking silences. Aristotle fails to integrate his passing ruling out of murder[11] into his more general account of virtuous and vicious conduct. Does the wrong of murder lie in the fact that the murderer breaks the law, that he takes more than his fair share of liberty, so fails to display justice in the narrow sense? Which sorts of assault and killing will a wise lawmaker forbid? Aristotle is silent on these questions. Perhaps they admit of no general answer, or perhaps prohibition is not the best way to go about limiting violence, reducing the extent of killing.

Hobbes, whose laws of nature have as their point the ending of the general war that shortens human lives, does not include "Do not kill" among his moral commandments. Hobbes realized the pointlessness of trying to lessen violence by commandments forbidding it, and the difficulty of formulating any rule concerning it that rational persons could accept. His rules, his theorems of peace, enjoin us to seek peace when there is hope of it, to lay down our "right of nature" when others do, to keep covenants, show gratitude, and cultivate a number of peaceable dispositions, to give peacemakers safe-conduct, to submit to arbitration, and so on, but there are no rules forbidding either lying or violent assault with whatever powers we have left once we have laid down our right to all. Hobbes sees the point of *all* of his "true moral philosophy" to be to lessen violence, and sees also that this must be done indirectly, not by laws telling us how violent we can be when and to whom.

Hume, who follows Hobbes in thinking that only a successful cooperative scheme can avoid the threats presented by the opposition of human passions, is virtually silent on the wrongs of assault and murder. His artifices redirect avidity, which he takes to be the only motive to violence that calls for (or perhaps that admits of) social redirection. Envy and revenge, he writes, may lead us to ravish goods from each other, but they operate only at intervals, and against particular superiors or enemies.[12] They do not therefore pose the general threat to society that avidity does, and Hume offers no remedies for such threats as they do pose. Of course

51

magistrates, once invented, will presumably make criminal many forms of assault besides assault in the course of robbery, but in doing that they will not be enforcing any of those basic moral constraints that Hume calls "the laws of nature." We no more find a Humean equivalent of the Sixth Commandment than we find a Hobbesian equivalent.

Did Hume think we must just tolerate the violence against persons that envy and revenge can motivate, that we must content ourselves with redirecting avidity, so avoiding avidity-motivated violence against persons? He regards envy as "an irregular appetite for evil,"[13] dependent on the workings of the principle of comparison that blocks the normal human sympathy that would lead us to rejoice in, rather than envy, another's joy. Envy is in principle avoidable, on Hume's version of our psychology, and even where it is not avoided, it can surely be got to take a nonviolent form, once social artifices direct natural ambition into nonviolent and socially constructive competition. But revenge is harder to avoid, contain, or transform, if Hume is right about our nature. He lists resentment and the desire to punish our enemies as primitive human appetites, as inevitable (in appropriate conditions) as lust. Resentment and vengefulness are passions we have and ones we sympathize with in others; they are regular rather than irregular human appetites for evil.

Resentment of "enemies" leads naturally to violence, and Hume's version of morality seems to contain no remedy for it. Gentleness is a "natural" virtue, but we will not expect it to be shown toward those whom we resent as enemies, as ones who have harmed us, or humiliated us. The best remedy for resentment will be removal of its grounds, not control of its expression. I think Hume saw that justice, and other "artificial" virtues dependent on rational cooperation, are powerless against deeply resentment-rooted violence, and this is the terrorist's sort.

Hume distinguishes from angry avenging the sort of calm deterrent punishment for lawbreaking that good magistrates will administer.[14] Those who see themselves to have been injured will want to avenge themselves, and will be prone to violence. Humean magistrates take over the punishment for injustice that otherwise victims might violently inflict, for that is one of their main functions. But since, as we have seen, it does not count as a Humean "injustice" to inflict bodily injury (unless that is incident to violent seizure) and since any revenge violence seems also ungoverned by any "laws of nature," then whatever magistrates do to try to retain their claimed monopoly of violent methods will count as something other than just "the execution of *justice*," if justice is restricted to what Hume calls the "three fundamental laws of nature, *that of stability, of possession, of its transference by consent, and of the performance of promises.*"[15] The magisterial function that will be exercised when laws forbidding civilian violence are enforced will be either (if what I have just argued is disputed) the *decision* as well as the execution of justice or that cooperation beyond what justice requires that Hume thinks magistrates rightly enforce when they arrange for public works such as harbor building and the disciplining of armies. Hume does not, like Locke, include one's person as part of one's property, and his laws of justice protect property rather than persons. If wrongs against the person are to be recognized by the magistrate, it will be by those optional extra cooperative schemes that Humean magistrates have discretionary powers to institute. Civilian violence against persons will take on the same sort of status as tax fraud or draft evasion – a matter of breach of a local magistrate's requirement, not break of a law of nature.

Magistrates will find terrorists guilty of criminal violence, if they succeed in arresting them, and if their violence occurs in the territory they govern. But since the terrorists in question rarely recognize the authority of these magistrates, they will have no cause to feel moral guilt for their violence on the grounds of its disobedience. It *is*, from the magistrates' point of view, uncivil disobedience, but terrorists will understandably not care about that.

The protest that stems from resentment of injury and indignity has a vital positive role to play in Hume's moral theory, a role that can perhaps guide us in our response to terrorist resentful violence. This is the role of drawing the attention of cooperators and mutual recognizers of rights to those who are dangerously excluded from their schemes of right-recognition and right-protection. In the *Enquiry concerning the Principles of Morals* Hume adds a significant new circumstance of justice, namely that all those with power to make their resentment felt be included in the cooperative scheme. If, say, women are excluded, despite their power to make their resentment felt, the scheme will be unstable, so not serve its purpose of increasing security. If women are excluded, or some race, class, or language group, then they must be expected to demonstrate their power to make resentment felt, in order to force entry to vital cooperative schemes from which they are excluded.

Exclusion is not itself an "injustice" to those excluded, as Hume construes justice and injustice. It may be not just inhumanity but also "inequity," and it certainly will be *folly* if the excluded do feel resentment and have power to make it felt. I think that we should understand terrorist violence as a demonstration of this power to make resentment at exclusion felt. The proper response to it is not counterviolence nor moral condemnation, but inclusion, at least in cooperative schemes we set up in order to listen to one another's grievances. The best response is removal of the grounds for the deepest resentment. That is no easy task, of course, but it is a task we make unduly hard for ourselves if we fetter ourselves with moral indignation. Hume, like Hobbes, realizes the pointlessness of moral injunctions to avoid violence against persons, especially when these are directed by those with security of life and with recognized rights against desperate, insecure persons, resentful at exclusion from our various clubs that "under shelter of our governors," allow us but not them to "taste at ease the sweets of society and mutual assistance."[16] The Humean "natural" moral virtues of humanity, equity, and plain prudence should prompt us to try to respond to the terrorism that demonstrates the power to make resentment of exclusion felt, by appropriately conciliatory moves.

As recent events show, one of the toughest challenges to the peacemaker is to find a mutually face-saving way whereby former group terrorists can, even when it suits their former opponents, be accepted into the community of states and candidate-states. Since this community includes some states reasonably seen as just as guilty of state terrorism as the group is of group terrorism, it seems unrealistic to demand a unilateral renunciation (and so admission) of terrorism by those hoping to make the transition from group to state. We need to find the right tactful incantations for the ceremony of graduation into legitimacy. History surely here can give us useful suggestions for tried-and-true face-saving diplomatic phrases.

A new Grotius might be content to postpone, perhaps indefinitely, the list of fixed rights of violence and nonviolence (for individuals and for more or less organized groups), to turn from the deontological moral language of patriarchs to a gentler moral language. She might try to codify the methods and discover the characteristics of successful peacemakers, of ones who might have a hope of bringing about at least long truces in all our wars and incipient wars within and across national boundaries – class wars, battles of the sexes, confrontations between militant religions, between hostile ethnic groups, between capitalists and socialists, pacifists and armed defenders, group terrorists and state terrorists, terrorists and "legitimate" forces. A list of the functional virtues of peacemakers would be a start, to be supplemented by a list of the functional virtues of the parents of peaceable but spirited children, the functional virtues of the successful teachers of nonviolent self-assertion to adolescents, the virtues of adult electors who choose strong, gentle leaders and reject macho bullies.

Lists of productive virtues, alas, do not tell us how to bring those virtues into being, any more than lists of rights tell us how to ensure respect for them. Lists of gentleness-producing and gentleness-preserving virtues would, however, at least purport to embody some empirical, history-tested knowledge about what does and does not produce violence, and gentleness. We would then be committed to trying to find out not just what produces gentleness in individual persons, but also what produces the parental ability to preserve and replicate gentleness, what produces the ability of some teachers and some leaders to strengthen and inspire it, and so on. For this empirical knowledge to come about, or increase, we will need, to ground our moral philosophy, benign remembering of historical examples, as well as social science and psychology. We will need information about what institutional structures, and chains of authority, have relatively good or bad records, records of nurturing gentle or violent people. We will need to study variants of the family and modes of governance there; to study schools and governance in them; to study different political parties and what sort of people flourish within their differing structures. We will be aiming at discovering the roots and soil of violence and gentleness, and at pooling what knowledge we have.

You have had from me mainly proclamations and protests, not worked-out plans or programs. You may also have had a little more verbal violence, and more moralizing or meta-moralizing, than one might hope for from a believer in a nonjudgmental morality, in a morality of nonviolence, in the ideal of a moral philosophy that would contain tested recipes for producing and sustaining gentleness, tested antidotes to violence. I have perhaps shown myself more hypothetically willing to forgive the terrorist than to forgive many of those who wax morally indignant about the terrorist. A completed moral philosophy of the kind I would hope we might get would contain recipes against the rage to moralize and to meta-moralize, as well as against other forms of violence. But I do not yet know those recipes. In the absence of moral knowledge, we all, like the terrorist, tend sometimes to fall back on homeopathic cures, and so on mere violence as a response to violence.

NOTES

I have been helped in revising this essay by comments made by many persons during the discussion at the Bowling Green conference, and by critical comments from Kurt Baier, Wulf Schiefenhövel, Christian Vogel, and anonymous readers for Cambridge University Press. By no means all their criticisms have been met in this revision. The topic is one that I find of daunting difficulty, and I expect to continue revising my views about it.

1   Doris Lessing, *The Good Terrorist* (London: Grafton, 1986), p. 146.
2   See *QQ: Report from the Institute for Philosophy and Public Policy* (University of Maryland) 7, no. 4 (Fall 1987).
3   Here I adopt the useful terminology used by Terrence Moore in his Ph.D. dissertation, "The Nature and Evaluation of Terrorism" (University of Pittsburgh, 1987).
4   For a discussion of terrorism by powerful states, see Noam Chomsky, *The Culture of Terrorism* (Boston: South End, 1988).
5   Annette C. Baier, "Trust and Antitrust," *Ethics* 96 (January 1986): 234.
6   Michael Walzer, *Just and Unjust Wars* (New York: Basic, 1977), p. 197.
7   See the contribution of Thomas Schelling to this volume.
8   If the deaths of the Pan Am passengers in the plane that was destroyed over Lockerbie, Scotland, in December 1988 were seen by the perpetrators as revenge for the deaths of the Iranians in the airbus mistakenly downed earlier by U.S. forces in the Persian Gulf, then this act of "terrorism" would be more like a punitive strike than is the typical terrorist act, as I have construed that. A kind of crude justice, one airbus full of innocents for another, would then have been involved.
9   Walzer, *Just and Unjust Wars*, p. 204.
10 Hugo Grotius, *Rights of War and Peace*, trans. A. C. Campbell (Westport, Conn.: Hyperion, 1979), chap. 20, sec. 2.
11 Aristotle, *Nicomachean Ethics*, trans. M. Ostwald (Indianapolis: Bobbs-Merrill, 1962), bk. 2, chap. 6, 1108a, 9–14.
12 David Hume, *A Treatise of Human Nature*, ed. L. A. Selby-Bigge and P. H. Nidditch (Oxford: Clarendon, 1978), pp. 487, 491.

13 Ibid., p. 376.
14 Ibid., pp. 410–11.
15 Ibid., p. 526.
16 Ibid., p. 538.

Chapter 4

Terrorism, rights, and political goals

VIRGINIA HELD

USAGE AND DEFINITION

An examination of usage is particularly unhelpful in deciding what terrorism is and whether it can be justified. Usage characteristically applies the term to violent acts performed by those of whose positions and goals the speaker disapproves, and fails to apply it to similar acts by those with whose positions and goals the speaker identifies. And usage much more frequently applies the term to those who threaten established conditions and governments than to those using similar kinds of violence to uphold them. There is a tendency to equate terrorism with the *illegal* use of violence, but of course the questions who can decide what is illegal and on what grounds are often the questions at issue.

Careful analysis can make progress in clarifying the issues surrounding terrorism and in providing a basis for recommended interpretations. We can recognize that drawing distinctions is difficult, and yet agree with Jenny Teichman when she says that "seemingly ambiguous kinds of violence can . . . be distinguished from one another." She suggests that "*revolutions* can be differentiated into the peaceful and the violent. . . . *Civil protest*, similarly, can be either peaceful or violent. *Guerrilla war* is simply small war. Whether *riots* are crimes or acts of war depends on the intention and the degree of organization of the rioters."[1] Whether or not one shares her ways of drawing these distinctions, one can agree with her conclusion that such distinctions are possible, and

59

important to make. "Terrorism" also, she believes, can be defined, despite being, in her view, "the most ambiguous concept in the list."[2]

Much recent philosophical discussion of the term "terrorism" provides sufficient clarification, and demands sufficient consistency, to make persuasive the view that terrorism is not committed only by those opposed to governments and their policies. "Terrorism" must be understood in such a way that states and governments, even friendly or democratic ones, can be held to engage in acts of terrorism, along with those who challenge the authority of and disrupt the order of such states and governments. But an adequate definition has not yet emerged in the philosophical literature.

In an article called "On Terrorism," R. M. Hare does not even attempt a definition.[3] Carl Wellman offers a wide definition: Terrorism is, he suggests, "the use or attempted use of terror as a means of coercion."[4] But this definition is so wide that, as he admits, it includes nonviolent acts that almost no one else would count as terrorism. Wellman writes: "I often engage in nonviolent terrorism myself, for I often threaten to flunk any student who hands in his paper after the due date. Anyone who doubts that my acts are genuine instances of the coercive use of terror is invited to observe . . . the panic in my classroom when I issue my ultimatum."[5] Although this particular ultimatum may well be an instance of the coercive use of terror, it does not, for most of us, constitute an instance of terrorism, and the very conclusion that on Wellman's definition it would have to is enough to suggest to most of us, I think, that his definition is unsatisfactory. Violence seems an inherent characteristic of terrorism, so that Wellman's "nonviolent terrorism" seems to be something else than terrorism.

Further, not only does Wellman's definition allow in too many acts that are implausibly counted as terroristic, it excludes others that should not be ruled out. For Wellman, "coercion, actual or attempted, is of the essence of terrorism."[6] He does not mean only that terrorism is itself coercive, as is violence, for instance, but also that it is a means to further coercion, as when terrorism against airline passengers is used by a given group to coerce a government into releasing certain prisoners.

To build the goal of coercion into the definition of terrorism seems mistaken. Among other difficulties it excludes what can be considered acts of expressive violence, as some acts can best be deemed. Some terrorism seems to be an expression of frustration more than a means to anything else, or it can have a variety of goals. Terrorism can be intended as punishment, or to call attention to a problem even when no ability to coerce anyone further is expected. If we say that punishment is coercive, we can still recognize that though one may have to coerce people in order to punish them, the two are not identical. Sometimes wrongdoers accept punishment voluntarily, and coercion is often not punitive, so the two terms have different meanings. In the case of terrorism whose purpose is to call attention to a problem, we can again agree that the violence involved is itself coercive, but not that it is for the purpose of further coercion. If an effort to coerce people to pay attention, to force them against their wills to heed the terrorists' message, is to count as an intention to coerce further, we would have to consider a wide range of free speech to be means of coercion, as orators and demonstrators speak and gather in public places in ways that others cannot easily avoid hearing and seeing. If forcing one's message on persons would be considered a means of coercion, rather than merely itself coercive, then so much free speech (and especially so much advertising) would be a means of coercion that the meaning of this term would lose its reasonable limits. Of course terrorism is not merely free expression, but what else it is is not necessarily a means of further coercion. The violence it involves is coercive, but it can be for the purpose of gaining a hearing for a view rather than for the further purpose of, say, extracting a concession from opponents.

One of the most useful recent discussions is that of C. A. J. Coady, though I shall disagree with his definition. He defines terrorism as "the tactic or policy of engaging in terrorist acts," and a terrorist act as "a political act, ordinarily committed by an organized group, which involves the intentional killing or other severe harming of non-combatants or the threat of the same."[7] The crucial component of terrorism, in his view, is intentionally targeting noncombatants. He does not think the intent to spread fear should be part of the definition of terrorism. Among his reasons is that, instead of spreading fear and demoralization, the terrorist act may give rise to defiance and a strengthening of resolve.

In response to this latter point, one can point out that although of course a terrorist act may fail to have the intended consequence of spreading fear, any act can fail to produce its intended effect. The issue is whether an intention to produce fear as well as damage should or should not be built into the definition of terrorism. Unless we do build it in, we may lack a suitable way to distinguish terrorism from other forms of violence. Coady says that if we refer in the definition to an intention to spread fear there will be problems in ascertaining what the intention behind the act was; I do not think such problems will be much more severe in the case of assessing the intention to promote fear than in the case of assessing the intention to harm noncombatants, and this latter intention Coady does build into his definition.

A difficulty with confining terrorism to those acts involving the intentional harming of noncombatants is that doing so will exclude actions that seem among leading candidates for inclusion, such as the blowing up of the marine barracks in Lebanon in October 1983. In this attack, in which a truck with explosives was driven into a marine compound and exploded, 241 persons, most of them American marines, were killed.[8] The drivers of the truck were killed as well. The marines were clearly the intended target. On Coady's definition, this act could not be an act of terrorism, and this seems arbitrary.

Additionally, on Coady's definition, such intentional harming of noncombatants by a resistance group as would be caused by, say, a long-term campaign of refusing to fill service roles like that of hospital orderly for an oppressing group would count as terrorism, and this seems implausible. Coady cites the work of the Brazilian revolutionary Carlos Marighela, whose handbook of urban guerrilla warfare, published in 1969, has been influential in Latin America with revolutionary groups. Marighela confines his discussion of terrorism to only two paragraphs; he means by it "the use of bomb attacks."[9] Though this is certainly insufficient as a definition, it contains a core that should not be dismissed, and that core does not seem consistent with a claim that an intention to harm noncombatants is a necessary component of terrorism.

Another difficulty here is the drawing of the distinction between combatant and noncombatant itself. Coady calls various claims that one cannot distinguish the two "absurd and obscene," but he unfairly loads his own descriptions of the distinctions.[10] He is surely right that inconsistency often operates here, as those who deny that the distinction can be made among their enemies in wartime fail to accept a comparable argument made by revolutionaries about *their* enemies. Still, the distinction is considerably more difficult to make, on both sides, than Coady admits, for reasons that will be touched on later.

Another useful discussion is Jenny Teichman's, though again, I shall reject the definition offered in it. Teichman concludes that terrorism is not a matter of scale, that it is a style or method of government or of warfare, and that it can be carried out by states as well as groups. "Terrorism," she writes, partially agreeing with Coady, "essentially means any method of war which consists in intentionally attacking those who ought not to be attacked."[11] She shows why those who ought not to be attacked may not be equivalent to the category of noncombatant, or that of innocent, as usually understood. Those responsible for the start and the conduct, as well as the carrying out, of violence are not the improper targets the definition rests on. The major difficulty with her definition, in addition to the excessive focus on some version of the combatant/noncombatant distinction, is that it builds a moral judgment into the definition, an approach that I and many others reject for reasons to be discussed later.

My own view of what terrorism is remains, then, close to what it was in an article I published in 1984, in which I focused on violence, rather than on terrorism itself.[12] I there defended the view that violence is "action, usually sudden, predictably and coercively inflicting injury upon or damage harming a person."[13] And I saw terrorism as a form of violence to achieve political goals where creating fear is usually high among the intended effects. For reasons similar to those subsequently argued by others, I limited violence and terrorism to harm to persons rather than to property; sometimes, though not always, one harms persons by harming their property, but the intention to harm persons must be present.

Judith Lichtenberg speculates on how terrorism *does* induce fear: Violence targeted at ordinary people makes ordinary people everywhere feel uneasy.[14] In the case of the attack on the marine barracks in Lebanon, the target was not ordinary people or noncombatants, but the aim to induce fear can also be present in such cases. The aim can be to induce fear among military personnel: Young American soldiers anywhere, and especially in the Middle East, can realize that the most expensive and sophisticated weaponry cannot protect them against the kind of attack that killed so many of their fellows.

I now think that we should probably not construe either the intention to spread fear or the intention to kill noncombatants as necessary for an act of political violence to be an act of terrorism. It does seem that both are often present, but not always. And there do not seem to be good reasons to make the latter a part of the definition while dismissing the former. Furthermore, there can be other motives. As Grant Wardlaw notes in his perceptive book on terrorism, "Whilst the primary effect is to create fear and alarm the objectives may be to gain concessions, obtain maximum publicity for a cause, provoke repression, break down social order, build morale in the movement or enforce obedience to it."[15]

I will not venture to suggest exactly what one or what combination of factors may be necessary to turn political violence into terrorism, but perhaps when either the intention to spread fear or the intention to harm noncombatants is primary, this is sufficient.

THE JUSTIFIABILITY OF TERRORISM

A second way in which usage and much popular and some academic discussion have been unhelpful in illuminating the topic of terrorism is that they have frequently built a judgment of immorality or nonjustifiability into the definition of terrorism, making it impossible even to question whether given acts of terrorism might be justified. Thus news reports frequently equate terrorism with evildoing. Politicians often use the term as an automatic term of abuse. The British author Paul Wilkinson, in a book on terrorism, characterizes terrorists as persons who "sacrifice *all* moral and humanitarian considerations for the sake of some political end."[16] Benjamin Netanyahu goes even further. He describes the terrorist as representing "a new breed of man which takes humanity back to prehistoric times, to the times when morality was not yet born. Divested of any moral principle, he has no moral sense, no moral controls, and is therefore capable of committing any crime, like a killing machine, without shame or remorse."[17] The philosopher Burton Leiser says that, by definition, terrorists consider themselves above law and morality; he equates terrorism with piracy and considers it invariably criminal and immoral.[18] Finally, Michael Walzer begins a discussion of terrorism with the assumption that "every act of terrorism is a wrongful act."[19]

Arguments against building unjustifiability into the definition of terrorism can follow similar arguments against holding that violence is by definition morally wrong. Not only is violence often used in ways usually accepted, as in upholding law, but one can easily cite examples of violence used against governmental authority where it makes sense to ask whether such uses of violence were morally wrong or not. The 1944 bomb plot against Hitler is one obvious candidate. Even if examples of possibly justifiable acts of terrorism, as distinct from other forms of violence, are for many persons harder to acknowledge, we should still be able to *consider* the justifiability of terrorist acts. We should be able to treat such questions as open, and this requires that we not imagine them to be answerable merely by appealing to a definition.

Many of those who use "terrorist" as a term of denunciation apply it, as noted before, to their opponents and refuse to apply it to the acts of their own government, or of governments of which they approve, even when such governmental action is as clearly violent, intended to spread fear, or expectably productive of the killing of noncombatants.[20] But one cannot effectively criticize the terrorism of those Third World revolutionaries who consider various terrorist acts to be admirable[21] unless one also criticizes the terrorist acts of campaigns of counterterrorism carried out by one's government and the governments of states one considers "friendly."[22] What to consider "original offense" and what "retaliation" is of course a matter of political judgment. Many of those engaged in acts considered terroristic by existing governments consider themselves to be retaliating against such unjustified and violent acts by those governments themselves as "reprisal raids" that predictably kill civilians.

In a balanced discussion of forms of violence, the philosopher Robert Holmes concludes that terrorism per se is morally no worse than many conventionally accepted forms of violence. Ordinary warfare often uses terror as a tactic, and we should remember that the terror bombings of Dresden, Hiroshima, and Nagasaki undoubtedly killed far more people than have been killed by all the terrorists, as conventionally so labeled, throughout the world in all of the years since.[23]

One can further argue, as does Richard Falk, that one cannot be sincerely or consistently opposed to terrorism unless one is also opposed to the "tactics of potential or actual warfare that rely on indiscriminate violence or that deliberately target civilians."[24] Since those who defend preparing for nuclear war are not willing to reject such tactics, their opposition to terrorism seems more propagandistic than honest. However, the mistake of selective application can be corrected, as we become accustomed to the term "state terrorism" and then reduce the bias so far manifest in usage concerning its application.

Some of those who define terrorism as the intentional harming of noncombatants conclude that therefore, either by definition or not, terrorism is always wrong.[25] Since we can rule out as inadequate the view that terrorism is by definition always wrong, let us consider only those cases where the judgment is not one of definition but independently arrived at. Then, is intentionally harming noncombatants always wrong, and terrorism always wrong because it involves this?

Let us consider some objections to the position that it is never justifiable to harm noncombatants. First let us take up the question of harming noncombatants in wartime, and focus on a recent example. Reports suggest that the Iran–Iraq war may have cost some 1 million dead, 1.7 million wounded, and more than 1.5 million refugees.[26] It is also suggested that Iran's decision to accept UN Resolution 598 calling for an end of the fighting was partly the result of a demoralization within Iran brought about by the Iraqi bombing of Iranian cities.[27]

Certainly, from a moral point of view, the war ought not to have been fought and other means to achieve this outcome should have been found. Iraq was at fault in starting the war and in violation of international law in its use of poison gas.[28] But once the war was under way, was violence used against noncombatants beyond the possibility of moral justification, if it did in fact hasten the cessation of violence? Since the Iraqi invasion of Kuwait on August 2, 1990, it has become commonplace to demonize the Iraqi leader Saddam Hussein, but it should be possible to evaluate specific actions.

An argument can be made that no absolute right of noncombatants to immunity from the violence suffered by combatants should be granted, especially when many of the combatants have been conscripted or misled into joining the armed forces. Recent reports indicate that many who serve in armies around the world are children. Iran's conscription age was lowered to thirteen, the Contra rebels in Nicaragua recruited boys as young as twelve, and these are not isolated examples. Some two hundred thousand members of the world's armies, according to a UN report, are youngsters. Sometimes they are forcibly rounded up; sometimes they are urged by parents "to enlist in armies to gain food, jobs or payments if the child dies in battle."[29] Such "combatants" hardly seem legitimate targets while the "civilians" who support the war in which they fight are exempt.

Now let us apply this objection to terrorism. Is violence that kills young persons whose economic circumstances made military service seem to be almost their only option very much more plausibly justifiable than violence attacking well-off shoppers in a mall, shoppers whose economic comfort is enjoyed at the expense of the young persons who risk their lives in order to eat and thereby defend the shoppers? It is hard to see here a deep moral distinction between combatant and noncombatant. If the combatant is a conscript, the distinction between combatant and "ordinary person" is often difficult to draw. And although one may certainly hold that any child is innocent, it is still not clear why the children of one group should be granted an absolute right of exemption from the risk of violence where no such right is granted to the children of an opposing group, *if* the violence is justified on other grounds. When the police use violence to apprehend a suspected criminal and an innocent child is killed in the cross fire, this is normally interpreted as an unfortunate tragedy, not a clear violation of the rights of the child. *If* an act of "unofficial violence" is otherwise justified and an innocent child is killed, it might, perhaps, be no more clearly a violation of the rights of the child. So we cannot conclude, it seems, that terrorism is necessarily always wrong even if the intention to harm noncombatants is always present.

This is not to suggest that we should simply abandon the distinction between combatant and noncombatant. It is certainly harder to justify harming noncombatants than it is to justify harming combatants, other things being equal, and we can try to combine this distinction with usefully drawn notions of "those responsible." But as Coady notes, "If a revolution is unjustified then any killing done in its name is unjustified whether of combatants or non-combatants."[30] And the same thing can be said of any repression of opponents of a regime. It is often more important to keep this in mind and to apply the judgments it provides than to rely on a distinction between otherwise legitimate and illegitimate targets.

Many of those who most bitterly denounce terrorism are entirely willing to sacrifice the innocent lives of hostages to uphold the principle that one should never negotiate with hostage takers.[31] They judge that in the long run fewer lives will be lost if one upholds this principle. But this risks harm to innocent hostages and may rest on justifications quite comparable to those of hostage takers, who are willing to risk harming innocent persons to bring about a political goal on the theory that in the long run, fewer lives overall will be lost if the goal is achieved than if intolerable oppression continues.

Judith Lichtenberg and the author of the report on terrorism in *QQ* suggest that we should refuse, in retaliating against terrorism, to sink to the tactics of the terrorist by risking the lives of the innocent.[32] But – though they do not draw this conclusion – such concern for the lives of the innocent might then indicate that we must be willing rather than unwilling to negotiate with terrorists. The argument is always that negotiating with terrorists now risks more loss of innocent life later, but of course the sincere defender of terrorism makes a parallel claim: that a risk to innocent life now will avoid the further loss of innocent life later that must be expected as a repressive regime continues its unjust and violent repression.

Most recent philosophical discussion avoids the mistake of making terrorism wrong by definition. Hare, Wellman, Coady, Holmes, and others agree that, as with violence, we ought to be able to consider whether terrorism can ever be justified. The question should be open, not ruled out by definition. But then, can terrorism be justifiable?

Burleigh Wilkins in a recent article argues that consequentialism provides weak defenses against terrorism.[33] To a consequentialist, terrorism would have to be justifiable if, on balance, it brings about better consequences than its alternatives. And though such consequentialists considered by Wilkins as Hare and Kai Nielsen think that terrorism is hardly ever justified, their arguments depend on empirical estimates that terrorism almost always produces results that are worse on consequentialist grounds than their alternatives. Others find the empirical claims on which such judgments rest to be questionable.

Reading the historical record is notoriously difficult. Some think, with Walter Laqueur, that terrorist violence has tended to produce "violent repression and a polarization which precluded political progress," rather than the changes sought by the terrorists.[34] The German philosopher Albrecht Wellmer, building on the critical theory of Habermas, finds of the terrorism of the Red Army Faction in Germany in the 1970s that although it "reflects and brings to a head the pathologies of the system against which it is directed," its net effect has been reactionary: It has provided legitimation for political repression and a defamation of the entire left.[35]

Others think, with Charles Tilly and Lewis Coser, that violent protests have been an almost normal part of the Western political process, and that they have often contributed to progressive developments.[36] Concerning effectiveness, Richard Falk points out that the bombing of the marine barracks in Lebanon is considered by some to be one of the most successful uses of force "in the history of recent international relations, leading a very strong power to accede to the demands of a very weak opponent."[37] The marines had been deployed in Lebanon as the major expression of an American intent to support the Gemayel government and, as a result of the bombing, were removed from Lebanon by President Reagan.

It may be almost impossible to predict whether an act of terrorism will in fact have its intended effect of hastening some political goal sought by the terrorists, or whether it will in fact do the terrorists' cause more harm than good. But as Wilkins asks, "Is there something special about acts of violence which makes them different from other acts where judgments about their consequences are concerned? We frequently do many things where the outcome is uncertain."[38] If existing conditions are terrible, "they might prompt a prospective terrorist to reason that *any* chance of altering these states of affairs is worth the risk of failure and the near certainty of harm to property or persons that violence involves."[39]

Furthermore, states use violence and the threat of violence to uphold their laws, and some use terrorism. Many theorists still define the state in terms of its monopoly on the use of violence considered legitimate.[40] But if violence can be condemned on consequentialist grounds it can be condemned in unjustified state behavior as well as in the behavior of a state's opponents. On the other hand, if violence or terrorism by the state *can* be justified, it may be as impossible to predict its success as to predict the success of the violence or terrorism of its opponents. Where a legal system violates the human rights of those on whom it imposes its will, the violence or terrorism it uses to do so is surely no more justified than the violence or terrorism used against it, and quite possibly it is less so. When the security forces of an unjust regime kill or brutalize detainees to deter future opposition, or shoot at random into groups of demonstrators, they engage in acts of terrorism. Even relatively legitimate legal orders on occasion violate the human rights of some; the violence or terrorism they use to uphold their authority against those they thus mistreat is not more justified than the violence or terrorism of their opponents. In both cases, predictions of success may be impossible to make accurately, but in another sense impossible to escape making.

In my view we cannot adequately evaluate social action in consequentialist terms alone.[41] The framework of rights and obligations must also be applied, and in the case of terrorism it is certainly relevant to ask: Are rights being violated, and can this be justified?

Against Hare and others who evaluate terrorism by applying utilitarian calculations, Wellman usefully considers the place of rights in evaluating terrorism. Wellman says that "certain fundamental human rights, the rights to liberty, personal security, life, property, and respect, are typically violated by acts of terrorism."[42] This means not that terrorism can never be justified, but that an adequate moral appraisal will have to take violations of rights into account along with any calculation of benefits and harms produced.[43]

Coady rightfully notes the prevalent inconsistency in many discussions of terrorism. The use of violence directed at noncombatants is judged justifiable on utilitarian grounds if carried out by one's own or a friendly state, as in many evaluations of the justifiability of bombing raids in wartime in which civilians can be expected to be killed. At the same time, when revolutionaries and rebels use violence that harms noncombatants, such acts are judged on nonutilitarian grounds to be unjustifiable violations of prohibitions on how political goals are to be pursued. As Coady observes, consistency can be achieved either by applying utilitarian evaluations to both sides or by applying nonutilitarian evaluations to both sides. He favors the latter, and concludes that terrorism is "immoral wherever and whenever it is used or proposed."[44] My own suggestion is for a nonutilitarian comparison of rights violations. It could reach a different conclusion.

One of the most difficult problems for political philosophy is the problem of how to evaluate situations where human rights are not being respected. What are persons justified in doing to bring about such respect, and how should these actions be judged? Should "bringing about increased respect for human rights" be evaluated in consequentialist terms? But then how should this consequence be weighed against any violations of rights necessitated by the action to achieve this consequence? If we say that no violations of rights are justified, even in this case, this can become a disguised recipe for maintaining the status quo. If we permit violations, we risk undermining the moral worth of the very rights for which we are striving to achieve respect.

My suggestion is that we not yield to a merely consequentialist evaluation, but that we strive for reasonable comparative judgments. In a well-developed scheme of assured rights, rights should not be traded off against one another, or judged in comparative terms. We do not usefully speak of more of a right to vote or less of a right to vote, but of a right to vote. And we do not usefully try to determine whether a right to vote is more or is less important than a right to nondiscrimination in employment. Where rights conflict, we may order them by priorities or stringency; this, however, is not a matter of maximizing, but of seeking consistency. Some rights may be deemed to have priority over others, or to be more basic than others, but our aim is not to engage in trade-offs. We seek, rather, to arrive at a consistent scheme in which all the rights of all persons can be respected and none need be violated.

In a defective society, on the other hand, where rights are not in fact being respected, we should be able to make comparative judgments about which and whose rights violations are least justifiable. Is it more important, for instance, for blacks in South Africa to gain assurance of rights to personal safety than it is for white South Africans to continue to enjoy their property rights undisturbed? While blacks are denied respect for their most basic rights, it seems worse to continue these violations than to permit some comparable violations of the rights of whites participating in this denial.

Such an evaluation is not a consequentialist calculation, but it does allow us to compare rights violations. It requires us not to ignore the violations involved in maintaining an existing system, since of course charges of rights violation should not be applied only to those seeking change, while those upholding an existing system are exempt.

I shall use the expression "effective respect for rights" to mean that an existing legal system recognizes the rights in question and effectively upholds respect for them. Of course this does not mean that violations never occur; no legal system can secure perfect compliance with its norms. It means that violations are on the whole prevented by adequate education, socialization, and police protection, and that those who commit such violations are apprehended and dealt with to a sufficient degree to make respect for the rights in question generally high. There is no escape from the fact that effective respect for rights is a matter of degree, but it is quite possible to make an accurate empirical judgment that it is absent when a legal system does not even recognize a right in question as a legal right. When using the expression "effective respect for rights," we should specify the type of rights in question; this can be done.

Let's consider the case where a certain type of right is recognized as a human right by the major international documents and bodies establishing international norms concerning rights.[45] When such a right is not recognized as a legal right for a certain group of persons in a given legal system, there will clearly then be no effective respect for those rights of those persons in that legal system. An example would be the right to nondiscrimination on grounds of race recognized as a right in articles 2 and 7 of the Universal Declaration of Human Rights adopted by the General Assembly of the United Nations on December 10, 1948. Under the system of apartheid in South Africa, especially before the reforms initiated by the government of F. W. de Klerk, this right was not recognized for South Africa's black population. Hence very clearly there was for blacks in South Africa no effective respect for this right.

Frequently, rights are recognized as legal rights in a given legal system, but respect for them is not effective because law enforcement agencies are corrupt or prejudiced, or the government is inefficient or unfair in its administration, and so forth. The empirical judgment that effective respect for rights is absent may in such cases be difficult to make, and the lack of effective respect for rights can be as serious as in those cases where the right is not even recognized in the legal system. However, an advantage for purposes of moral theory in choosing a case of the latter kind, where a human right is being violated and is not even acknowledged to be a legal right, is that there can be so little dispute at the empirical level that effective respect for rights is absent. So let us consider this kind of case, imagining two groups, A and B, and supposing that the failure to recognize the human rights of the members of group B as legal rights in legal system L is advantageous to the members of group A, in this case, and disadvantageous to the members of group B, insofar as further benefits and burdens accrue to them in exercising or in failing to have the rights in question. However, the evaluation of comparative justifiability of rights violations will not be made on the basis of these further benefits or burdens.

Now let us ask whether it can be morally justifiable to violate some rights to achieve effective respect for other rights. First, an aside: If there are legal rights in conflict with human rights such that we can judge that these legal rights ought not to exist, then what appears to be a violation of them will probably not be morally unjustified. That kind of case will not present the moral difficulties I wish to consider.

The difficult case is when achieving effective respect for the fundamental human rights of the members of one group, which rights ought to be respected, requires the violation of the fundamental human rights of the members of another group, which are also rights that seemingly ought to be respected. If terrorism can ever be justified, it would seem to present this kind of problem. Where there is a lack of effective respect for the fundamental human rights of the members of one group, and *if* there is a reasonable likelihood that limited terrorism will significantly contribute to bringing about such effective respect, and no other effective means are available, can it be justifiable to violate the fundamental human rights of those who will suffer from such terrorism? Their rights to "life, liberty and security of person," as specified in article 3 of the Universal Declaration, are likely to be violated by any act of terrorism. Can this possibly be justified?

Let us specify two situations. In the first, S_1, the members of group A have a human right to x and they enjoy effective respect for this right in a given legal system, while the members of group B also have a human right to x, but suffer a lack of effective respect for this right. In situation S_2, in contrast, both the members of A and the members of B have a human right to x and they enjoy effective respect for that right. Obviously S_2 is a morally better situation than S_1. It is the process of getting from S_1 to S_2 that is in question.

We can, it seems to me, make a number of comparative judgments. First, nonviolent methods not involving violations of human rights would certainly be morally superior to violent methods, other things being equal. Defenders of nonviolence argue, often convincingly, that nonviolent pressures are in fact more successful, and lead to the loss of fewer lives than do violent methods, in moving societies from situations such as S_1 to situations such as S_2. It seems obvious that nonviolence is morally superior, if it can succeed.

I consider myself an advocate of nonviolence, by which I mean that one should recognize strong prima facie principles against the use of violence, and always place the burden of proof, in a justification, on the violent course of action if it is claimed that violence is needed to prevent or to correct serious wrongs or violations of rights. More important, one should continually champion what Sara Ruddick calls "a sturdy suspicion of violence."[46] One should strive to invent and to promote nonviolent forms of action, and should try one's best to make nonviolent approaches successful. It is often to this aim that our best efforts can be directed: to create and to sustain institutions that permit, encourage, and are responsive, when appropriate, to nonviolent forms of control or protest, thus deflecting tendencies on any side of a conflict to resort to violence.

To advocate nonviolence is to argue that there are prima facie principles against the use of violence to uphold a legal order as well as to challenge it. It may well be justifiable to intervene forcefully to prevent, say, violent assault, but force is not the same as violence, and violence usually need not and should not be used. The state has *many* means besides violence of upholding its legitimate authority and bringing about the effective respect of rights, and such nonviolent means should be developed far more than they have been. Strong prima facie arguments against violence should also apply to groups seeking changes in political and legal arrangements. Nonviolence is not acquiescence; it can be a stubborn refusal to cooperate with injustice and a determination to resist oppression, but to do so nonviolently. Feminists have added greatly to the case for nonviolence. As the author of one collection of essays writes: "Put into the feminist perspective, nonviolence is the merging of our uncompromising rage at the patriarchy's brutal destructiveness with a refusal to adopt its ways."[47]

In important ways, the terrorist often shares the worst macho aspects of his targets, mirroring the fascination with violence and the eroticization of force characteristic of the culture he attacks.[48] However, after this has been said, comparative judgments are still needed. If a judgment is made that in certain circumstances violence to uphold law is justifiable, cannot a judgment as plausibly be made that in certain other circumstances, violence to bring about respect for rights can be justifiable? And if violence can be justifiable, can terrorism, on occasion, be also? State terrorism to destroy legitimate movements of liberation exists. Can terrorism as a considered method to overcome oppression with as little loss of life as possible be, in contrast, less unjustifiable than state terrorism?

Gandhi is reported to have said that "it is best of all to resist oppression by nonviolent means," but also that "it is better to resist oppression by violent means than to submit."[49] In his book on Gandhi, William Borman asserts that Gandhi "repeatedly and explicitly makes statements preferring violence to cowardice."[50] Gandhi wrote that "my nonviolence does not admit of running away from danger and leaving dear ones unprotected. Between violence and cowardly flight, I can only prefer violence to cowardice."[51] This leaves us with the task of making comparative judgments concerning the use of violence by all those unwilling or unable to adopt "the summit of bravery," nonviolence, and preferring, on their various sides of any given conflict, violence to flight. It is these comparative judgments with which I am concerned in this essay.

Let us return to my example of trying to move from S_1 to S_2. If a judgment is made, especially in special circumstances, that nonviolence cannot succeed, but that terrorism will be effective in moving a society from S_1 to S_2, can engaging in terrorism be better than refraining from it? Given that it will involve a violation of human rights, can it be better to violate rights through terrorism than to avoid this violation?

Table 1 outlines the situations and the alternatives. Alternative 1 is to maintain S_1 and to refrain from terrorism; alternative 2 is to employ terrorism and to achieve S_2. Both alternatives involve rights violations. The questions are: Can they be compared and can either be found to be less unjustifiable?

It has often been pointed out, in assessing terrorism, that we can almost never accurately predict than an outcome such as S_2 will be achieved as a result of the terrorism in question. But I am trying to deal with the moral issues *given* certain empirical claims. And *if* the empirical judgment is responsibly made that the transition is likely to achieve S_2, which situation is clearly morally better than S_1, and that no other

Table 1

	Alternatives		Assumptions
Alternative 1:	{	S$_1$ maintained No terrorism (no T)	Change from S$_1$ to S$_2$ requires terrorism Members of both groups have rights not to be the victim of terrorism
Alternative 2:	{	Terrorism (T) S$_2$ achieved	Terrorism will violate such rights of members of A, will spare members of B

Considerations			For group A	For group B
Alternative 1:	{	S$_1$ {	Human right to x Effective respect for this right	Human right to x No effective respect for this right
		No T	No violations of rights vs. T	Violations of rights to x
Alternative 2:	{	T	Violations of rights vs. T	No violations of rights vs. T
		S$_2$ {	Human right to x Effective respect for this right	Human right to x Effective respect for this right

Notes: S$_1$ is the situation in which members of group A have a human right to x and enjoy effective respect for this right in the legal system, while members of group B have a human right to x but no effective respect for this right and hence suffer violations of it. S$_2$ is the situation in which members of both groups have a human right to x and enjoy effective respect for that right.

means can do so, can alternative 2 be better than alternative 1? Rights will be violated in either case. Are there any grounds on which the violations in alternative 2 are morally less unjustifiable than the violations in alternative 1?

It seems reasonable, I think, that on grounds of justice, it is better to equalize rights violations in a transition to bring an end to rights violations than it is to subject a given group that has already suffered extensive rights violations to continued such violations, if the degree of severity of the two violations is similar. And this is the major argument of this essay: If we must have rights violations, a more equitable distribution of such violations is better than a less equitable distribution.

If the severity of the violations is very dissimilar, then we might judge that the more serious violations are to be avoided in favor of the less serious, regardless of who is suffering them, although this judgment could perhaps be overridden if, for instance, many different though less serious violations were suffered by the members of group B, a situation that could outweigh a serious violation for the members of group A. But generally, there would be a prima facie judgment against serious violations, such as those of rights to life, to bring about respect for less serious rights, such as those to more equitable distributions of property above what is necessary for the satisfaction of basic needs.

The case on which I focus, however, involves serious violations among both groups. The human rights to personal safety of oppressed groups are, for instance, frequently violated. If a transition to a situation such as S_2 involves violations of the rights to personal safety of the oppressing groups, why would this violation be less unjustifiable than the other? Fairness would seem to recommend a sharing of the burden of rights violation, even if no element of punishment were appealed to. If punishment is considered, it would seem more appropriate for those who have benefited from the rights violations of the members of a given group to suffer, in a transition, any necessary rights violations than to allow the further rights violations of those who have already been subjected to them. But punishment need not be a factor in our assessment. We can conclude that though nonviolence is always better than violence, other things being equal, terrorism carried out by the group that has reason to believe it can only thus successfully decrease the disregard of rights where such disregard is prevalent is less morally unjustifiable than terrorism carried out by the group that maintains such disregard.

That justice itself often requires a concern for how rights violations are distributed seems clear. We can recognize that some distributions are unfair, and seek to make them less so. Consider the following: The right to personal security, of freedom from unlawful attack, can be fully recognized as a right in a given legal community, and yet of course some assaults will occur. The community's way of trying to assure respect for such rights is likely to include the deployment of police forces. But if almost all the police forces are deployed in high-income white neighborhoods and almost none in low-income black neighborhoods, so that the risk of assault for inhabitants of the latter is many times greater than the risk for inhabitants of the former, we can judge without great difficulty that the deployment is unfair. Or if we take any given level of effort to protect persons from assault, and if cuts in protection are then necessary for budgetary reasons, and the cuts are all made in areas already suffering the greatest threats of attack, we can judge that such cuts are being made unfairly.

The basis for such judgments must be a principle of justice with respect to the distribution of rights violations, or of risks of such violations.[52] This is the principle to which I am appealing in my argument concerning terrorism, and it seems clear that it is a relevant principle that we should not ignore.

What all this may show is that terrorism cannot necessarily be ruled out as unjustifiable on a rights-based analysis, any more than it can on a consequentialist one. Depending on the severity and extent of the rights violations in an existing situation, a transition involving a sharing of rights violations, if this and only this can be expected to lead to a situation in which rights are more adequately respected, may well be less morally unjustifiable than continued acceptance of ongoing rights violations.

NOTES

I am grateful to the many persons who made helpful comments when this article was presented in preliminary forms at a philosophy department program at the Graduate School of the City University of New York; at a conference of the Greater Philadelphia

Philosophy Consortium; at the Conference on Violence, Terrorism, and Justice at Bowling Green State University, November 18–20, 1988; at a conference on Law and the Legitimization of Violence at the University of Buffalo; and at presentations at Colgate University and at Hampshire College: especially to Joseph Raz, Hans Oberdiek, Annette Baier, Jonathan Glover, Peter Simpson, C. A. J. Coady, Thomas Headrick, Bart Gruzalski, and Huntington Terrell.

1 Jenny Teichman, *Pacifism and the Just War: A Study in Applied Philosophy* (Oxford: Blackwell, 1986), pp. 89–90.
2 Ibid., p. 90.
3 R. M. Hare, "On Terrorism," *Journal of Value Inquiry* 13, no. 4 (Winter 1979): 241–49.
4 Carl Wellman, "On Terrorism Itself," *Journal of Value Inquiry* 13, no. 4 (Winter 1979): 250.
5 Ibid., p. 252.
6 Ibid.
7 C. A. J. Coady, "The Morality of Terrorism," *Philosophy* 60 (January 1985): 52.
8 Department of State, *Patterns of Global Terrorism: 1984* (Washington, D.C.: Government Printing Office, 1985). The State Department classifies this attack as an act of terrorism.
9 Carlos Marighela, *Handbook of Urban Guerrilla Warfare,* in Marighela, *For the Liberation of Brazil,* trans. John Butt and Rosemary Sheed (Harmondsworth: Penguin, 1971), p. 89.
10 Coady, "The Morality of Terrorism," p. 59.
11 Teichman, *Pacificism and the Just War,* p. 96.
12 Virginia Held, "Violence, Terrorism, and Moral Inquiry," *Monist* 67, no. 4 (October 1984): 605–26.
13 Ibid., p. 606. For a useful discussion of the concept of violence, see C. A. J. Coady, "The Idea of Violence," *Journal of Applied Philosophy* 3 (1986): 3–19.
14 See *QQ: Report from the Institute for Philosophy and Public Policy* (University of Maryland) 7, no. 4 (Fall 1987): 2.
15 Grant Wardlaw, *Political Terrorism* (Cambridge: Cambridge University Press, 1982), pp. 41–41. See also Aziz Al-Azmeh, "The Middle East and Islam: A Ventriloqual Terrorism," *Third World Affairs* (1988): 23–34.
16 Paul Wilkinson, *Political Terrorism* (London: Macmillan, 1974), p. 17 (emphasis added). In a more recent book, Wilkinson does not build the moral judgment quite as directly into the defi-

nition. He defines political terrorism as "coercive intimidation. It is the systematic use of murder and destruction, and the threat of murder and destruction in order to terrorize individuals, groups, communities or governments into conceding to the terrorists' political demands" (Paul Wilkinson, *Terrorism and the Liberal State* [New York: New York University Press, 1986], p. 51). Then, on the basis of a useful though not unbiased survey of terrorist activity, he concludes that terrorism is "a moral crime, a crime against humanity" (p. 66).

17   Benjamin Netanyahu, ed., *Terrorism: How the West Can Win* (New York: Farrar, Straus and Giroux, 1986), pp. 29–30.

18   Burton Leiser, *Liberty, Justice, and Morality* (New York: Macmillan, 1979), chap. 13. Leiser considers the Palestinians to have provided the foremost examples of terrorist acts. Israeli "reprisals" and the children and noncombatants killed in them are not mentioned.

19   Michael Walzer, "Terrorism: A Critique of Excuses," in *Problems of International Justice: Philosophical Essays*, ed. Steven Luper-Foy (Boulder, Colo.: Westview, 1988), p. 238. His position is effectively criticized by Robert K. Fullinwider in "Understanding Terrorism," pp. 248–59, in the same volume.

20   The essays collected in Netanyahu, ed., *Terrorism*, provide many examples.

21   See John Dugard, "International Terrorism and the Just War," *Stanford Journal of International Studies* 12 (1976): 21–37.

22   On this point see especially Richard Falk, *Revolutionaries and Functionaries: The Dual Face of Terrorism* (New York: Dutton, 1988).

23   Robert L. Holmes, "Terrorism and Other Forms of Violence: A Moral Perspective" (Paper presented at the meeting of Concerned Philosophers for Peace, Dayton, Ohio, October 16, 1987).

24   Falk, *Revolutionaries and Functionaries*, p. 37.

25   See, e.g., Coady, "The Morality of Terrorism"; Leiser, *Liberty, Justice, and Morality*; and Jan Schreiber, *The Ultimate Weapon: Terrorists and World Order* (New York: Morrow, 1978).

26   Fox Butterfield, *New York Times*, July 25, 1988, p. A1.

27   Bernard Trainor, *New York Times*, July 19, 1988, p. A9.

28   Ibid.

29   *New York Times*, August, 7, 1988, p. A8.

30   Coady, "The Morality of Terrorism," p. 63.

31 See, e.g., Leiser, *Liberty, Justice, and Morality*, p. 395.

32 *QQ: Report from the Institute for Philosophy and Public Policy* 7:2.

33 Burleigh Wilkins, "Terrorism and Consequentialism," *Journal of Value Inquiry* 21, no. 2 (1987): 141–51.

34 Walter Laqueur, *The Age of Terrorism*, rev. and expanded ed. (Boston: Little, Brown, 1987).

35 Albrecht Wellmer, "Terrorism and the Critique of Society," in *Observations on "The Spiritual Situation of the Age": Contemporary German Perspectives*, ed. Jürgen Habermas, trans. A. Buchwalter (Cambridge, Mass.: MIT Press, 1984), p. 300.

36 See Charles Tilly, "Collective Violence in European Perspective," in *Violence in America: Historical and Comparative Perspectives*, ed. Hugh Davis Graham and Ted Robert Gurr (New York: Bantam, 1969) pp. 4–45; and Lewis A. Coser, "Some Social Functions of Violence," *Annals of the American Academy of Political and Social Science* 364 (March 1966): 8–18.

37 Falk, *Revolutionaries and Functionaries*, pp. 34–5.

38 Wilkins, "Terrorism and Consequentialism," p. 150.

39 Ibid.

40 The classic statement is Max Weber's: "The state is considered the sole source of the 'right' to use violence. . . . The state is a relation of men dominating men, a relation supported by means of legitimate (i.e. considered to be legitimate) violence" (*From Max Weber: Essays in Sociology*, trans. and ed., H. H. Gerth and C. Wright Mills [New York: Oxford University Press, 1958], p. 78).

41 See Virginia Held, *Rights and Goods: Justifying Social Action* (New York: Free Press/Macmillan, 1984; Chicago: University of Chicago Press, 1989).

42 Wellman, "On Terrorism Itself," p.258.

43 Ibid.

44 Coady, "The Morality of Terrorism," p. 58.

45 See, e.g., Committee on Foreign Affairs, comp., *Human Rights Documents* (Washington, D.C.: Government Printing Office, 1983). For discussion see, e.g., James W. Nickel, *Making Sense of Human Rights* (Berkeley: University of California Press, 1987).

46 Sara Ruddick, *Maternal Thinking: Toward a Politics of Peace* (Boston: Beacon, 1989), p. 138. See also *Rocking the Ship of State*, ed. Adrienne Harris and Ynestra King (Boulder, Colo.: Westview, 1989).

47 Pam McAllister, Introduction to *Reweaving the Web of Life: Fem-*

inism and Nonviolence, ed. Pam McAllister (Philadelphia: New Society, 1982), p. iii.

48   See, e.g., Robin Morgan, "The Demon Lover," *Ms.* 17, no. 9 (March 1989): 68–72.
49   Quoted in McAllister, Introduction, p. vi.
50   William Borman, *Gandhi and Non-Violence* (Albany: State University of New York Press, 1986), p. xiv.
51   Quoted in ibid., pp. 252–3.
52   This argument is in response to a comment by Rogers Albritton.

Chapter 5

The political significance of terrorism

LOREN E. LOMASKY

I

Q: Why do Japanese commandos fire Czech submachine guns at
    Puerto Rican passengers departing an Air France flight in an
    Israeli airport?
A: To strike at American imperialism.

It could be a bad riddle. Instead, it is one of the numerous
guises in which contemporary terrorism presents itself. Although the instance[1] may seem especially bizarre, it contains
many of the elements common to terrorism as practiced during the last third of the twentieth century: A party nursing
a grievance lashes out violently and unpredictably against
targets bearing only the most tenuous connection to the object of its animus. No melioration is brought about by the
strike, nor could any rationally have been anticipated by
those who organized the operation. After bodies are bagged
and reporters depart, political life proceeds much as before.

The subject of this essay is how to understand and evaluate
the phenomenon of terrorism. An immediate obstacle that
presents itself is that any purported definition of "terrorism"
will itself be laden with moral and political baggage. Most
individuals who employ violent means in their political activities prefer to speak of themselves as "urban guerrilla,"
"revolutionary," or some such. Their admirers and supporters generally comply. Thus the bromide "One person's
terrorist is another's freedom fighter." One need not accede

to the implied relativism to acknowledge the absence of firm and generally accepted criteria of application for "terrorism" and its cognates.

However much this absence may concern philosophers and other political taxonomists acting in their professional capacities, it has remarkably little echo in the *vox populi*. When TWA ticket counters or Israeli schoolchildren are sprayed with bullets, when newspaper heiresses are held hostage, Turkish diplomats murdered, or airliners destroyed in flight by plastic bomb explosions, the events are routinely and unproblematically understood by the media and their audience to be terroristic. That is not an unimportant datum. Every day innumerable people are victimized by violent as-sault or natural calamity. Only rarely do these events escape the back pages of local newspapers. Yet when destructive activity dons the garb we recognize as terrorism, it ascends to extraordinary prominence. Ordinary citizens and their leaders believe that terrorism is portentous, that it is *news*. That belief is self-justifying. Events that happen halfway around the world and that directly involve only a relatively small number of heretofore obscure people take over tele-vision screens everywhere. For some reason, terrorist assault seems to *matter*. Its perceived significance is, however, totally disproportionate to any measurable effect on mortality tables or the stability of political regimes. If analysts have reason to care about definition, it is because other people care about terrorism for quite different reasons.

II

Terrorism, as commonly understood, is a species of private enterprise, albeit not the sort that Better Business Bureaus usually commend. Although states may instigate or other-wise promote terrorist attacks, the actions are carried out by individuals who are not (or at least do not present themselves as being) functionaries of a governmental apparatus.[2] That may seem to prejudice the issue, to imply that there is some-thing especially odious about murders that do not enjoy the imprimatur of a sovereign member of the United Nations. No such ascription is intended. In a century that has witnessed Nazi genocide, Stalin's Gulag, and the immolation of Cambodia under the Khmer Rouge it would hardly seem to need mention that states are unsurpassed wielders of deadly force.

To withhold the term "terrorism" from the activities of secret police or armies is not to proffer excuse or mitigation. Rather, it is to return to the question why terrorism should seem to be so worthy of note. All the casualties of terrorism in the Middle East, arguably the most fertile ground for its exercise, represent only a minute fraction of the number of persons killed in the recently concluded Iran–Iraq war. Although statistics are, for obvious reasons, unavailable, one may surmise that there has not been so much as one day during the previous two decades, the decades during which "international terrorism" rose to great prominence, in which the number of homicides committed by free-lance operatives has equaled the number of killings carried out by governments. Why then should we concern ourselves with terrorist activity? Assessed from a detached consequentialist perspective, fixation on terrorism may appear an indulgence.

Terrorism so understood is not the official activity of governments, but it nonetheless possesses distinct political significance.[3] Unless an individual or group represents itself as acting in the service of a political ideal or program, it will not be deemed terrorist. Charles Manson was not engaged in terrorism,[4] but the Symbionese Liberation Army was. The Mafia may routinely excite terror in individuals to secure its ends, but that does not render it terrorist in the intended sense. Again, no special imputation of moral noxiousness is either asserted or denied.

Although terrorism is a political phenomenon, its targets need not enjoy any political prominence. By far the majority of terrorist raids are aimed at individuals who are distant from positions of power and authority: airline passengers, for example, or children at play. Only occasionally is the object of attack a military unit or a high official of the despised government. In part, no doubt, that is because these individuals tend to be less easy to reach and better able to respond in kind to the employment of deadly force than private citizens. However, it is by no means obvious or even likely that choice of target is entirely a matter of expediency. A systematic program of assault on civilians constitutes a *different* sort of political enterprise than does a campaign to assassinate diplomats or to ambush military patrols, and surely terrorists are not oblivious to that fact. For one thing, it is a program that will elicit a different degree of attention from those of us who are civilians and who recognize that, but for fortune, it is we who might have been fodder for the terrorists' ambitions. It is also, in ways that will subsequently be developed, uniquely expressive of a distinctive political ethos. Thus, it is reasonable to suspect that the occurrence of civilian casualties is not merely adventitious to the practice of terrorism, and that the oft-repeated characterization of terrorism as incorporating *indiscriminate* violence can be misleading. Terrorists' failure to discriminate in their choice of victim, or rather, their failure to discriminate on the basis of standard political categories, is itself a defining feature of their enterprise.

III

Can we say, then, that terrorism is to be described as the use or threat of violence by private parties, exercised primarily on other private parties, in order to bring about desired political objectives? This understanding is called into question by available data. One of the most palpable facts about terrorist activity is the vastness of the gulf between efficacy and aspiration. In almost none of the instances of terroristic activity that come to widespread attention is there any genuine likelihood that the assault on person or property will serve to advance the claimed political ends. It is inconceivable that the Lod airport attack might have overthrown or even deflected the aims of the governments of Israel, Japan, or the United States – and, crucially, the unlikelihood was eminently knowable at the time. The murder of a dozen athletes in Munich in 1972 did not even put a halt to the Olympic Games, let alone persuade the government of Israel to alter its policies in a direction favored by Black September. Indeed, if terrorism exerts any detectable effect on the platforms and activities of governments, it is to steel them in their resolve to resist and eliminate the aggressors. Those governments that show themselves lax in pursuing the counterattack on terrorism are typically replaced by more repressive regimes of firmer will. Surviving members of the Italian Red Brigades, Baader-Meinhof, Montoneros, Tupamaros, and other such groups will attest to that fact.[5]

Two attempts at explanation suggest themselves. First, one can hypothesize that terrorists typically act with the intention of bringing about those political ends to which they declare allegiance; they are, however, in the grip of mistaken beliefs about political causation and are incapable of correcting those misbeliefs. Second, one can maintain that terrorists generally aim at *expressing support* for political outcomes without, however, intending thereby to *bring about* those outcomes. It is the second of these hypotheses that seems better to fit the data. Although some evidence suggests a tendency toward psychological abnormality among terrorists,[6] it does not justify a conclusion that terrorists generally lack a faculty for making straightforward causal judgments. Individuals persistently unable to apprehend the sheer implausibility of toppling regimes by gunning down assorted tourists are unlikely candidates for successfully carrying out complex quasi-military operations. In the absence of specific evidence to the contrary, it is reasonable to impute to terrorists no lesser rationality than that which social analysts routinely ascribe to other actors and which, in any event, is requisite for the conduct of their operations. Rational agents are not systematically unable to distinguish efficacious from inefficacious activity.

Indeed, it is probably the conviction that terrorists are, irrespective of their moral credentials, rational agents much like the rest of us that leads many theorists markedly to misdescribe terrorist activity. C. A. J. Coady describes terrorism as "a means or technique for the pursuit of political ends"[7] but fails to present evidence that would suggest that terrorism actually does advance avowed political ends – unless one construes those ends as something quite different from the ostensible purposes routinely cited by terrorist perpetrators as rationales for their activities. Carl Wellman defines "terrorism" as "the use or attempted use of terror as a means of coercion."[8] This is both too wide and too narrow. It is too wide in that it includes a vast range of governmental, criminal, and quite licit private activity.[9] It is too narrow in that it plainly fails to apply to instances such as the Lod airport massacre in which the three gunmen made no demands, issued no timetables, but merely opened fire. Also, there have been many instances of terrorism in which no group took "credit" for the incident, let alone presented an agenda of political demands.[10]

Nonetheless, the line taken by Coady and Wellman is common in the literature on terrorism. Despite considerable evidence to the contrary, terrorists are characterized as determined seekers of political ends by violent means. This may be the result of a misleading exercise in empathy. "What would lead *me* to contemplate, let alone carry out, the murder of uninvolved men, women, and children?" is the implicit question. For most of us the answer would either be "Nothing!" or "The pursuit of an end so momentous, so far-reaching, that failure to achieve it would be no less than a moral catastrophe." Merely to render terrorism thinkable, we must conceive of it as directed toward the attainment of an end that cannot be secured via less costly means but that *is* likely to be advanced through the employment of violence. Terrorism becomes fathomable, more easily located within the realm of recognizably political activity, if the terrorist is taken to be engaged in at least the same genus of behavior as that which we might elect were our circumstances sufficiently desperate.

Understanding should be sought via a different route. Specifically, we do better to focus on the attitudes *expressed* by terrorist activity than on the outcomes thereby achieved. It is not only the terrorist who engages in primarily expressive activity; many altogether familiar and benign activities practiced by ordinary men and women are not outcome-oriented. Consider, for example, fans seated in their bleacher seats who, in virtue of being fans and not merely spectators, cheer for their favored team during a sporting event. It is possible – barely possible – that the fans' behavior is to be explained as predicated on their belief that the marginal expected return to one more cheer justifies the cost imposed on their vocal cords. That, though, is exceedingly farfetched. (It becomes even more so if they are seated not in the bleachers but in front of their television screens.) We misidentify the situation if we regard it as the calculated result of an application of means–end rationality. For the vast majority of fans, cheering is not a cost but rather a benefit, not an investment in outcomes but a consumption good. One cheers because one wishes to express support for one's team and not because one is attempting to secure some further desired outcome.

The example is innocuous, perhaps too much so to stand as a credible analogue to the terrorist's activity. One that may seem more applicable in virtue of the higher stakes involved is the believer's voluntary acceptance of martyrdom. Individuals who refuse to contravene an article of faith even at the cost of their lives are expressing fidelity to that faith without thereby attempting to bring about some *further* religiously valuable outcome. Indeed, if such forfeiture of life is designed to advance an end beyond that of simply remaining firm in allegiance, then it is disqualified as a genuine act of martyrdom. For example, one who accepts being killed so as to secure a ticket to paradise or to gain further converts to the faith has, according to the theory of martyrology, failed. We may legitimately wonder in any particular case (as does Becket in T. S. Eliot's rendition) whether the individual has actually acted as a martyr. However, we simply fail to understand what martyrdom is if we do not conceive it as an expressive rather than outcome-oriented action.[11]

In similar fashion, terrorism should be understood as activity *supportive* of political ideals, but it need not be deliberately crafted to *bring about* favored outcomes. That is not to rule out by definitional fiat instances of terrorist activity pursued with the intention of bringing down a regime or causing it to alter its policies in a preferred direction. Clearly there are some cases of outcome-oriented terrorism, such as when hostages are taken in order to secure ransom money to be pumped back into the cause or to secure the release of imprisoned comrades.[12] Note, however, that these are intrinsically subsidiary to the main thrust of the terrorists' activity; there would neither be comrades to free nor need for money to purchase weapons were there not some prior agenda to be supported. Although terrorist activity assumes innumerable guises, it is primarily, though not exclusively, expressive in nature rather than a long-term investment in political outcomes.

It follows that utilitarian appraisals of terrorism are generally beside the point. The utilitarian, here as elsewhere, commends a cost–benefit analysis in which the costs of any particular action are estimated and then compared with the expected return (where that figure is calculated as the probability-weighted sum of the various possible outcomes). The usual caveats about one's likelihood to misestimate both costs and benefits when one's passions are engaged, damage that may be done to the actor's own generally salutary dispositions, influence on others of precedents one establishes, and so on will be duly noted.[13] Perhaps the utilitarian analyst will conclude that a sober reckoning of consequences demonstrates that terrorism is hardly ever justified; perhaps not. In either case, the bookkeeperly accounting is irrelevant. It presupposes that the terrorist's acts are engineered to produce desired political outcomes, and we have found reason to reject that understanding.[14] Rather, terrorism is to be appraised by criteria appropriate to acts that are intended to express support for envisaged scenarios but that do not thereby aim at bringing them about as consequences of the act.

That may seem to stack the deck against the terrorist. Expressive activity, one may suppose, is intrinsically of less account than are projects that directly aim at results external to the performance. One may be justified in incurring a modest cost to post a get-well card to an ailing friend, discounting entirely any therapeutic benefit that may result, but that sum is entirely disproportionate to the resources that could reasonably be expended to achieve a cure for the illness. Similarly, it is at least an open question whether one may countenance the sacrifice of the (nonconsenting) innocent when that is the price that must be paid in order to eliminate some manifest political evil. However, to sacrifice the innocent merely in order to *proclaim* the presence of an evil or to *denounce* it may seem frivolous. In both a figurative and a literal sense, expressive activity may be deemed "inconsequential."

That judgment, though, is too quick. Expressive activity need not, from the perspective of the agent, present itself as trivia, as "merely" expressive. The act of "bearing witness" to what one takes to be a moral truth is itself normatively considerable. The example of the martyr is to the point here, and although few of us may possess the stuff of which martyrs are made, we can at least recognize the depth of conviction from which the martyr acts and, under appropriate conditions, admire that expression.[15] Such recognition would not be available were it not the case that we subscribe at least in some measure to the martyr's ethic. Few of us are prepared to douse ourselves with gasoline and light a match to protest a war we hold to be grossly immoral, yet we would, I think, accuse ourselves (and others) of moral insensitivity if the perception of such an injustice never elicited protest – never, that is, except when it has been calculated that the protest will be efficacious in the requisite degree toward eliminating that unjust state of affairs.[16] There are some evils elimination of which, as a logical matter, is impossible. We mourn, retribute, commemorate, honor, memorialize, lament, commiserate over that which is irretrievably past. An entirely forward-looking consequentialism can make no sense of these familiar contours of the moral landscape except to thrust them into a Procrustean bed from which they emerge as prophylaxis directed toward future eventualities that do remain under our control. In good Procrustean fashion, the fit is achieved only by dint of sacrificing crucial bodily parts.

It would be foolish to deny that expressively motivated activity is indeed often consequential. Typically, however, these results are achieved only because the act that generates them was not contrived with them in mind. Many individuals may be inspired by the martyr's example to take up the cause for which he or she died, but the inspiration would be obliterated were they to become convinced that the martyr accepted death precisely in order to multiply the number of disciples. I may be steeled in my determination to resist future moral horrors through participation in rites of remembrance commemorating past victims of other catastrophes, but if my engagement in those rituals is exclusively directed by my personal program for self-improvement, then I shall almost certainly fail to achieve the desired outcome.[17] Manipulative rationality has its successes but also its liabilities, chief among them that manipulation perceived is, in large measure, manipulation defused.

Terrorists have their manifestos and agendas, but more centrally, they carry with them their grievances. Although the former are usually unreadable and unintelligible, the latter must be given credence if terrorist phenomena are to be understood. By "given credence" I do not mean endorsed but rather acknowledged. Rage and righteous indignation are among the most powerful emotions in the human breast, and they would not be such were they easily confined to that domain. One who is engaged by some circumstance, justifiably or otherwise, is someone who is disposed to express that sentiment on a conspicuous canvas.

To be sure, those generally inclined to deplore violence will find it easier to sympathize with individuals who practice pacific modes of protest or who elect to employ their own bodies as the appropriate canvas rather than practice their art on the anonymous passengers of an airliner. Nonetheless, terrorists do not present themselves simply as psychotics

95

unable morally to distinguish between burning leaves and burning people. We are informed by the killers of children that they kill precisely because their own children are denied their birthright; they are at war with all because public hostility or indiference constitutes, as the terrorists see it, a declaration of war against their own people. Because the cause for which they are willing to die – and kill – is of such gravity, they deem it mandatory to underscore the nature of the enormity they denounce with acts of a particularly flagrant and attention-commanding character: kidnapping civilians, littering an airport with bodies, transforming a recreation site into an abattoir. This sort of proportioned response to perceived injustice is entirely beyond the capacity of psychotics. It does not follow, of course, that terrorists are morally superior to psychotics. They are, however, different. And if to construe terrorism as primarily a species of expressive activity is to leave the deck stacked against terrorists, these are the cards that they have wittingly dealt.

Like terrorists, many of their respondents are best understood as operating in a predominantly expressive mode. One can hardly fail to note a disproportion between, on the one hand, the nugatory capacity of terrorist activity to disrupt political structures and, on the other hand, the fevered commentary it elicits. Former president Reagan declared international terrorism to be the United States' foremost public enemy and announced a policy, notoriously repudiated by the subsequent performance of his administration, to brook no negotiation with terrorists or their supporters. Mrs. Thatcher's response to Irish terrorism incorporated, among other measures, substantial curtailment of traditional British liberties of the press. Sober-minded persons of seasoned political judgment adopt near-apocalyptic tones when discussing the impact of terrorism. In words reminiscent of Jonathan Edwards on sin, journalist and historian Paul Johnson contends:

Terrorism is the cancer of the modern world. No state is immune to it. It is a dynamic organism which attacks the healthy

96

flesh of the surrounding society. It has the essential hallmark
of malignant cancer: unless treated, and treated drastically, its
growth is inexorable, until it poisons and engulfs the society
on which it feeds and drags it down to destruction.[18]

In order to understand terrorist phenomena it is necessary to
understand how they can summon such striking responses.

It would, of course, be myopic to deny that terrorism has
imposed severe costs within Western (and other) societies.
These costs, however, have fallen far more heavily on individuals than on political institutions. An airplane crash
exacts a considerable human toll whether it is the result of
malfunctioning equipment or a concealed bomb. Governments survive the latter as easily as they do the former. One
might expect, then, that terrorist incidents would call forth
the sort of expressions of regret and mourning that accompany natural disasters, or the indignation that accompanies
the commission of a heinous crime. These latter events, however, lack any significant political dimension. What requires
explanation is the general perception of terrorist activity as
politically portentous. A purely consequentialist account will
be as inadequate for understanding the response to terrorism
as it is for understanding the motivations undergirding the
practice of terrorism. Terrorism is politically significant because of what it *represents* and not just because of what it
brings about. Accordingly, the normative appraisal of terrorism must take seriously that representational dimension if it
is to perceive what, from a political perspective, is most truly
insidious about terrorism.

IV

A political order, whatever else it may be, is an order. That
is, it necessarily embodies socially recognized distinctions
such as those between citizen and alien, licit and illicit actions, states of peace and war. Where such distinctions either
have never arisen or have entirely broken down, politics does
not exist. Instead, one is confronted with the Hobbesian state

of nature in all its brutish unloveliness: "In such a condition, every man has a right to every thing; even to one another's body. And therefore . . . there can be no security to any man."[19] For Hobbes, the establishment and preservation of security was the únique *telos* of politics, from which all prescriptions for institutional design geometrically followed as theorems. Even if one does not embrace the Hobbesian conception of the quest for order as the culmination of politics, it is at least its beginning. Absent firm distinctions between *mine* and *thine*, distinctions initially grounded in the separateness of individuals' bodies and then naturally extending to their actions and the instruments through which and for which they act, no other goods that civil society may hold forth will be attainable.

This sketchy characterization of political first principles is not meant to be controversial; rather, I take it to be entirely platitudinous. It is precisely because the status of order as a political desideratum cuts across contestable ideologies and aspirations that it can serve as a basis for contrasting the *political* with the *contra-political*. Anarchism resides – barely – within the realm of political alternatives, but nihilism does not. The anarchist maintains, maintains emphatically, that the natural distinction between individual wills has normative consequences, chief among them being the inherent repugnance of sovereignty exercised by one person over another. Nihilism is different. The nihilist acknowledges no such normative consequence of the separateness of persons and thus takes everyone and everything to be fair game, at least in the negative sense that no criteria are admitted by means of which the fair can be distinguished from the foul.

Despite the historical association, often tendentiously overstated and misdescribed, between terrorism and anarchism, terrorist activity is fundamentally nihilistic. It is the deliberate employment of principles of language and conduct corrosive of political order. Analysts work to taxonomize terrorisms as of the left or of the right, as nationalistic or internationalistic, but these categorizations possess at most a superficial validity. At bottom, terrorism is essentially contra-political. To commit oneself to a career of terror is to shuck off in particularly violent and blatant fashion the restraints that divide civil society from the state of nature. This, rather than bare mortality statistics or measurable disruption of regimes, renders terrorism especially noteworthy, is that which prompts in both learned commentators and the general public a fascination that combines fear, loathing, and wonder. Terrorists lift, though more through their aspirations than through any direct effect of their deeds, a corner of the curtain screening us from the Hobbesian jungle.

That terrorists present themselves as free-lance operatives (whatever the degree of sub rosa support they may receive from sovereign states) is to the point, though not because their acts are more destructive of life and welfare than those openly carried out under the aegis of governments; as noted earlier, it is the reverse that is usually the case. Nor are bloody deeds rendered less intrinsically vile by the circumstance of their issuing from states. Violence, we may agree, is deplorable whatever its provenance – but that is precisely reason to be concerned to limit the number and variety of sources from which it emanates. The institution of government is, in its most primary function, a means for the limitation of violence. No acute study of history is needed to make us aware that this aim, even in the best of times, is realized only imperfectly. Because governments persistently prove themselves to be lukewarm or worse in their fidelity to the task of checking violence, we have reason to attempt to achieve a politics that will instill in them more restraint in their dealings both with their own citizens and with foreign countries whom they take to be competitors. The liberal tradition of political inquiry from Locke through Rawls is, in no small measure, characterized by the quest for principles through which such restraint may be secured. We may also aspire to transcend the limitations that seem inherent to national sovereignty through the establishment of supranational order-conferring political structures, although the record of organizations such as the League of Nations and United Nations affords to these hopes little encouragement.

What is *not* called for, what would surely forfeit the limited degree of tranquillity we might reasonably expect to enjoy, would be a democratization of the right to perpetrate acts of violence such that each person, in pure Hobbesian state-of-nature fashion, would enjoy carte blanche to purge his or her grievances on the bodies of others.

Terrorism overtly expresses rejection of a politics that would limit the domain of authorized violence. To be sure, terrorists are neither the only nor the most prolific practitioners of nonstate violence. Professional criminals as well as common thugs daily take it upon themselves to pursue their aims through coercive means. The toll in lives and property they cumulatively exact is many times greater than that achieved by terrorists. Although I have no wish to minimize the moral evil of the former, it is nonetheless the case that ordinary crime must be understood to differ in kind from the activity of terrorists. The criminal attempts to secure through illicit means ends basically identical to those that others pursue inside the law: money chief among them, but also power, status, and a sense of achievement. Criminal activity operates within the interstices of the political order and is parasitic upon it. Where crime succeeds it does so in virtue of the fact that those upon whom it preys are, by and large, law-abiding. The standard felon does not will the collapse of civil order but, to the contrary, is pleased to take a free ride on the benefits it affords. Terrorism is different. It is the expression of disdain for the institutions of civil society in general and, specifically, for the goal of limiting the practice of violence. Terrorists do not aim to free ride but rather to destroy. Although in practice they may have little effect, the ideal they express is nihilistic.

Terrorists are sometimes spoken of as "guerrillas," as individuals engaged in internecine warfare against the established order. This characterization is erroneous. Although terrorists bear some affinity to insurgent forces, the opposition in which they set themselves is more radical. Civil war seeks the demolition of political authority for the purpose of constituting in the vacuum thereby created an improved authority. Because civil war entails a temporary retreat into the state of nature, some political theorists (Hobbes and Kant, for example) judge it to be always impermissible. Others, chief among them Locke, approve civil war, but only in conditions of utmost exigency and only to restore an order against which the current regime has itself cast the first stone. Both rejection and qualified approval issue from the same political logic. Government is instituted for the limitation of violence. Civil war is its catastrophic breakdown. Thus, on one account, it is inadmissible. However, governments can themselves become ferocious initiators of violence against persons. Therefore, maintains the other account, armed rebellion waged against gross governmental excesses is licit. Both unambiguously endorse political order, either as it in fact exists or as aspiration. Civil war is, then, the enterprise of attempting through the use of military means to replace an odious order with one that is morally (more) satisfactory. It, unlike terrorism, is outcome-oriented. The guerrilla, to be sure, avoids pitched battles until a shift in the balance of forces renders that tactic feasible. However, guerrilla warfare is genuinely warfare, that is, a politics by other means. Rebellion without any hope of melioration is not civil war; it is murder or suicide or both. Terrorists may entertain in their hearts a fantasy of the established order being laid low and subsequent securement by themselves of political control, but fantasy, even when punctuated by bullets, is not warfare.[20]

Another aspect of terrorism's contra-politics is its adherence to a policy of affirmative action for potential victims. It renounces conventional distinctions of person and place. Although soldiers or high officials of the despised regime may become targets of bombs and bullets, cruise ship passengers, office workers, men and women at prayer in a synagogue, or children asleep in their beds qualify equally well as candidates. By declaring open season on persons everywhere, terrorists underscore their rejection of familiar political categories and the limitations on violence they embody.

Although in a loose sense terrorists practice political assassination, their killings have a more esoteric flavor. Individuals are not singled out for death in virtue of the particular offices they hold, any specific complicity in the design or execution of governmental policy, or perceived wickedness attaching to their own personal conduct. Terrorists propound a sort of doctrine of original sin within which liability to the damnation they wield is universal. Ordinary assassins, by way of contrast, discriminate in quite conventional ways, holding particular individuals accountable for their own alleged misdeeds or their active participation in unjust institutions. Assassination, although an avowedly political deed, resembles ordinary crime in this way: It implicitly accepts the legitimacy of political order even as it contravenes its dictates. Assassins are, so long as they remain merely assassins, attempting to remove one officeholder or a class of officeholders in order that they be replaced by better people pursuing more acceptable policies. Within the natural law literature there exists an extended discussion of the nature of tyranny and the conditions under which tyrannicide is justifiable. All this is implicitly rejected by terrorists. They carry no specific animus against the passengers of the airliners on which they plant bombs; any other assorted collection of travelers would have done as well. Those whom fortune provides as victims are merely handy targets, ciphers for their use. Political assassination is usually an evil, but it is one of a different nature than terrorism.

When armies clash, lives are lost. Some people maintain that these killings are justified when the conditions of a just war obtain. It is not my intention either to defend traditional just war theory or to offer a replacement. In an age in which national armies are conscripted from the general citizenry and entire cities are placed in bomb sights, a doctrine of justice in warfare may have become obsolete. Still, there is a point to the distinction between soldiers and civilians, the former but not the latter being fair game for assault. The point should by now be familiar: This is a distinction responsive to the concern that violence not be unbounded. There can be little doubt that this would be a better world were there no soldiers' uniforms signifying "I am a proper target – and dispenser – of deadly force." However, that is a prospect utopian at best. If violence cannot be eliminated, it remains a matter of urgency to limit both its domain and its intensity.[21] Marking off some persons, even if entirely arbitrarily, as "soldiers" and others as "civilians" may not instantiate the highest ideals of a refined morality, but it possesses the minimal virtue of expressing a conviction that *some* people are off limits. Terrorism, by contrast, represents the endorsement of unconstrained liability to violence.[22]

Shall we then endorse the common characterization of terrorism as the employment of *indiscriminate* violence in support of political ends? That characterization is sometimes accurate, as when a random assortment of airplane passengers is blown from the sky. In such a circumstance, what matters to the terrorist is that there *be* victims; it does not matter *who* those victims are. On other occasions, though, terrorist targets are quite carefully and deliberately selected. But just as the politics of terrorism is to be understood as a contra-politics, so too are the discriminations of terrorists a kind of contra-discrimination.

When a dozen athletes are kidnapped in an Olympic village and then murdered, the terrorist has achieved, achieved with exquisite precision, an inversion of the customary categories of political order. It is precisely because the Olympic Games represent an ideal of comity among nations and competition without violence or hostility that they present themselves as a uniquely enticing opportunity for disruption. To have disrupted in similar fashion a conclave of the Hell's Angels would not have paid so rich a dividend.

The bullet placed in Pope John Paul II by Agca was similarly symbolic, as is the deliberate slaughter of children. Instances of this terrorist motif abound. Among all the passengers on the *Achille Lauro*, wheelchair-bound Leon Klinghoffer was deliberately selected for a bullet in the brain and dumping into the Mediterranean.[23] It was the elderly Lord Mountbatten, and not some active politician, who was dispatched by a bomb while on a fishing holiday. Terrence Waite, emissary

of the archbishop of Canterbury, entered Lebanon to negotiate the release of victims of kidnapping; that rendered him,
according to the terrorist's logic of inversion, eminently suitable for disappearance into the netherworld from which he
had hoped to free others. The point seems to be that just
those individuals (or venues) who, according to conventional
categories, are most properly removed from the play of
deadly force must be subjected to it.

The terrorist's assault on political categories is accompanied by a corresponding assault on language. As if by
instruction from the Queen of Hearts, words are turned
topsy-turvy to signify whatever the terrorist wants them to
mean. A ragtag group of covert killers refers to itself as an
"army": for example, the Japanese Red Army, the Irish Republican Army, or, with uncharacteristic modesty, the Italian
Red Brigades. Easily vanquishing all other competitors in the
contest for most preposterous designation is the "Symbionese Liberation Army," which, at the time of its kidnapping of Patricia Hearst, was comprised of eight members!
Whatever may have prompted either the formation or the
naming of this group, it cannot be doubted that it was neither
Symbionese[24] nor an army, nor had it anything whatsoever
to do with liberation.

With equal imaginativeness, individual members of these
organizations refer to themselves as "soldiers," "urban guerrillas," "insurgents," or, most popularly, "freedom fighters." Terrorist homicidal assaults are described as "battles"
or "operations," and often are characterized as having been
undertaken in "self-defense." Individuals who have the mis-
fortune to be captured by terrorists are tried as "enemies of
the people" in "people's courts" and, when found "guilty"
– a foregone conclusion in a world in which none are innocent
– are not simply killed but rather "executed." This transval-
uation of language is not merely incidental but instead is
very much of a piece with the general political nihilism that
underlies terrorism. It is to invoke political and juristic terms
that underlie civil society's quest for order and to bend them
to the purpose of maximizing disorder. Although it is not

surprising that terrorists want to include semantics among their quarries, one is hard pressed not to raise an eyebrow when the world's press shows itself woodenly content to parrot their mal-locutions as if there were nothing whatsoever fanciful or perverse to them.

V

The preceding observations have aimed at generality. That which is common to various terrorist organizations rather than that which distinguishes them has been the primary focus of attention. That is not to maintain that differences among the groups are purely nominal. Terrorists differ in their political orientation: While many situate themselves on the left, right-wing terrorism is present and, in some countries, the predominant form. Many kill out of nationalism, others in the name of proletarian internationalism. Some terrorist organizations, such as the PLO, possess in good measure the panoply of states, while others, such as the Symbionese Liberation Army, are no more than a tiny collection of misanthropic misfits. A few groups enjoy considerable state support, a sophisticated infrastructure, and a high degree of stability, while others are no more than a blip in yesterday's news. Some terrorists routinely extort for profit and become virtually indistinguishable from participants in conventional organized crime, while others live as ascetics dedicated to the pursuit of their "ideals." And so on, and so on. Although these vicissitudes are of considerable significance to those whose job it is to catalog or to blunt particular campaigns, they can be set aside in an investigation of what it is about terrorism *as such* that renders it such a high-visibility, politically meaningful phenomenon.

I have argued that terrorism, the terrorism that plays itself out in newspapers and on television screens to rapt audiences around the world, is to be understood as activity that is primarily expressive in character rather than outcome-oriented. What it expresses is virulent and unregulated opposition to the preconditions of successful civility. If this description is accurate, then the normative verdict follows directly. Nearly all of us have a fundamental stake in the preservation of political order within which alone the pursuit of nearly all human goods is rendered feasible. Therefore, we have strong, indeed conclusive, reason to concur with Johnson's description of terrorism as a cancer to be excised. This is neither hyperbole nor vapid apocalypticism. Rather, it is to grasp with acute comprehension the animus of terrorism and to respond in strict proportion.

Some seek excuse or mitigation for the terrorist by contrasting the body count for which he or she is responsible with the considerably greater toll exacted by governments or even with the nonviolent actions of private men and women: "The amount of terror inflicted by 'terrorists,' no matter how dreadful, is a thimbleful compared to official, legally-sanctioned terror. . . . [M]ore terrorists wear three-piece suits, ride in Rolls Royces, and sit in the seats of corporate power and government than lurk in dark alleys."[25] This judgment may issue from an inconsiderate consequentialism that takes its bearings entirely from the statistics entered in official records. Alternatively, it may bespeak a relativism that is not far distant from the nihilism of the terrorist: When some people die from bombs and others from air polluted by factories, who is in a position to assess on whom the greater blame is to be placed? The disinclination to judge may, in rare cases, spring from a deep well of pity and humility, but far more often it is symptomatic of moral impotence. It can also carry a reflexive significance: One for whom the pen rather than the bomb is the preferred instrument of expression may elect to express his or her own contempt for the wearers of three-piece suits by contrasting them unfavorably with the terrorist.

Terrorists have grievances. That is so whether they are individuals dispossessed from the land of their ancestors or the bored and spoiled children of professional families. Possession of grievances in no regard distinguishes terrorists from the remainder of humanity: Bad luck and injustice are, to one degree or another, the common human lot. One of the great curiosities of a certain desiccated strain of Western liberalism[26] is its perpetual willingness to excuse the inexcusable just so long as it issues from those who possess official standing as being among the downtrodden;[27] it takes as the foremost of moral virtues a conscientious refusal to "blame the victims." To the extent that this instinct arises from the sublimation of unease consequent on finding oneself in a favored social and economic position, it is of psychological but no analytical interest. However, this liberal reflex can also present itself as the product of a concern for distributive justice. Those who either are among the dispossessed or act as proxies on their behalf are not entirely shielded from criticism; they may, for example, be reprimanded for acting excessively or imprudently when they respond violently to social iniquities. However, in light of the evident failure of nonviolent strategies to secure redress, violence committed by those who seek meritorious ends must be sympathetically appraised. The terrorist is viewed as a sort of contemporary Robin Hood, outside the law but responsive to its best impulses.

This is radically to misidentify the logic of terrorism. Unlike Robin Hood, who, as the legends have it, practiced an outlawry that was scrupulous in the distinctions it enforced between the guilty and the innocent, between usurper and victim, terrorists either ignore such distinctions entirely or else turn them on their head. The enemy is only incidentally particular individuals who cross the terrorist's path; more fundamentally it is civil order. Because it is only within the ambit of such order that the pursuit of justice becomes feasible, the terrorist undercuts in intention and deed all basis for redress of wrongs. This is yet a further implication of the terrorist's contra-politics. Political theorists since Aristotle have been virtually unanimous in their understanding of politics as directed by a concern for melioration of bad luck and misfortunes consequent on wrongful human conduct. They have recognized that those who suffer most from the collapse of order are, almost inevitably, the poor and the weak. Insofar as terrorists repudiate this tradition, they lack

107

standing as advocates of a program of social justice. Whatever the liberal may believe, the terrorists' ends are not those
of any liberalism, no matter how attenuated and apologetic.

If self-identified progressive consciences have failed by and
large to convey a clear sense of the normative standing of
terrorism, print and, especially, electronic journalists have
not performed conspicuously better. The abduction of an
airliner or occupation of an office building by an unrestrained
band of zealots is, in their perception, above all else a good
story, and journalists have proved themselves willing to bear
considerable financial as well as moral costs to enhance their
coverage:

> In some instances, terrorists seem to have been paid by the
> media. In the Beirut crisis of 1985 – the hijacking of
> TWA 847 – US networks allegedly paid over $1 million a week
> to assure their monopoly over access to the hostage spec-
> tacular. ABC reportedly paid Amal $30,000 for sole access to
> a hostage interview session and $50,000 for the "farewell
> banquet."
>
> What did the media get in return for this investment? They
> received tapes from hostages in which they reported feeling
> fine, that the captors were nice people, and massive doses of
> propaganda. Only later was it revealed – as after the Tehran
> siege – that the hostages had by no means felt good and that
> some had been severely mistreated. . . . The terrorists were
> aware of the competition between the American networks in
> which a few additional points in ratings meant huge increases
> in advertising revenues; they put their knowledge to good use.
> As a British correspondent noted at the time: "It was done
> quite consciously. There were graduates of media studies from
> American colleges at meetings at Nabih Berri's house in West
> Beirut while tactics were being worked out." . . . Some of the
> hostages bitterly resented the activities of the networks in Bei-
> rut, referring to ABC as the "Amal Broadcasting Corporation"
> and NBC as the "Nabih Berri Corporation."[28]

It has often been noted that this sort of journalistic feeding
frenzy represents an inducement for the perpetration of yet

additional terrorist attacks as well as incentive to choreograph those attacks in especially novel and garish fashion so as to hold the rapt attention of an easily jaded audience that would otherwise turn back to sitcoms. I have no wish to deny that providing an inducement for terrorism, whether in the form of publicity or cash, is morally culpable. Additionally, though, this kind of coverage is condemnable on grounds internal to journalistic practice. It is the function of the press to report the news, not to create it. Moreover, the press is responsible for applying its professional skills so as to provide its readers and viewers bona fide information, as opposed to serving as indiscriminate shills for desperate men and women who wish to deliver themselves of diatribes. A journalism both cavalier with facts and bereft of moral judgment is meretricious.

Some will contend that journalists have little choice but to act as they do, that they cannot claim for themselves a Solomonic wisdom to tailor the news as they see fit but must rather pass on to their audience whatever statements they are given. It is the task of the public and not the press to attempt to ascertain where the truth may lie. The objector contends that a free press does not engage in censorship, however odious the information with which it is presented.

The response is jejune. Journalism, like politics, is a practice that necessarily incorporates selection and discrimination. No reporter mindlessly passes on all that he sees and hears. A filtering process is inevitable; all that is in question is which criteria will be employed to distinguish news from chaff. Journalism done well discriminates between confused and clear, reliable and unreliable, informative and misleading, portentous and trivial. When these criteria give way to titillation for the sake of added rating points, journalism becomes indistinguishable from entertainment. The public deserves to be afforded the information it needs to comprehend the flux of world events, to form political judgments, and to be able to take action to avoid dangers. A free and responsible press provides such information, but that is quite distinct from plying a servile pen or camera. That reporting be free and untrammeled is a venerable principle of journalism; but so too is the principle that advertisers are to pay and not to be paid.

In fairness, journalistic distortions of the nature of terrorism are not entirely a manifestation of cynicism. Newsworthiness is not a platonic form but rather a function of human interests. Because the public is fascinated by terrorists, so too – and properly – is the press. The fascination is, in large measure, the fascination of dread. It is more than a little chilling to be confronted by individuals who seem conspicuously to lack the concerns and restraints that one has thoroughly internalized and on which sociality rests. That is why psychopathic killers such as Ted Bundy and Jack the Ripper attract considerable attention and analysis. Individuals who play out their violent role on an international stage may achieve yet greater prominence. There exists a tension between the repulsion one feels toward their deeds and one's desire to understand them as men and women ultimately not all that unlike oneself. To the extent that their motivations and designs are ones that we can sympathize with, if not share, these people need not be viewed as unremittingly threatening to the kind of life we cherish. If we allow them to speak their minds at length, and if we attend to what they have to say, perhaps the strangeness will be exorcised. Thus the tendency of the press – and not only the press[29] – to display terrorists fatuously as ordinary people, albeit with an extraordinary gripe.

Terrorists may, for all I know, indeed be ordinary, but *terrorism* is not. It is not merely a politics that gets out of hand: Cook County but somewhat more so. Rather, terrorism represents the radical rejection of civil accommodation. It takes the Hobbesian state of nature not as the problem but as the solution. Whether terrorists do or do not love their children, whether they weep when they hear the melodies of their homelands, is irrelevant to the appraisal of terrorism. To suppose otherwise is to fail to take seriously the political significance of terrorism.

The political significance of terrorism

NOTES

I am grateful to James Child, Robert Evans, Raymond Frey, Gerald Gaus, and an anonymous Cambridge University Press referee for helpful criticism.

1 Assault by three members of the United (Japanese) Red Army at the Lod airport, May 1972.

2 As I write, the trial of Kim Hyon Hui has opened in South Korea. According to the indictment and her own statements, while acting as an agent of the government of North Korea she planted the bomb that destroyed a (South) Korean Airlines jet near Burma in 1987. What renders the case especially fantastic is that many South Koreans voice the suspicion that she was in fact acting under orders from a *South* Korean government that hoped thereby to profit at the polls from a resurgence of anti-Communist sentiment. Whichever may prove to be the case, it is worth noting that the responsible government found it in its interest to feign an ordinary (i.e., private) terrorist attack. See *Wall Street Journal*, March 8, 1989, p. A10.

3 The way in which terrorism is political does, however, diverge radically from ordinary modes of political activity, so much so as to render terrorism the antithesis of normal politics. Section IV describes the contra-political nature of terrorism.

4 I am assuming that Manson's fixation on the deep meaning of Beatles' lyrics and the like was too jumbled and solipsistic to count as a political program.

5 The 1983 suicide attack on the U.S. Marine barracks in Lebanon is often cited as an example disconfirmatory of the thesis that terrorism is futile. President Reagan responded to the death of 241 marines by removing the American military presence in Lebanon. Although I do not deny that this event was politically consequential, the particular context within which it occurred renders it with virtual textbook clarity an exception that proves the rule. Unlike isolated terrorist attacks occurring in a country at peace, the barracks bombing was a distinctly military operation carried out in a country riven by rival armies and with only a nominally functional government. It was directed at forces maintaining only a reluctant and peripheral commitment to the hostilities, and did not threaten that coun-

try's own political institutions. In sum, the barracks attack was only tangentially terroristic. Therefore, the U.S. departure from Lebanon cannot serve as a counterexample to the thesis that terrorism – as distinct from civil war, revolution, etc. – almost never succeeds in advancing the political aims it ostensibly serves. See Richard Falk, *Revolutionaries and Functionaries: The Dual Face of Terrorism* (New York: Dutton, 1988), pp. 34–5.

6 See, for example, Martha Crenshaw, "The Psychology of Political Terrorism," in *Psychology: Contemporary Problems and Issues*, ed. Margaret G. Hermann (San Francisco: Jossey-Bass, 1986), pp. 379–413.

7 C. A. J. Coady, "The Morality of Terrorism," *Philosophy* 60 (1985): 55.

8 Carl Wellman, "On Terrorism Itself," *Journal of Value Inquiry* 13 (1979): 250.

9 Indeed, Wellman writes, "I must confess that I often engage in nonviolent terrorism myself, for I often threaten to flunk any student who hands in his paper after the due date" (ibid., p. 252). This implausible confession represents an extreme example of the theorist's inclination to render terrorist activity continuous with that performed by agents of less sanguinary mien.

10 As I write (March 1989), no one has come forth to claim responsibility for planting the bomb that destroyed Pan Am Flight 103 in the skies over Lockerbie, Scotland, some three months previously.

11 I have argued in a series of papers written with Geoffrey Brennan that ordinary voting behavior should be understood as predominantly expressive. See G. Brennan and L. Lomasky, "Institutional Aspects of 'Merit Goods' Analysis," *Finanzarchiv* 41 (1983): 183–206; "Inefficient Unanimity," *Journal of Applied Philosophy* 1 (1984): 151–63; "The Impartial Spectator Goes to Washington: Toward a Smithian Theory of Electoral Behavior," *Economics and Philosophy* 1 (1985): 189–211; "The Logic of Electoral Preference: Response to Saraydar and Hudelson," *Economics and Philosophy* 3 (1987): 131–8; "Large Numbers, Small Costs: The Uneasy Foundations of Democratic Rule," in *Politics and Process: New Essays in Democratic Theory*, ed. G. Brennan and L. Lomasky (New York: Cambridge University Press, 1989), pp. 42–59.

12 For example, the hijacking of the *Achille Lauro* (1985).

13 For a characteristic utilitarian appraisal see R. M. Hare, "On Terrorism," *Journal of Value Inquiry* 13 (1979): 241–49.

14 Strict utilitarians may be unmoved, maintaining that the propriety of any action is a function of the value of its consequences, irrespective of whether that action is performed with the intention of bringing about those consequences. From this perspective, an inquiry into the motivational structure of terrorist (or other) activity is strictly irrelevant to its normative appraisal. Terrorists, martyrs, baseball fans, Wall Street arbitragers – the actions of each are to be evaluated via the same consequentialist standard. It would take us too far afield to place this monolithic conception of moral evaluation under scrutiny. I merely note in passing that the frequency of predominantly expressive performances across many ordinary – as well as extraordinary – practices in which we engage constitutes one reason among many to be suspicious of the credentials of utilitarianism as an all-purpose moral decision theory.

15 In the sense intended here, martyrdom is not understood as an exclusively religious calling. Indeed, some martyrs may also be terrorists, as was Bobby Sands, who starved himself during May of 1981 as an act of allegiance to the cause of the Provisional Irish Republican Army.

16 An admirable statement of this viewpoint is Stanley Benn, "The Problematic Rationality of Political Participation," in *Political Participation*, ed. Stanley Benn et al. (Canberra: Australian National University, 1978), pp. 1–22.

17 I concede that indirect strategies such as that commended by Pascal to would-be wagerers may occasionally succeed. Note, however, that they do so only insofar as they are able to transform straightforwardly outcome-oriented activity into something else. Much illuminating discussion of this theme is found in Derek Parfit, *Reasons and Persons* (Oxford: Oxford University Press, 1984), especially in chap. 1, "Theories That Are Directly Self-defeating," pp. 3–51.

18 Paul Johnson, "The Cancer of Terrorism," in *Terrorism: How the West Can Win*, ed. Benjamin Netanyahu (New York: Farrar, Straus, and Giroux, 1986), p. 31.

19 Thomas Hobbes, *Leviathan*, ed. Michael Oakeshott (New York: Macmillan, 1962), p. 103.

20 I do not maintain that there invariably exists a sharp line separating terrorists from guerrilla combatants and other genuinely political actors. The Palestine Liberation Organization, unlike, for example, the Japanese Red Army, is a group that can be thought of as straddling the fence. Although it has control of no territory within the land it claims and avoids engagement with Israeli military forces, it aspires with some realistic prospect of success to statehood and possesses a genuine political program that it endeavors to advance. The PLO has (recently) established a government-in-exile and, significantly, enjoys the aboveboard sanction of existing governments. Thus it is not mistaken to regard the PLO and, especially, some of its constituent elements as a terrorist force, *nor* is it mistaken to think of the PLO as engaged in the pursuit of genuinely political ends.

21 Nuclear warfare is especially horrifying because of the amount of destructive force it unleashes but also because it largely obliterates all distinctions between soldier and civilian. To a lesser extent, the same thing is true of chemical warfare.

22 Armies traditionally have been exclusively male organizations. More recently, under the twin spurs of changes in the technology of warfare and feminist criticism, women have been afforded entry into military careers. In the United States and several other Western countries, women may serve in armies but are neither liable for conscription nor allowed to assume combat roles. Feminists criticize these exclusions, especially the latter, holding them to be arbitrary and perpetuative of sexual stereotypes. One may concede that there is some force to this critique while nonetheless maintaining that even a thoroughly arbitrary exclusion from combat status has compensating advantages: better that some classes of the citizenry be held immune from bloodletting than that everyone be rendered vulnerable.

23 Abu Abbas, director of the *Achille Lauro* hijacking, during a November 1988 conclave of the PLO jocularly observed of Klinghoffer, "Maybe he was trying to swim for it." Evidently, the expressive potential of terrorism extends to the wry. See *New Republic* 199 (December 5, 1988): 10.

24 According to Walter Laqueur, "The name 'Symbionese' was defined as 'body of harmony of dissimilar bodies and organisms living in deep and loving harmony and partnership in

the best interest of within [sic] the body'. Its emblem was a seven-headed cobra, a 170,000-year-old sign signifying God and life" (*The Age of Terrorism*, rev. and expanded ed. [Boston: Little, Brown, 1987], pp. 244–5).

25 Martin Oppenheimer, "Defining Terrorism," reprinted in *Terrorism: Opposing Viewpoints*, ed. Bonnie Szumski (St. Paul: Greenhaven Press, 1986), pp. 87–8.

26 I here use the term "liberalism" not in its ancient and honorable sense but rather in that which George Bush intended when he hurled it at his 1988 presidential campaign opponent, Michael Dukakis, and which the latter so nimbly sought to evade.

27 I say "official standing" because the list of approved causes is highly selective and, so far as any objective measure of disadvantage might indicate, quite capricious. Palestinians and, to a lesser extent, Northern Irish Catholics receive considerable sympathy and support while, for example, Tibetan and, until recently, Kurdish populations targeted for genocide have been largely ignored in Western media. Lebanese Maronites, though verifiably a beleaguered minority, are almost always reckoned on the side of the oppressors. As in baseball, one can't tell the players without a scorecard.

28 Laqueur, *The Age of Terrorism*, pp. 124–5.

29 Consider the testimony offered by the pilot of the unfortunate TWA flight 847: "I breathed . . . a silent prayer of thanks that the hijackers were so family oriented. They cared deeply about their wives and children, so they understood that it was difficult for me to be separated from my family. . . . If there was one thing the hijackers like to talk about, besides Khomeini, it was their families. One day one man was positively giddy because he had earned a few days off and was going to be able to spend some time with his wife and two children. . . . Those were the times when I felt most strongly that, in spite of the situation we found ourselves in, we were all brothers in the family of man" (John Testrake, *Triumph over Terror on Flight 847* [Old Tappan N.J.: Fleming Revell, 1987], p. 149).

Chapter 6

Terrorism and morality

JAN NARVESON

DEFINITIONS

The interest in terrorism is centrally due to its involving a particularly distasteful subset of what is already a fairly distasteful group of human actions, namely violent ones. Which ones are they?

The term "violence" has known ambiguities. A murderer who stabs or shoots his victim has performed a violent act, certainly. But should we say the same thing of a murderer who lulls his victim to permanent slumber with a gentle and pleasant-tasting poison? Does the victim of a would-be murderer who defends himself by killing his assailant commit violence? I will not attempt to capture the precise nuances of ordinary language here, if that is indeed possible, but instead will simply identify as "violence" those intentional human acts whose immediate aim is the infliction of pain, bodily harm, damage, severe distress, or death on other persons. Law enforcers who shoot and kill in the course of their duties, however justified in doing so, will be said in this sense to have defended themselves with violence – probably not something that would ordinarily be said. Thus violence may, in principle, be either unjustified or justified, either evil or good in its upshot; calling an act "violence" does not morally judge it, in the usage adopted here.

To term terrorist acts a "subset" of violent ones may be misleading in one major respect. Much of what is generally regarded as terrorism consists not directly in the performance of violent acts but in the *threat* of such performance. As a terminological convenience, I will include those threats as cases of terrorism, even if none of the threatened violence actually occurs. The serious threat of it is sufficient.

Terrorist violence has two further features of special interest: It is (1) *politically* motivated and (2) directed at persons who are threatened not on their own accounts, but with a view to influencing further persons, in particular those with power, official or otherwise, to affect the political arrangements of the community in question. Terrorist victims are agreed by the terrorists to be "innocent," in a sense to be considered further.

A third feature often associated with terrorism will *not* be regarded as part of the definition here: namely, that it is performed by persons in an "unofficial" capacity. I will instead take it that terrorism can also be practiced by armed soldiers of an established government, police officers, or other agents of purportedly legitimate governments. Indeed, it may be that by far the greatest proportion of the acts in question is so performed. Much of what is said in this essay may seem to presuppose that intimidation by such officially acting persons is not terrorism, but that is not by intention. Rather, as will be observed, the point is that the problems involved in dealing with terrorism of that kind are considerably different, and considerably more difficult, than those involved in responding to terrorism by privateers or "insurgents," as Alex Schmid and Janny de Graf usefully term them.[1] In fact, much insurgent terrorism has been regarded by its practitioners as a reasonable response to what they perceive to be a sort of state terrorism practiced by those they are opposing.

The difference between state terrorism and insurgent terrorism is that states use terrorism in order to *prevent* changes in the currently prevailing political arrangements, whereas insurgents use it in order to *effect* changes in them. But the strategy is the same. What distinguishes terrorism is that its victims are distinct from (though not necessarily discrete from, for they may be included in) the set of persons whose actions the terrorists are trying to influence. For this reason, the victim has little or no influence on the conduct of his assailant. Pointing out, for example, that she is innocent or has little to do with the power structure the terrorist seeks to affect will typically do no good. The victim of terrorism is a pawn, perhaps the star case of Kant's category of using persons as "mere means."

Ideologically speaking, the "ism" of terrorism is not the thesis that terror is a good thing in itself – that would be something more like sadism. Terrorism is more nearly the view that terror *may* be used for political and moral ends. I say "more nearly," though, because this isn't quite it either. The public may be concerned to terrify those who might otherwise commit assorted evils into desisting from such acts. Those are political and moral ends, I suppose, and yet we don't think of such activities as constituting terrorism.

One might object that these are *legitimate* uses of "terror," a response that raises anew the problem of obtaining a neutral characterization of terrorism, one that does not logically prejudge it. However, we can perhaps evade this problem by pointing out that the aim of inspiring people *in general* with terror isn't what institutionalized punishment is about: Only malefactors and would-be malefactors are the intended objects of any "terror" involved. This fails to be terrorism, then, because the people, if any, who would be terrified by the threat of punishment are the very people whose behavior we are trying to influence. If others are terrified, it is at the prospect of being wrongly enmeshed, as when the innocent are punished. But given the facts, the state would agree that those cases are mistakes, miscarriages of justice. One avoids the expected harms by simply refraining from doing the punishable acts. The victim of terrorism doesn't have this recourse, for the terrorist does not visit evils upon the innocent by mistake, but by design. What the victim might have been intending to do doesn't interest the terrorist as such; he is after other game.

In characterizing terrorism as the view that terror "may" be used for political ends, we raise a further question: Does the terrorist actually think that his use of terror is *morally OK*? Or is it that he thinks that even though it is definitely not morally OK, it is nevertheless available to be used? Probably some terrorists would say the former and some the latter. There is something to be said for the view that those who say the latter are confused. However, that is an issue we needn't go into, for what we want to know is whether terrorism *is* ever morally justified, whatever its perpetrators may think. If it ever is, then whether a part of the justification of terrorism is that it is done with "moral motives" is perhaps not of crucial importance. I will, in fact, as a working hypothesis ascribe to the terrorist an explicit moral motive: namely, that of believing his cause to be just, whether or not he would want to put it that way. This will be, I think, the most favorable case. Those whose motives are downright evil could be condemned on that ground even if we thought their cause just; if so, that would be an extraneous interfering condition.

TERRORISM AS POLITICAL

Terrorism, as understood here, is a political action or sequence of actions. As the name implies, the strategy is to inspire the "target" population with terror, by means of random acts of violence: meaning by "random" that they may fall upon anyone in a sizable class of persons, at any time, are done without specific warning, and are done in an utterly impersonal manner. The perpetrators, though unknown as individuals, are understood to be acting as the agents of some group whose political purposes provide the motivation. Such acts could be done for no reason at all, of course – by homicidal maniacs, say. But terrorism as we understand it here is political: It does have at least an ostensible purpose, that of forwarding some political program, which may range from the "liberation" of specific groups or individuals from what it claims to be oppression, all the way to general social revolution leading to some new form of social organization. The point of using terror is to influence people who are in a position to do something to achieve the terrorists' ends. It may be a sort of extortion: "Free the Xs, or we will kill many more of the Ys!" Or it may be a more general sort of coercion: "We will continue this until you support the revolution."

Invariably there is a publicity aspect to the terrorist attack, drawing the attention of as many people as possible to certain alleged wrongs. Frequently also there is an intention of punishing for those wrongs: "We are going to do to the so-and-sos what they did to our people," either on a specific occasion or in general. In the latter vein, victims are sometimes alleged to have been "executed" (examples: the one-time premier of Italy, and certain West German businessmen). Terrorism is also often combined with armed robbery, the organization simultaneously procuring funds for its program and also holding that the banks are agents of the oppressive capitalist state, or whatever, and thus deserve what they get from the terrorists.

Related activities might include the use of particularly terrifying weapons in war, such as nerve gas or chemical weapons or (no doubt coming in the future) "death rays," or of suicide attacks such as the ones that killed hundreds of American and French soldiers in Lebanon early in 1984 – or indeed, of nuclear weapons. However, we will not be considering the context of official war here, and the suicide attacks concern us only in their terroristic aspect, rather than in their use as a strategy in war. Soldiers at the front in an army in wartime expect to be attacked, by surprise and otherwise, and the terror they may feel, of both the known and the unknown, is part of the business. But it is not what we are considering under the name "terrorism." (On the other hand, guerrillas operating behind the lines by randomly attacking the civilian population might well count as terrorists in our sense.)

Mention of the motive of punishment, specifically of retribution, brings up a problem about adherence to the foregoing characterization of terrorism. For if A's motive in doing violence to B is to wreak retribution upon B for something B has supposedly done to C, then it would not as such count as terrorism in that narrow definition. Yet a good deal of what is generally considered terrorism does fall into this general category: That is, the victims are not wholly irrelevant, as such, to the cause being espoused.

However, we may perhaps accept such cases in the following two ways. (1) Though a tsarist official, say, who was the target of an attack was thought by his assassins to be guilty of horrendous crimes, it was also true that the motive of visiting violence upon him was to bring down the regime of which he was a part, by inspiring *other* supporters of the regime with terror. That the particular official selected as a target may have been guilty of particular crimes was, in many cases, a part of the motivation for violence, but only a part, and that not perhaps the major one. (2) Further, although the terrorist may think that the officials in question are guilty of terrible things, the fact is that they are not, as things stand, *legally* liable for punishment under the established legal system. The terrorist takes the doing of what he claims to be justice in his own hands. This certainly imposes on his targets a sense of terror as defined: the threat of violence that is unexpected and very difficult to have any control over. And if we suppose that acting in a generally accepted manner as the agent of what is recognized to be the current government carries with it any sort of moral legitimacy at all, then these cases also raise the question of justification in an important way.

Consider a citizenry that feels it has been ill-used by a particular official. Some of the citizens organize and carry out a plot to assassinate this official; but they make it clear that they have no intention of bringing down the constitution or perhaps even this particular government. They instead are simply trying to punish this man for what he has allegedly done, in the belief that the regime isn't likely to do so. Beliefs of the latter kind might be part of a larger belief-set implicating the regime more broadly and pointing to a need for more substantial change. If so, that would motivate what we are considering "terrorism" here, but in the absence of such a belief-set, those cases will not count as terrorism in the sense intended here. Tyrannicide is different from terrorism, then, even though the two often go hand in hand, and despite the fact that "tyrannicide" in the broad sense of eliminating a regime that is oppressive (or sustaining in power one that is regarded as just but under threat) is the larger motive of all terrorism in the sense we are employing here.

WAR IN THE SHADOWS

Certainly terrorism is related to war. The terrorist sees himself as engaged in a sort of "war," an informal war in which he is a shadowy participant rather than one in clearly defined uniform, but still a sort of war, aimed at political objectives.

Terrorist attacks cannot be specifically advertised in advance, for if they were they would fail, since their perpetrators would then be apprehended or would be engaged in open battle, which they would necessarily lose. Yet it is essential that it be known by the public, and especially by the agency whose actions are to be influenced by the terrorists' program (normally a government), which organization was responsible. For if recognition is omitted, then nobody can be influenced by the occurrence of a terrorist act to make the proposed changes. And this would destroy the act's status as a political act, thus eliminating any pretense of moral justification.

These two facts constitute a sort of paradox, or at least a source of internal tension: Terrorism can be neither mere murder, which is purely private, without (intended) political significance, nor war, which is entirely public and overt, but which the terrorists would normally be incapable of winning. Murderers would be no match for the police if they were to act in public, like an army; they can be successful only by remaining undiscovered. Armies are intended to be (more than) a match for their opponents, and can be successful only if they are. Thus, terrorists must be in some way public if they are to succeed, yet also secret, since they cannot be strong enough to win in a war, which is a public operation. They operate in "twilight," as it were, rather than either in total darkness or in broad daylight. We expect movies about terrorist organizations to have a lot of shadowy, ill-lit scenes in them; it's an appropriate symbolism.

Does this itself raise a question about the legitimacy of terrorism? Is the use of clandestine, secretive methods of itself morally dubious? It's hard to see that it is. During wartime, we expect armies to attack in secrecy if they can, perhaps at nighttime, to use devices for keeping the armed persons or, say, their airplanes invisible, and so on. What we should perhaps say about this is that what makes terrorism so prima facie objectionable is its essential feature of attacking the presumptively innocent; any further criticisms in respect of its shadowy ways can hardly, by comparison, make the difference between moral permissibility and impermissibility.

THE EVIL OF TERRORISM

Where does terror stand in the hierarchy of moral evils? It is widely regarded as quite peculiarly awful – worse, perhaps, than just about anything else. But on reflection, that is not so very obvious. If we look only at its threatened evils in themselves – being blown to bits, summarily executed, arbitrarily and uncomfortably detained for considerable periods, and so on – we will find that although they are, of course, ghastly, they are not in general strikingly worse in themselves than many others. Torture, for example, is a plausible candidate for a worse evil. (Terrorism can involve torture, of course, but it typically does not.) What terrorists do to people does not exceed in degree of physical damage what is quite normally done by soldiers in wartime, by private criminals, or for that matter by motor vehicles in accidents.

It has become something of a commonplace of the literature that the degree of suffering and death from the latter greatly exceeds that inflicted by terrorists: A normal year's automobile accidents in any sizable Western country probably exceeds all the insurgent terrorist damage to life and limb there has ever been. Moreover, the number of lives lost to such terrorism is a mere fraction of those lost to ordinary murderers, at least in North America; another commonplace of the literature is that the probability of an ordinary citizen's being murdered by a gangster in Detroit is about seven times that of his counterpart in Belfast's being murdered by a terrorist.

We should not forget, though, that both are dwarfed by the wholesale evils of state-inflicted violence – by the Holocaust, Stalin's reign of terror, or the Pol Pot regime in Kampuchea, and so on. It is a fact of life – discouraging, perhaps, but not entirely surprising – that isolated, small-scale acts of terrorism get disproportionately more press than such enormities. The present essay, indeed, concentrates on the least significant of these horrors, from the purely quantitative point of view. Victims of internal state violence fall, usually, to trumped-up causes. Its victims are rarely quite "random." Citizens of reasonably decent states have little fear of such things, whereas they are at risk of the sort of terrorism I am interested in here. How much this difference matters is an interesting question, which I will touch on (but not settle) later on.

It is true that terrorism involves a *peculiar* evil – namely terror. This peculiar evil seems to consist especially in three things.

1. *Sense of risk.* First, for the affected public at large, there is the uncertainty of life it engenders: an increased probability of persons unknown visiting evils upon us without our being able to anticipate them. At any moment, a bomb might go off in the department store we are peaceably shopping in, or our abode might cave in under the force of a blast. For persons held hostage, there is the awful uncertainty of their immediate fate, and in particular its being at the whim of people who seem devoid of the usual human sympathies, persons who are quite possibly psychologically unstable, even irrational – individuals, in fact, who seem to be just barely "persons" at all.

2. *Powerlessness.* Secondly, these risks, no different in kind

and considerably less in degree than those facing the front-line soldier in wartime, differ from the soldier's case not only in that we have no control over the fact of being put at those risks, but also in that we have no way even of knowing that we have assumed them. "Any individual or individuals, ir-respective of anything they may or may not choose not to do, can become the objects of terror. Nor is there any com-pliance behavior that would reduce the probability of their falling victim to terror."[2]

The volunteer soldier has the first of these, the sense of risk, and even the conscript has the second: He at least knows when he is getting into the situation of high risk, and whence it will come. Until that time, he is not appreciably less safe than the normal citizen. But it is precisely that "normal cit-izen" who is put at risk by terrorists. Their attacks can come at any time, anywhere – while we are going about our daily business, or asleep in our beds, for instance – and there is nothing we can do to alleviate the insecurity. Nor, once taken victim, is there much we can do personally to affect release, for the terrorist isn't interested in us, as such, nor in anything we have control over. *Qua* victim of terrorism, we are being used; our fate is entirely in the hands of others. These things especially are what make up the peculiar evil, the "terror," of terrorism.

3. *Apparent absurdity*. A further feature often adds to the agony of this phenomenon from the point of view of the ordinary person. This is what we might call the putative absurdity of terrorism as a method of achieving the terror-ist's aims. Sometimes this is because those aims are so vague that the terror in question can hardly qualify even as an *intended* means of achieving them: If we have no idea what it would be for mankind to live "at one with nature," or whatever, then the suggestion that a good way to reach that condition is to murder a few random innocent people doesn't even get off the ground. As one writer puts it, "To kill in the name of unspecified and unspecifi-able benefits is to kill for no reason at all."[3] (This is the terrible lesson of Marxism's militant side, in retrospect: To

engage in terrible evils when one doesn't really know what one is doing is a tragedy.)

Even when the terrorist's ends are fairly clear, it is often unclear how he could suppose that his terrorist activities conduce to those ends. The sense that we might be not only sacrificed to an abhorrent or silly cause, but pointlessly sacrificed on top of it, adds to our disconsolation at the prospect of being victimized in this way. We feel that our lives would be wasted – and not even by ourselves, but by someone else – treated as jetsam, things of no account that can be not only damaged and wrecked but even *thrown away*. This is an outrage reasonably placed somewhere near the top of ways not to be treated.

What is so awful about terrorism, then? It is, I take it, much the same thing as what is awful about ordinary crime: violence and the threat of violence to peaceable persons, persons attempting to go about their lives in the pursuit of harmless, nonthreatening, and normally useful purposes. "Perhaps the reason to be appalled," as one writer observes, "is indeed not that society and law are in danger. We roll with the punch of terrorist attacks, and society carries on. . . . Perhaps the real cause for worry is much more analogous to the auto accidents. . . . It is simply a major nuisance to have to dodge bombs or to have to fear kidnapping." The nuisance in question is much intensified by the fact that it is caused by fellow humans who "mean to do us harm,"[4] and worse, who mean it in a way that leaves us with peculiarly little control over the situation. Still, a very great nuisance it is, and our rational concern about it should be proportionate to the degree of nuisance in question.

In classifying it as nuisance, I may seem to be taking sides on what is, obviously, a major matter: namely, whether the purposes for which the terrorism is employed do justify it. The assumption is that in general they do not. However, I do not assume that terror is never justifiable for any purpose: Nuisance is sometimes something we may just have to put up with, and the same thing could turn out to be true of terrorism. Let us see.

VIOLENCE AND MORALITY

Certainly the complications of definition I have considered, among various things, suggest a need for a more general treatment. In order to know where terrorism falls on the moral spectrum, we need to have a fair idea about where other uses of violence fall. And to do this, we need a well-grounded moral outlook or theory. The subject is a large one, of course; but we get nowhere on the present case of violence unless we at least indicate generally where we stand on the adjacent cases. When, then, is violence justified – if it ever is – and why? Let me first put the general case.

Morality

Morality, in my view, is a set of behavioral requirements and inducements that are (1) societywide: Everyone is to be subject to, to live up to the rules that are (2) (to be) universally reinforced: Everyone is also to participate in their reinforcement, by an assortment of (3) *informal* methods: No central, official agency defines and enforces them.

One can study the currently existing morality of a given society. But a *justificatory*, philosophical theory of normative ethics should tell us how such a set of rules can be rational. And this in turn, I am persuaded, can only mean considering how it can be rational for all people to do what this recipe says they are to do, namely, to live up to the rules, and take part in getting everyone else to do likewise. Notably this reinforcement will consist in promoting *internalization* of the rules: that is, in inducing each person (and oneself) to be motivated from the inside to be the sort of person who does what those requirements require and to have the sort of character that the general point and structure of those rules make it desirable to have.[5]

Moral justification: the "social contract"

I believe an upshot of this argument is that a rational morality must be understood along the lines of a "social contract," in the following sense: It has to be a reasonable expectation of each participant that she or he will do better if all people live up to those rules than if they have no rules at all, or if they have any of various others, though some others might be just as good. The "if" clause is what makes it contractarian: The obligation to conform applies, *provided* others do likewise; it ceases, at least prima facie, if they do not. The reasonable expectation of doing better, living what one regards as a better life overall, is what makes morality rational when and if it is.

There are ample conceptual difficulties in this idea, to be sure. But instead of discussing them generally, I will consider the argument's application to the case of violence. Whether this succeeds or not, it should make an interesting subject of investigation.

VIOLENCE AND THE SOCIAL CONTRACT

The social contract outlook puts a very great pressure against the use of violence in attaining those miscellaneous ends by which we variously identify the good life, for the obvious reason that for A to do violence to B is for A to do to B what B does not want done to her, namely, to worsen B's situation, without compensation and without consent. That we are not to pursue our routine life purposes by violence is the first rule on the social contract agenda, a requirement without which no proposed morality could reasonably fulfill anyone's schedule of life interests. This is true even of warrior classes, whose pursuit of war would be impossible except against a background of substantial peace and cooperation, at least among the warriors' own support groups; and it is the more obviously true of ordinary people such as you and me.

Just as we can "agree to disagree" about many things, so we can agree to put up with acts that entail a high likelihood of inflicting various kinds of damage to ourselves in special cases. Boxers in the ring do so, within carefully defined limits. So do gamblers, who voluntarily risk their financial interests. And so on. What won't do, however, is to have people doing these things to us *without our leave*. And those who use violence do just that, attacking their victims without warning, without mercy, and without recourse.

In the Hobbesian tradition, to which I incline, those who violate the social contract put themselves back into the state of nature in relation to society. When we encounter actions by individuals in what was supposed to be a civilized society that depart from the norms of agreed practice, some degree of reversion to that lawless condition has been made – at least *some* bets are off. The question is, how many? Clearly we need to envisage degrees of departure and contemplate appropriate corrective measures that are proportionate to the degree of departure. For this purpose, a suitable rough measure is provided by the "retributive" view on punishment: We may do to the other approximately what he has done to us. (Whether we actually *should* do what I am here suggesting we *may* do is, however, quite another matter. The retributivist says we positively ought to do this; I am proposing only that we may do so.)

The justificatory procedure here goes like this: Whenever anybody intentionally does anything, we attribute to him a generalization to the effect that acts of that description (the description under which he acts) *may* be done by anybody, and thus the effects of those acts on others (when there are some) may legitimately be visited upon him. It does not matter whether this individual explicitly makes any claims of that kind. We "attribute" this claim to him not as a further effort to scrutinize his interior psychology, which frankly doesn't, as such, matter to us, but rather with a view to constructing a reasonable basis for interaction. Such a basis is, by definition, a mutually reasonable one: one to which both of us can give rational assent, from our respective – and probably diverse – points of view.

When someone deviates from a reasonable rule, then, we suppose him not, at first, to have abandoned *all* of morality but only some segment of it, leaving much, and in particular the more important because more basic features of it, in operation. This gives us a base line for reasonable response:

Moral bets are off, back to the nearest base line to which it is reasonable to suppose (from what we know of our agent's collateral behavior) he is still willing to adhere. If he cheats at cards, we cease playing cards, but we don't pull out our 45s and shoot him.

Where what our agent has done is to perform a major act of violence against us, then, the reasonable rule is that we may respond up to that level at least. A great many bets are off with such an individual, since what he does affects so major a portion of our lives. And for one who uses unlimited violence, *all* bets are off, we are in the unlimited Hobbesian condition, and in principle there is nothing we may not do to him. What we do to him may or may not be motivated by retaliation. The point here is only that he may not complain even if that is our motive and even if we consider retaliation prima facie disreputable, as indeed we should. But how, in view of his terrible behavior, does *he* get to complain about that?

JUSTIFYING VIOLENCE: THE OPTIONS

Here is a list of situations that might be (and, sometimes or often, have been) held to justify violence. I suggest that our social contract outlook will lead to the following ordering of types of cases, from most to least plausible as justifications of violence:

1. Preventing immediate injury to self – sheer self-defense
2. Preventing immediate injury to others – sheer other-defense
3. Preventing longer-range threats to life, to self or others
4. Preventing or rectifying loss of legitimate liberty by self or others
5. Providing conditions of a minimally acceptable life when no other means is possible (even though others have not clearly deprived one of such conditions)
6. Promoting a *better* life for oneself, some favored group, or humankind at large, beyond the "minimally acceptable"

level mentioned in (5). (A variant of [6] would be providing a level of life *as good as* that enjoyed by some other group or individual, or bearing some other proportion to it.)

This list, I should make clear, concerns the *ends* for which violence might be justified. Two further kinds of consideration will need to be assessed, however. One is whether the means employed are acceptable in the circumstances, even if the ends are in order. We shall want to insist that the violent means be *necessary*, in some sense needing clarification; that they be of likely efficacy; and that they be reasonably proportionate to their ends. Many of the major questions about terrorism concern these further questions. I will be taking them up in a later section ("Justice in Means").

The other consideration concerns the special category of punishment. This too I consider in a later section ("Punishment").

At present, my question is, which if any of these proffered justifications is capable of justifying violence? I will argue that (1)–(4) are basically acceptable, that (6) is definitely not acceptable, and that (5) is the hard case, but that fundamentally it must be considered marginally acceptable if at all.

THE ACCEPTABLE JUSTIFICATIONS: VIOLENCE AS DEFENSE

Assuming that the requirement of reasonable proportionality in one's use of violence is observed, (1) and (2) provide the clearest cases of justified use of it: We may employ some degree of violence to ward off some degree of threatened violence, if necessary. This is an immediate correlate of the fundamental plank of the moral platform about violence: Those against whom retaliatory violence is used in (1) or (2) are persons who are acting in violation of its basic provisions. What degree of violence do those two conditions justify? I have elsewhere suggested that what is allowed is, eventually, *whatever is required to do the job*, though initially one's preventive violence should not exceed what is threatened.[6] As argued earlier, if the attack is expectedly fatal, then fatal force may if necessary be employed; if less, then less.

What about cases of type (3)? Suppose I claim to be protecting someone from a threat that is not immediate: How much may I do? May we engage in preventive warfare, "getting" them before they "get" us? Not, at least, unless the evidence is strong that they do pose a real though temporally distant threat of harm, *and* there is no economical and nonviolent way of effectively allaying this threat. (I further explain the intended sense of "economical" later in this essay.)

In fact, the question what constitutes "defense" is likely to be the foremost source of dispute in these matters. Defending ourselves against someone advancing with a lethal weapon with evident intent to do damage is one thing. But what about defense of what we conceive to be our basic rights and liberties? A's threat to dismember B on the spot is certainly a threat to B's liberty, just in virtue of being a threat to B's life and limb. But what about threats to B's property, or B's desired way of life? I take the right to property to be an offshoot of, indeed an inference from, the general right to liberty.[7] But reasonably deciding what is ours may be difficult indeed – and much the more so when the liberty in question is a "collective" liberty of some large group.

This relates to terrorism in a direct way. Suppose the terrorists claim to be promoting the "liberation" of some sizable group. Then we must ask: Is the current regime threatening the members of that group with a degree of force that justifies such an extreme response as the execution of anyone? And even if it is, who may then be executed?

Let us concede that the situation sometimes is that extreme. There is sometimes an ongoing pattern of state violence – even, in some cases, what can reasonably be considered state terrorism. Peaceable means of influencing this regime are unavailable, indeed suppressed by the regime in question. Does this license violence? Yes. But does it and could it license *terrorism*? This is less promising. The violence that an act of initial violence authorizes is directed against

the aggressor, not persons who are presumptively bystanders. Most important, there is the case where the terrorists'
objection to those they attack is that they have *done* nothing
to rectify the injustices of which the terrorists complain. I
will return to this central type of case, noting here only that,
prima facie, this is not sufficient to justify violence. "Nothing" is the normal base line of interaction: It is precisely what
people normally do owe us, and we them. It is when they
threaten to treat us worse than that that we may have cause
to react with violence.

THE PROBLEMATIC JUSTIFICATION: NEED

Meanwhile, what of cases of type (5) or even (6)? There is,
first, a fundamental line to be drawn between (1)–(4) on the
one hand and (5)–(6) on the other. For in (1)–(4), at least
those against whom violence is used are, as I say, themselves
in violation of the reasonable rules of morality. But when we
come to (5), let alone (6), there is a problem. It is not clear
that morality does or can require us to guarantee each other
even the "minimum essentials of a decent life" – especially
if "decency" is left to the whims of current ideological fashion
for its definition.[8]

Here there is enormous disagreement in the literature,
some holding that there is a fundamental right to an equal
share of the world's natural resources, at least, or possibly
even of its socially produced goods. The case for the former,
on social contract grounds, is dubious enough; but the latter
entails a problem of major dimensions. For if I claim a right
to what *you* have produced, in order to keep *me* alive, then
I do *not* appeal to a common value. You didn't produce it in
order to feed me, but to feed yourself, or some loved one,
or to do any number of other things with it. I have no fundamental claim on your resources. I can offer my services in
some way, in return for sustenance. With any luck we shall
make a deal. Or I may appeal to your humanity and sympathy, and, again with any luck, you are likely to respond.
But if I choose to satisfy my needs by violence, then it is hard

to see why you are not justified in responding in kind. Your case becomes one of defense. My need is something to which you, being human, are likely to respond with sympathy; my threat, however, is something else.

If the only way to keep from starving is to use violence, may we then use it? Rather than answer this question straightforwardly in the affirmative, as too many do, it seems to me that we must rather say something like this: that we may have a situation in which nothing can be said about rights and wrongs, because we are below the minimal requisites to provide a basis for expecting humans all to benefit from cooperation. And this is, indeed, something for the more fortunate of us to bear in mind. But it is by no means the same thing as granting a "right." Rights require universal respect; but in the case of this putative "right," the basis for such respect is importantly lacking.

It doubtless behooves the better-off to consider the plight that might be faced by the resourceless, and in particular that it could certainly motivate violence by them even if it does not justify it. To forestall this, or in preference to extensive schemes of protection, the better-off might well turn to a scheme of guaranteed minimal means of life, in exchange for a renunciation of violence as a recourse. This, indeed, may be the correct underlying description of what all technologically developed states have in fact done. If so, of course, this particular possible motivation for political terrorism is not a live option – a point of considerable importance, as will be seen later on.

THE UNACCEPTABLE JUSTIFICATIONS

Whatever we say of this extreme (and rare) situation, we must draw a very strong line between (5) and (6). Using violence against individual A merely in order to improve the condition of individual B from some already tolerable condition to some better one is not, on the face of it, morally acceptable; using it where life is at stake, on the other hand, is another matter. The latter is in the realm of the under-

standable and the excusable, if not the justifiable; the former
is below that level altogether.

Two sorts of motive are here rejected. One might be called
"self-improvement." Old-fashioned imperialism is one example, the motivation being sheer aggrandizement of the
conquering party. The motivation of simply having more
than the other fellow is another.

Thus consider the goal of securing a homeland for the Jews,
which inspired, as I understand it, a fair amount of outright
terrorism in the 1940s[9] and continues to motivate extensive
violence to the present day. Those against whom violence
was originally employed in order to wrest their lands for this
purpose had done no wrong by any reasonable standard;
they simply happened to be in the way. Here was a group
of people who wanted to live together, as a group, and to
do so at a particular place, what is now Israel. But that place
happened to be already occupied by other people, who had
been there hundreds of years and whose title to the land was
clear by any reasonable standard. The morally appropriate
way to proceed here is to go and make an offer, prima facie.
Yet the reasonable idea of proposing to buy out those people
doesn't seem to have been taken very seriously, even though
it is likely that such a real-estate campaign would have met
with a considerable measure of success. But no, the Jews
simply *had* to have a "homeland" in this particular area, their
claim to which was largely a function of religious beliefs and
of exceedingly murky and remote history.

Is it reasonable to suppose that the rules on which diverse
people will interact would permit people to use violence
against the persons and properties of others for *such* reasons?
A negative answer to this question seems remarkably obvious. Had not the Jews themselves complained of being
victims of religious discrimination in precisely such respects
for centuries on end? To go on about the historic and divinely
inspired mission of the Jewish people and suchlike is simply
to sweep the fundamental issue under the carpet. Such
things may be said to fellow Jews, but they cannot reasonably
be said to persons of entirely differing faith and traditions,

by way of explaining to them why you are forcibly depriving them of their centuries-old property.

That the considerable terrorism practiced by Jewish extremists in the process of creating modern Israel was not morally acceptable, then, seems clear enough. Do I get to go out and blow people to pieces because I like their land better than the bit I already have, or even because I currently don't have any? Or because two thousand years ago people from *our* team lived there rather than people from the tribe of those who occupy it now (and for many preceding centuries)? How helpful is it to go into the details of extremely early history at this level?

What is much disputed in some portions of the literature, however, is what some regard as a distinct motive: equality, say of material condition or welfare. But this too must be rejected as a justification of violence. There is no reason at all why people should be thought to have equality as any kind of common end, and it is patently clear that they do not. Most people – though, to be sure, by no means all – presumably wish to be as well off as possible, whatever the resulting relation between themselves and others in this respect. A social contract among everyone and everyone else cannot assume that people have motives they do not have. And among those who happen not to share the passion for equality, no good reason for requiring everyone to restrict his or her ends to those compatible with someone's idea of "equal condition" is discernible – not to mention that the idea affords no clear and uniform definition that makes any sense anyway.[10]

PUNISHMENT

When a disutility is inflicted on someone on the ground that that person is in turn guilty of a violation of one of the reasonable moral restrictions, how are we to view this event? Some theories on this matter, those of a broadly "retributivist" cast, have it that punishment is something like an end in itself, such as that of effecting a proper moral "balance" between offender and victim. Others, however, see punishment as a kind of extension of defense: In threatening those who propose to use violence against innocents, we are in effect defending those innocents. If we have, as most of us think and as I will argue next, the right to defend ourselves, then so long as our proposed system of punishment meets the restrictions on means, it too would be justified.

Punishment as an end in itself, however, is extremely problematic from the contractarian perspective. But it is sometimes in effect viewed as a sort of compensation to the aggrieved party. Whatever the merits of that idea, compensation itself is certainly supported by the contract scheme. If that scheme gives me a right to x, and you take x away from me, then the terms of the contract will be met if you can and do restore x to me. And that is a motivation that does loom fairly large in terrorist annals.

POLITICS

The thesis I have been defending, utilizing the list surveyed and the ensuing discussion, is that violence is justified exclusively on the basis of defense against violence: namely, violence against life and limb, and against freely pursued courses of life that do not in their turn inflict violence against others. As it stands, this conclusion may seem too narrow, confined as it is to the case of individuals against individuals. Yet much violence, and all terrorism, are for political ends. One could well ask whether I should include further entries on my list to cover violence for the purpose of bringing about just political situations. By way of anticipation, my reply is that alterations of that kind either are necessary for the defense of what is already argued to be defensible, or are not. If not, then those political alterations may not be pursued by violent means. To maintain a right to, say, political independence for its *own* sake, and independently of any of the causes already considered, is to ask what is unacceptable: to ask that others give way, and even allow the use of force in order to ensure that they give way, to the pursuit of ends

137

they do not share and have no evident stake in. Government pretends to benefit all. But when it imposes political unity on the peaceable but reluctant, it does not do so, and it loses its claims to legitimacy. Government, and therefore politics, are, in short, to be put in the category of means and not ends.

TERRORISM: TWO PROPOSED JUSTIFICATIONS

What is the terrorist's case? How does he purport to justify his savage actions? Sometimes the actions in question are claimed, as I have noted, to be *executions*, punishments. This claim, as noted, takes us somewhat outside the narrow area of terrorism, but we are including it for the reasons given at the outset. The other and more important rubric is that of securing justifiable political change. I shall consider each by turn.

Terrorism as punishment

If the claim is that the violence perpetrated amounts to execution or the like, we have in turn two questions:

1. Is capital punishment really morally justified for the alleged deeds being "punished"? In particular, does it apply in the case of the particular victims actually killed, who are usually not personally guilty of those alleged crimes, or, arguably, of any crimes at all?

2. Is it appropriate for the execution to be carried out outside the standard legal system, specifically the legal system of the society to which the killers belong?

The first of these questions involves us in the general issue of capital punishment. We can hardly take up that issue here, except to note, first, that many would deny that capital punishment is ever justified, even for horrendous crimes; but second, and more crucially, that it is inherent in terrorism's methods that the persons "executed" are normally not guilty of anything that their societies or governments *consider* to be crimes at all, let alone capital ones. Nor, ordinarily, are they guilty of anything the terrorists would consider to be capital crimes.

Besides that, few among those who do advocate capital punishment would allow that it may suitably be carried out in the absence of laws explicitly providing for and regulating it. If the point of law is to defend our rights, then it is irrational to favor the public toleration of procedures that completely dispense with the procedural safeguards of the law for such matters as the assessment of guilt for capital crimes – literally matters of life and death. Thus there is here a tension between the two questions just raised: Even if the acts done by the "executed" persons were awful and should have been illegal – often quite dubious – the fact that they were not illegal is not easily dismissed. To be executed for an act that was regarded as permissible by one's society, and perhaps even as one's downright duty as an agent of the government of that society, is very likely, at a minimum, to be *unfair*, as being a violation of what lawyers refer to as "natural justice." The victim is "tried" and "executed" on the basis of "laws" not knowable in advance; neither she nor anyone else is given the chance to refute the "charges" on the basis of which she is condemned. Thus it is difficult for terrorist "executions" to be anything but travesties of justice in purely procedural terms.

Difficult, yes – but not really impossible. If a public execution can ever be right, then it can hardly be denied that a private execution *could*, in principle, be substantively right. The victim may in fact have done acts that really deserved capital punishment, even though this fact is not recognized by public law or in the public courts. If so, however, the justification for bypassing the legal system would have to be that the system is corrupt, its laws in need of overhauling, its officials incompetent, debased, or irretrievably biased, or that it simply is not possible under the circumstances (no publicly ascertainable evidence being available, e.g.) to bring that particular person to justice. If the former kind of claims about our system are being made by the terrorist organization, we should have to get into the evaluation of those changes and thus into general political philosophy. In the absence of such justification, we would provisionally have to rule the terrorists in the wrong – and, as will be argued further later on, the fact that they were unwilling to argue it in public prior to acting isn't going to help their case any.

In the case where the evidence isn't publicly available, the terrorist clearly doesn't have much chance of persuading us. We shall value the safeguards of public procedures above the dubious "protections" inflicted by the terrorists in the name of whatever values he claims to promote.

All in all, we cannot reasonably be expected to tolerate a society in which anything as important as the deprivation of life is simply left to the judgment of private persons acting on their own advisement, even if in the interests of what they allege to be good public purposes. To live in such a society is to walk in terror indeed. Meanwhile, let us move to the other and more fundamental of the proposed justifications of terrorism.

Terrorism as a means of social change: two questions

When the victims of terrorists are simply killed rather than claimed to be "executed," those victims are being used as means to political or social change. If such justifications are to be seriously pressed, we must again ask two basic questions:

1. Are the changes the terrorists are trying to bring about really improvements over the status quo? This corresponds to the familiar requirement in the just war tradition that the war must be fought for just cause.

2. Would terrorist methods of bringing about those changes be justified even if the first question were answered in the affirmative? This brings up the just war tradition's *jus in bello* requirements of "proportionality" and "discriminateness."

Serious consideration of these questions, I shall argue, raises a formidable barrier to the moral acceptability of terrorism. For both (1) and (2) must be answered in the affirmative if it is to be justified; yet question (2), I shall argue, could hardly ever be rationally so answered. Our naturally low opinion of terrorism is, I shall argue, justified. Let us see why.

THREE CONDITIONS ON JUST ENDS

If the claim is that terrorism will bring about improvements in our political or social arrangements, what constraints are there on such claims? I propose three.

1a. We may say for starters that the proposed scheme of improvements must be *coherent* – must make sense.
1b. Next, the changes on behalf of which violence is employed must genuinely be improvements, sufficient in degree to outweigh the costs involved in making them.
1c. And third, not just any old improvement will do. Rather, the improvement must be specifically an improvement in the *justice* of the society in question. A change that gave everyone in the society a piece of cake next Sunday would not justify the killing of anyone, including those who could have provided such an improvement but, meanies that they are, refused to do so.

Coherence of aim

The first requirement is that the proposed change in our society at least be describable, in a coherent and clear enough way so as to form a basis for rational concrete action. After all, if we can't *understand* a proposed change, how can we reasonably believe it to be an improvement?

This would hardly be worth mentioning were it not that even this very minimal condition is not often met. Consider, for instance, the wave of bomb throwing at the turn of the present century on behalf of what was billed as "anarchism," a program having apparently two main objectives: to abolish government and to bring about a communistic redistribution of wealth. Right. And how does one go about achieving such a redistribution in the absence of government? Nobody knew. The two aims were, practically speaking, incompatible.

The agents of any serious political action – not to mention killing people – are going to have to do better than that in specifying their ends, if there is to be any hope of their activity's achieving justification via these ends. It is not easy to think of a more unjust act than that of taking someone's life on behalf of a program so vague or incoherent that we would have no idea what it would be like even if we attempted to institute it with the best of intentions and overwhelming support. (Here one thinks of Marx, who devoted his life to advocating revolution but almost no time at all to telling us what the new situation was supposed to be like.)

Improvement

All violence against persons and their justly acquired property – which I take to be, morally speaking, essentially an extension or aspect of personhood – is, I take it, on the face of it wrong, and so requires special justification. Obviously violence on behalf of a change that is no better than what we already have would be unjustified. The argument is by simple dominance: S_2 would then differ from S_1 only in that some innocent people are worse off, for example, dead. An improvement, at a minimum, is required.

How much of an improvement? If a change is to be brought about by high levels of violence, then the improvement to be achieved by these means must be substantial. Thus, suppose that a certain change might decrease the waiting period for criminal trials by an average of three days per case. May anyone be killed in order to bring that change about? Surely not. However, where the regime being objected to is itself engaging in wholesale slaughter, in widespread intimidation, suppression, and so on, then the principles broached in this essay clearly put *levels* of violence of the order employed by terrorists on the list of morally contemplatable options.

Really significant improvements are required, then; but of what kind? Here we get into deep waters. How are we to judge proposed "improvements" in "social systems"? And how do we weigh the worth of persons sacrificed against the proposed improvements? This last question is widely responded to by rejecting the claim that we can do it at all. But the situation is not so simple. We will shortly take up the "discriminateness" requirement of classical just war fame. However, our next restriction is also clearly relevant to it.

The restriction to contexts of justice

Why confine the range of improvements to improvements in justice? The answer, I think, lies in this: A political system is essentially a system for allocating such goods and services – if any – as may be legitimately allocated by coercive methods. Where no coercion formerly exists, the introduction of coercion must be objectionable from the point of view of all concerned. For nobody is then preventing others from living the lives they see fit, given their resources. A situation in which this is no longer the case, which is necessarily what we have when coercion is introduced, must therefore be Pareto inferior to one that lacks coercion. And Pareto inferiority is the hallmark of the irrational when it comes to social systems.

JUSTICE IN MEANS

Supposing our cause is right, we next turn to the issues concerning means. I shall divide the issues raised by this second question among three further ones. We may continue relating the discussion to the just war tradition by thinking of the first two as relating to the traditional "proportionality" requirement, the third to that of "discriminateness."

2a. *Necessity*: Would other methods involving less or, preferably, no violence be possible?

2b. *Efficacy*: Is the proposed violence likely to be an *effective* way to bring about those changes?

2c. *Permissibility*: Even if terrorism would work and nothing else would, is it morally permissible to bring changes about by those means? Or must we simply live with the situation, under the circumstances?

Necessity and efficacy

Clearly we shall object to the use of violence on behalf of any change, however justified, if that change *could* have been achieved, at least with comparable readiness, by nonviolent methods. Similarly, we shall object to a method with such hideous costs if it is also certain to be inefficacious, even if any other method of achieving that end is equally so. (Pacifists would omit this last clause. I will discuss their view later ["Pacifism"].)

How would a case for the necessity of violence be made, where political ends are at issue? The first consideration that comes to mind is whether the terrorist's case has had a chance to be heard by those in power. In a democracy, with its electoral procedures and its institutions of free speech, it seems that the claim that it has not had such a chance would be hard to sustain. Indeed, many would suggest that the presence of democracy in the political system in question would automatically render violent methods of major change unjust. We will consider that case first, and then turn to the more prima facie plausible case of nondemocratic institutions. Since we must apply both questions for any given case, 2a and 2b will be considered in tandem for the two importantly different cases of democratic and nondemocratic institutional background.

DEMOCRATIC CHANGE

Democracy is rule "by the people." Political changes are to be brought about by public discussion against the background of a free press and via election of legislators by uncoerced voting, open to the entire public. Certainly, a prime stimulus to terrorist activity has been the absence of such methods in various societies. Sometimes terrorism has been the result of frustration owing to inability to get a case for proposed changes effectively into the democratic process. Still, on many other occasions it has in fact been perfectly possible for groups that resorted to terrorism to publish their views and run candidates in an election. When these alternatives are not taken, why aren't they? Undoubtedly it's because the group is sure it would lose in a free election, if indeed it could get the public to take its views seriously in the first place. Do we in that fact alone have sufficient reason to object to terrorism? I think not. For the terrorist group may feel, in fact, that only by outrageous actions can it get its views "taken seriously."

If terrorism is resorted to in the context of presumptively democratic political institutions of the familiar contemporary type, then the terrorist must suppose that his case goes beyond what is within the reasonable scope of democratic methods. He must, then, appeal to principles more fundamental than democracy. Are there such principles? Of course there are. All of those considered here in "Justifying Violence: The Options" are so. But if he does claim to appeal to more fundamental principles, we must ask how he is going to manage to find a principle more fundamental than that condemning violence against nonaggressors – which seems to be the very essence of the terrorist's procedures.

Consider the matter from the contractarian point of view. Obviously no one could want just any and every matter settled by an election: Whether or not Joe Smith should be hanged in the public square tomorrow for the general amusement is, I take it, not a subject that should come to a vote in the first place. But in a considerable range of cases (how extensive a range is a matter of enormous dispute) various alternative programs each have something to be said for them, and yet something must be done. In such cases it is hard to deny the attractions of a system that, generally, does the things that at any rate more people favor than any alternative, and that permits everyone to attempt to persuade those of another point of view from his own. And in any case, if most people are against a certain change, then the only way of getting it brought about is by force or duplicity; and then we should all be exposed constantly to the employment of violence, deception, or both – surely an intolerable state of things for persons concerned to pursue their chosen ways of life. For though another alternative might be better for us, if others find it worse for them and we can't convince them, while only public action would make either alternative possible, then we must either accept the one we like less or fight; and although some things are worth fighting for, the condition on which fighting for them is *morally* acceptable is that they are worth fighting for on the basis of or in defense of a principle that is acceptable from *everyone's point of view*. But so long as the matter lies within the aforementioned range, that condition is not met. When many different resolutions are inherently legitimate, and some public resolution is essential, then if a majority is against what we want even after we have had opportunity to persuade it otherwise, the likelihood of that condition's being met is, one must conclude, virtually nil. Indeed, the justification of democracy, if it is justified, is precisely that what we can all agree on when we cannot agree on any particular outcome is the selection of the democratic method of arriving at a particular outcome. So if anything like terrorism were to be justified in a democracy, it would have to be because democratic principles were being somehow misapplied: Either the matter wasn't properly exposed to the machinery of democracy or else things were done by that machinery that ought not to be so done.

But which things are those? In the absence of very extensive agreement about that point, we shall not be in possession of a secure rejection to terrorism in principle against any even moderately democratic state.

In sum, the argument that terrorism is necessary because prevailing political institutions do not enable the terrorists' case to be heard is implausible in the democratic context. If the ways in which their case *can* be heard do not suffice, then it is improbable that terroristic methods will contribute to its acceptance to a degree making it likely that their political aims will be realized. One would think the opposite more probable: A public made aware of someone's case by terroristic acts is likely to condemn the case along with the acts.

THE NONDEMOCRATIC CASE

Consider, then, the cases in which fair election procedures are not available: Might there then be a case for terrorism? Here we must draw a line between violent revolution and terrorism.[11] Whereas both involve the use of violence and a likelihood of innocent persons' falling victim to it, they differ in that the terrorist deliberately inflicts it on the innocent. In both cases, of course, the factor of likelihood of success must be looked at seriously. The question is whether terrorism differs importantly in this respect.

Let us suppose that the changes proposed are such as to justify measures so extreme as attacks on innocent persons to get them adopted (we will assume for the sake of argument that there can be such cases). But this justification will be lacking if the measures in question have, nevertheless, no chance of success. Such users of violence would be killing innocent people for no good reason, and the lives of their victims would be simply wasted. No possible pretense of justification remains in that case.

A word of caution is in order. We have here been speaking mainly of "insurgent" terrorism, which we may define as terrorism aimed at *changing* (some aspect of) the political status quo. ("State" terrorism, by contrast, is aimed at *maintaining* that status quo.) Yet it is inherent in the insurgent terrorist's enterprise that its activities are unlikely to succeed, especially on behalf of large-scale, permanent social change. For we are supposing that military power lies in the hands of the current state, which our hypothetical dissident regards as the enemy. If the dissident group is so small that it must resort to terrorism rather than overt military activity – a method that presupposes a substantial base of support, in both money and numbers of followers – then either it must be quite unpopular or its support populace must be very weak. If it is unpopular, then it can effect no changes of a type requiring large-scale acceptance. And if this tiny group were to step forward and identify itself so as to assume the reigns of government, its members would automatically make themselves the targets of the existing police, if there are any, *and*, one might add, of any other groups that happened to have a few guns or bombs at their disposal. If terrorism is proclaimed to be legitimate for group X, then groups Y and Z will be sure to think it legitimate for them, too. The situation may degenerate into one of general violent chaos, and the public is unlikely to have much sympathy for any of the contenders under the circumstances. The melancholy case of contemporary Lebanon comes to mind.

Thus if our tiny group is to be effective on behalf of large-scale change, it will have to be so by influencing the public. But will the public sympathize with a group whose method of advertising its aims is to blow innocent people to bits? This will no doubt influence people, but is this how we win friends? This, I hasten to add, is not an a priori rejection of the possible efficacy of terrorism. It is simply an important general consideration about likely efficacy. Roughly, the conclusion is that unless one is working for a cause already popular, then these methods will essentially ensure that it won't become so.[12]

INFLUENCING THE REGIME

I have here been speaking of widespread social change. But sometimes the purpose of the group will be much narrower. There may be government officials with the power to influence the specific policy the terrorist wants to bring into effect. Could not a well-planned terrorist campaign influence those officials to take the desired steps? It is difficult to avoid the conclusion that it might and, indeed, that in many cases it has.

Should governments *allow themselves to be influenced* by such means? This question, though obviously relevant, is somewhat academic in the case of the sort of regimes we are considering here, namely undemocratic ones. Since such regimes have normally gotten into office by violence in the first place, they are likely to be responsive to such methods. Nevertheless, some nondemocratic regimes may be responsible ones; in their cases, as well as in the democratic regimes familiar to us, the question is serious. Terrorism is obviously a public evil, not only because of the particular people who are killed or injured, but also because of the climate of insecurity it creates. Any responsible official will be concerned to avoid such attacks if possible. Yet if officials give in to the demands of one terrorist group on one occasion, will this not encourage other groups, on the same or other occasions? And where will it end? This is the terrible dilemma faced by officials. They can perhaps quell the particular danger mounted right now, but only at the risk of encouraging similar behavior in future. Terrorism in this form is a kind of blackmail, and raises much the same issues. Even in these special cases, the probability of success must be low because of the enormous public interest in keeping it low.

The most that responsible officials can do, after all, is to try to get the terrorist group to come forward and air its grievances in the public forum, and to give them a fair hearing. Of course, it is characteristic of a nondemocratic state that this is precisely the sort of thing it will not do – indeed, will instead do its best to prevent. Still, the regime ought to have made a fair hearing possible anyway. Even in a nondemocracy, means of giving alternative views serious hearing should exist. But to say this is to indulge in hand-wringing. When the prevailing institutions make serious discussion of alternative policies and structures impossible, then they are at fault, and if those institutions extensively violate other rights, in addition, then the case for violent action *against their responsible officials* is uncomfortably strong. But extending the range of targets to innocents is another matter. Whether that too can be justified, even in the outrightly undemocratic cases, remains to be seen.

Thus one must conclude that terrorism is extremely difficult to justify on strategic grounds, in the nature of the case. If its causes were plausible, terrorism as a means to promote them would be unnecessary, and when it is used, it is virtually assured of failure except for the most limited and immediate of purposes. Of course it will also produce hatred and suspicion of the terrorist group, rather than sympathy and support – another major factor working to ensure nonsuccess. Yet all of these factors are fairly obvious, and must surely be known to any terrorist groups that pause to reflect. Which, evidently, they often do not.

From this we must infer that much terrorism is quite properly regarded by the public as a "lunatic fringe" activity. Its initiators may pretend to be serious social reformers, to be working for just causes and thus worthy of the mantle of moral respectability; but in fact, the phenomenon turns out, all too often, to be of psychiatric rather than moral purport. What to do about terrorism, of course, remains a problem. But whether terrorism is morally justified seems scarcely to be an *issue* in many cases – scarcely a subject upon which reasonable people may differ.

We may, of course, differ about the ends to which terrorism is used: Whether society should, in the interests of justice, be changed in fundamental ways, and whether a particular group has been mistreated and ought to get a better shake, are certainly discussable subjects. The argument here, however, has turned primarily upon whether terrorism as a means to the promotion of those ends can ever be justified. In arguing that it virtually never can, a fair amount of weight has been put on the fact that it is highly unlikely to succeed in promoting them.

DISPENSING WITH EFFICACY

Now some might argue that efficacy cannot be a fundamental moral consideration in any case. For one thing, terrorism is not always inefficacious. But even when it is, is there not something grand and impressive about a noble though futile gesture on behalf of a good cause? And doesn't every terrorist think that he has a good cause? No doubt there is, and no doubt he does. But when the gesture consists in murdering or maiming innocent people, and terrorizing great numbers of others, the attribution of "grandness" is surely misplaced.

Let's look at it from the point of view of those innocent people – bearing in mind that morality, in the contractarian view, requires a universally acceptable basis of principle. How are we to get universal consent for junking the distinction between innocence and guilt that terrorism requires? And worse, what about the ignoring of likelihood of success in favor of grandeur? Even one who shares the goals of the terrorist will balk at the suggestion that he or she should be willing to be sacrificed *needlessly* for that cause. Like any act of criminal folly, however base its motivation, a terrorist act is likely to succeed in momentarily getting some space on page 1 in which the cause will come in for mention (unfavorable, one would hope). In a rare case, someone might think that result justifies the sacrifice of his or her life. But the terrorist doesn't ask his victims whether they would agree to the sacrifice: On the contrary, it is part of the very idea of it that their wishes on the matter are ignored. This makes the prospect of universal consent pretty desperate. But not, as I will shortly argue, impossible.

ARE THERE MORALLY IMPERMISSIBLE MEANS?

The last question on our list was whether terrorism *could* be permissible even if, as is extremely unlikely, all of the conditions mentioned have been met: The cause is just, no other alternative is available, and the means used really would be effective. Is the terrorist now justified, at any rate? Many think not. We have seen that terrorism inherently involves the grave risk of death or injury to evidently innocent people, those who, in a military context, would be termed "noncombatants." Now in the military case there is indeed risk of killing noncombatants, and plainly that is something that both sides ought, if possible, to avoid. But it is often impossible to avoid, as we all know; and when it is impossible, such killing is sometimes justifiable.

What makes it so, however, is that in a war the armies on each side are defending themselves from attack, and the army of the side with the just cause (if any) is defending an entire nation from attack as well. But terrorists are not "defending" either themselves or anyone else from attack or aggression, in general. In wanting to promote general social causes, the terrorist is most unlikely to be able to identify specific "victims" of unjust "attacks." Can it ever be right to promote general social justice by deliberately killing innocent people, even if doing so *would* promote those causes?

Here we have a question of moral arithmetic. We can imagine cases in which it would be possible to predict that if we kill N innocent people, then M innocent people who would have been killed by the enemy will not be killed: Killing the N innocents saves the lives of M innocents. Now suppose, what is invariably true in terrorist cases, that *none* of the Ns would have been among the Ms: None of the people we kill in our contemplated terrorist attack are among those who would have been killed in the foreseeable future by the oppressors we are trying to get rid of. It is easy to see that where N is not greatly different from M in size, the terrorist tactic ought not to be used. When fighting fire with fire, the fire you fight must threaten to do much more damage, if unchecked, than the fire you fight it with. (Imagine burning down the house of Jones, which was not in danger, in order to prevent the precisely similar house of Smith from catching fire.) But what if M is much greater than N? What if a hundred innocent lives are saved for every innocent life sacrificed?

Some thinkers on these matters insist that even then the

terrorist tactic is unjustified. To the question "Should the Numbers Count?" for instance, John Taurek answers in the negative.[13] But the answer is not plausible. That there is a case to be made along these lines at the intuitive level is clear enough if we contemplate an increase in the ratio of Ms to Ns. (This tactic has, for instance, fazed Robert Nozick and Charles Fried, to name two erstwhile defenders of "side constraints."[14] Suppose it is not just a hundred, but thousands or millions or even billions who will be saved for every innocent person sacrificed? Of course these situations are extremely unlikely – in the case of terrorism, their probability is, I have insisted, close to zero. No current terrorist can have adequate reason for thinking that such a ratio obtains in his case. But if it were to obtain, then what?

PACIFISM

One way of ruling considerations of numbers out of court is to embrace the principle that all violence is forbidden, as a matter of principle. We could follow the pacifist's principle and refrain from harming anyone, guilty or innocent, regardless of consequences. Though this is a rather large subject, it is clear that from the contractarian point of view of the present inquiry, pacifism as a matter of sheer principle is a nonstarter. That no one may use force for any purpose is violently unreasonable in those terms, and to embrace such a principle unilaterally is to open the door to evil.

Nor, I think, is it reasonable to deny that the perpetrators of terrorist acts often *deserve* to get their heads blown off. But it is possible to argue that violence, even when done to the guilty, in the long run breeds more violence. Tyrants of all sorts, including the local versions that terrorists are while they do their deeds, may be frustrated by refusals to cooperate with them even if no actions aimed at hurting them are taken; bringing them down by force will only create more problems than it solves, says the pacifist.

But these claims are hardly obvious. It sometimes is clear

that lives are saved by quick, decisive, and violent action. It is far less clear that an indiscriminate policy of nonviolence will do as well, at least in any moderate-length run. For in the long run, it isn't just that *we* are all dead, but that our friends, spouses, children, and others we value are too. And this isn't *fair*. If I have my choice between the cold-blooded agent of some ill-reasoned outrage lying bloodied on the earth and decent, harmless people doing so, then I shall opt for the former, not the latter; indeed, I owe it to the innocent that I adopt this preference and act on it. This, it seems to me, is largely independent of the pacifist's insistence that his is the "way of peace" – or if it is, then one must doubt that peace is all it's cracked up to be. Humankind down through the ages has insisted, not on peace, but on a just peace. I doubt that any other sort is really attainable, but I am inclined to think, first, that even if it is, it may not be worth having, and second, that at any rate nobody has any business forcing us to choose it at the cost of most or all of what we hold dear.

This last point is the crucial one. We may grant that in most and conceivably all cases, there might be effective nonviolent policies that would do the job – and could perhaps even be found, *if* we were to devote incredible amounts of time and effort, much of it wholly out of accord with our tastes in living, to training for the task of meeting such eventualities in the nonviolent ways in question. But the attacker has no *right* to that level of effort from us. Pacifism, as so conceived, violates the "economical" constraint proposed in my discussion of morally permissible uses of violence. People have the right to the least violent response to their threats and attacks among those responses that we have at our disposal without undue cost and disruption of our preferred legitimate ways of life. Going beyond this gives others, and in particular the violent, the right to disrupt our lives and impose large costs on us; but it is a major point of morality that it is precisely such impositions that people are *not* entitled to make.[15]

NUMBERS AND THE SOCIAL CONTRACT: THE
MORAL ARITHMETIC OF TERRORISM

Here again we may apply our contractarian idea to advantage. Some may think that no matter what the ratio is, we could not possibly get the consent of all to the idea that they should run a risk of being deliberately and heartlessly killed in order to save the lives of many other people. For we are not assuming altruism. On the face of it, it is not in Jones's interest that he should be killed in order that others may live. True. Nevertheless, it quite possibly *is* in Jones's interest to live in a society in which the likelihood that he lives has been made immensely higher by the fact that he *could* possibly be killed, in certain special circumstances – among which the case of defensive war stands out most strikingly. What the moralists I have in mind are forgetting is that when we are dealing in probabilities, as we necessarily are in the present context, then it must be presumed both that anyone *might* be a victim of terrorism *and* that anyone might also be a victim of the oppression the terrorist is, in our imaginary case, proposing to alleviate by his terrorist acts. Thus each person must ask this question: Am I willing to reduce the probability of being killed by terrorists to zero from some very tiny amount, if the cost of this reduction is that I face instead a hundred times higher probability of being killed or otherwise severely maltreated by tyrants? Now vary the "hundred" as you like: a thousand? a billion? It is evident that we shall at some point reach a negative answer to that question. We all want to live our lives, and so are necessarily concerned that those lives not be endangered by circumstances wholly foreign to them.

Some lives are inherently risky: Mountain climbers and Grand Prix drivers, for instance, are aware that their life expectancies are shorter than those of ordinary folk. But we are talking here of risks *not* naturally entailed by the particular sort of lives we choose to live. Still, the fact that people voluntarily climb mountains and such – indeed, that some of them even volunteer for suicidal missions, in extreme circumstances – is important. It shows that longevity is not, for most people, the supreme value. Even if it were, we sometimes must balance one risk of death against another. The classic maneuver of burying one's head in the sand is unlikely to maximize life expectancy. On the face of it, we should choose to minimize those risks, whatever they may be. And by hypothesis we are here comparing two unjust risks, two different ways of being unjustly killed. Clearly, we should opt for the lower of two such risks if we had our choice. And it is conceivable that accepting the risk of death as a victim to terrorists is the better choice, in extreme circumstances. We accept this risk readily in emergency situations. The terrorist may well claim that the situation he acts in *is* an emergency situation. He's probably wrong about this, but not necessarily; and if he's right, then we could see our way to accepting his terrible acts.

Thus, it seems to me, we cannot take the line of "high principle" urged by pacifists or other advocates of "moral side constraints." We must grant the terrorist that it would be logically possible for circumstances to arise in which his methods could be justified. We need not grant, however, that any of the actual terrorists we know anything about have such a case. For all practical purposes, terrorism may still be a moral nonstarter.

ARE THERE ANY "INNOCENTS"? NON-DOINGS AS DOINGS

In the foregoing discussions, I have been presuming that there is such a thing as an "innocent" person: that we can in general draw a reasonably workable line between those who are and those who are not guilty of anything that might possibly deserve the sort of violence employed by terrorists. But this presumption might be denied – indeed, denial is a familiar tactic in the terrorists' rulebook. Is there anything at all to his claim in this respect?

Plainly there is only one way in which it could possibly be defended. The sorts of terrorist victims we are especially concerned with here are neither murderers nor even officials in the regimes to which the terrorist group may be objecting. They have not, in the usual sense of the word, *done* anything. If the noninnocence claim is to be made at all plausible, then, it must be this very non-doing that is being objected to. Why, asks the X-ist, have you sat by and allowed us to be crushed under the Y-vian juggernaut? (Substitute your favored example.) "After all," continues the X-ist, "you *could* have done something. Since you didn't, you must take the consequences."

This raises the usual difficult questions about the active–passive distinction, among many others. John Stuart Mill, notoriously, held that "to make any one answerable for doing evil to others is the rule; to make him answerable for not preventing evil is, comparatively speaking, the exception."[16]

Yet he thought this rule compatible with holding people liable for jury duty, military duty, and so on; moreover, he argued that "even selfish abstinence from defending them against injury . . . [is one of the] fit objects of moral reprobation, and, in grave cases, of moral retribution and punishment."[17] Perhaps. But however we may feel about the principle, such "punishment" for "abstinence" could hardly extend to violent death from, say, a car bomb. If I refuse to testify against a murderer, who then goes free and murders again, I am certainly blameworthy, but I am not guilty of murder – only the murderer is that. And those who would generally abolish the line between killing and letting die, or more generally causing and allowing harm, are, I fear, abolishing freedom across the board. For of course we are all guilty of doing less than we conceivably might for humanity, or even for such narrower causes as preventing violence and assorted other forms of injustice. How much better the world might be if everyone were constantly as vigilant as typical terrorists would presumably have us be is anyone's guess – my own is that it would be far, far worse, frankly – but that we have a duty of any such kind under the social contract is wholly implausible.

But we are not done with this matter quite yet. For the

terrorist, it must be remembered, is not in fact punishing his particular victims for the "crime" of ignoring him. The punishment we all get from him is a slight increase in the *probability* of being visited with violent death or immediate threat of it. The particular victim is not sentenced to death. Rather, a large class of which the victim happens to be a member is being sentenced for neglect; and its penalty is that all members of it are subjected to this small but nonzero probability. Does this matter? We shall see.

GETTING ONE'S CASE HEARD

An essential of democracy, we have noted, is that one be able to present one's case, get a hearing. If we consider the global situation regarding terrorism in the recent past, it is, I think, this factor more than any other that is cited as possibly justifying terrorism, and has in fact motivated much of it. The Palestinians come prominently to mind. Only the publicization of violence, either by them or (less often, it must be admitted) by others against them, seems able to get the public even to notice their case, let alone do anything about it. That their terrorism has been born of frustration should be clear enough.[18]

Whether that frustration justifies the acts in question is, of couse, another matter. *Tactically* speaking, it most likely does not. A great many Palestinians and Israelis, and assorted others, would certainly be alive today, and both groups probably better off in many respects, were no terrorist tactics ever to have been used by Palestinian political groups. Certainly world opinion, especially in the West, would be much more favorably disposed toward them – *if* world opinion took any note of them at all, which of couse is the problem, from their point of view. Nor, we must admit, is it likely that the major Palestinian political aims would have been realized during the last forty years if only nonviolent methods had been employed. The people would surely be much better off, materially; they would, on the other hand, remain, as they are now, without much hope of the level of political group independence they aspire to. And until the rights and wrongs of their and the Israelis' claims are clarified to the general satisfaction, it is obviously difficult to blame them. Were they so clarified, on the other hand, there would most likely be no problem of terrorism from that quarter.

EVIL AS A GOOD?

Shifting our perspective quite a bit, consider now the following, as we might say "existentialist," justification of terrorism: "People's lives are too comfortable now, and this makes their values too shallow. They need to be reminded of their mortality, their vulnerability, from time to time. Terrorism nicely fills this need. Anyone might be a victim, at any time. Yet the actual probability of being such a victim is extremely low, so it's not as though we endangered large numbers of people. We merely stir people a little, make them aware of their human limitations. Maybe this will also soften their hearts a bit toward the oppressed, whom we are, of couse, ultimately trying to help. That's a bonus, from this point of view, but really no more than that."

Does this imagined justification actually go any way toward justifying? Even without terrorists, we are all in fact liable to many dangers that remind us of our mortality. At this very moment, we might have cancer and be dead in six months; this afternoon while crossing the street any of us might get run over by a car. There's no limit. And since, as our existentialist agrees, the terrorist's own contribution to this reminder is minute by comparison with all other sources, it seems that he is in a dilemma: Either his own contribution is totally unnecessary or it's grossly inadequate. Showing that we need, for some alleged spiritual benefit, a marginal increment in existential risk of *just* the amount our terrorist will induce is surely an impossible task!

Still, we are plainly beyond the realm of "demonstration" here. No proponent of any such argument can reasonably be expected to supply the asked-for metric. What he perhaps could be asked to supply, however, is an answer to the question whether he really thinks such an argument could be brought forward in any court of moral appeal on behalf of terrorism. And the answer must surely, again, be in the negative. Where we think that certain types of mayhem, such as those created in what we think are just wars, are morally justified, we regard those who inflict it as heroes, or at the very least as people doing their duty as citizens. But how could terrorists ever be so regarded?

For those to whom such arguments have appeal, there is in any case a ready solution: the *Tenth Victim* solution. In this movie of some years back, a collection of individuals formed a club, devoted to restoring excitement to otherwise humdrum lives by randomly selecting hunters and victims, whose roles in the game were, respectively, to hunt down and the kill the victims, and to attempt to prevent this by first killing the hunters. But a strict rule in this club was that third parties were in no way to be endangered by the activities of members. To a fairly tough-minded morality, this club's activities are in principle morally acceptable, though few societies, no doubt, would actually allow it (even Russian roulette, after all, is outlawed in modern societies, along with dueling). This prohibition is plausible just from the consideration that the "strict rule" in question is likely to be impossible to adhere to in practice. But obviously what would be so justified could not be terrorism, which essentially violates the strict rule in question by its defining modus operandi. And I do not see how an "existentialist" justification can do as well without abandoning any pretense to real moral justification.

Thus Leopold and Loeb, and the Nazis, to take two suitably odious twentieth-century examples, engaged in a kind of activity that was essentially elitist, in a sense that contractarian morality is incapable of tolerating. Moral "elites" are invariably self-appointed; but to be acceptable from a general point of view, that "appointment" would have to be ratified by all. And which potential victims would ratify it, even if they were ready to join a club of the *Tenth Victim* type?

RESPONSES TO TERRORISM

When faced with terrorism, what legitimate responses are open to us? Dealing with terrorists is inevitably frustrating, because they necessarily have the initiative. The terrorist's fundamental method of operation is to take advantage of the vulnerabilities we incur in civilized life. People go about their daily business unarmed and unwatchful for the likes of terrorists because they have enough trust in each other to be able to have daily business without such continual cautions. This trust contributes enormously to the efficiency of life: We can get our business done much more satisfactorily if we can forgo the necessity to be always arming ourselves against contingencies of the kind that the savage – the gangster, the psychopath, and all those others who would get their way by force – presents. Into this peaceful and highly advantageous situation steps the terrorist, who can succeed only because we are not all continually on the watch for him. He has no respect for our lives, and no respect for the principle of confining violence to those who have done violence. In addressing ourselves to the question what we *should* do by way of response to terrorist activity, then, we enter territory well beyond the competence of this writer. But here we can at least inquire what we *may* do.

Let us assume that the avenues of peaceful political change have been sufficiently open and sufficiently explored, and that the terrorist has rejected them. (Needless to say, I do not want to be interpreted as claiming that this assumption is generally true; I would think it is more nearly the opposite.) But where this assumption holds true, then the terrorist has declared war, in his peculiarly underhanded way. In such circumstances, I take it to be clear enough that there is hardly anything we may not do to *him*. In declaring the lives of others of no account, the terrorist automatically authorizes the rest of us to hold *his* life of no account. He is in Hobbes's state of nature with respect to us. Not only may we do any kind of violence to him that offers a prospect of success in freeing ourselves from his grip, but there is no intrinsic reason why we should stop at fraud, double-dealing, and the rest of it.

There are, to be sure, *extrinsic* reasons why we often and perhaps generally should not engage in such things. Thus the German police, in dealing with the terrorists raiding the Israeli Olympic team in 1972, opened fire while the terrorists thought themselves on safe transit from the country, as arranged by the police themselves. But they missed, which failure resulted in the terrorists' wiping out of the Israeli athletes. The police might have done better to keep their promises. Still, this is not because they morally *owed* the terrorists that duty, as they would to any normal person.

The restriction on all such resort to what would otherwise be immoral methods is, however, that innocent persons not be adversely affected. We may not freely kill random innocent persons in the process of killing terrorists. And therein lies a major problem. The terrorist is likely to hold, as we have seen, that there *are* no "innocent persons." And he often puts innocent lives at risk from situations of relative impregnability himself. He does so for the sake of some class of persons whom he identifies with his cause: For example, he may act in order to free previous terrorists currently languishing in the prisons of governments that are likely to be sensitive to the situation of the hostages the terrorist has taken. What are we to do? The terrorist announces that he will let the hostages go if we free the currently imprisoned terrorists. If we succumb to his demands, we unleash on the future world still more terrorist activity; nor are we sure that he will actually free the current hostages. The argument in favor of a policy of "not dealing with" terrorists is strong: saying no, waiting them out – but thereby prolonging the risk to the hostages in the case at hand.

Another thought might occur to one. If several former terrorists are those our current terrorist wishes to free in exchange for releasing his current hostages, we might ask why we should be much concerned with *their* lives? By their former activities, those individuals have already violated the canons of civilized life, and will do so again if released (which indeed is precisely why the current terrorist wishes to get them released). They are not "innocent persons," the putting at risk of whom we must be extremely concerned about. The thought that might occur to us, then, is to propose to the current terrorist that unless he releases his hostages, we will begin shooting the presently imprisoned terrorists, one by one; or at a minimum, that for any hostage killed by the terrorists, we will kill one of the prisoners. The draconian logic of this response is likely to strike home to the terrorist. This would be a "bargaining chip" of a kind he doesn't currently expect, because it is of his own kind. Yet it harms no innocent persons, and runs a fair likelihood of being effective.

Those who worry about the morality of such a response may do so on the score of its possible formal illegality. But then, we might simply put all convicted terrorists under a conditional sentence of death: If their colleagues stay in line, they live; but if innocent persons are killed by those colleagues, then the convicted terrorists are subject to execution. Obviously this is a tactic that would have to be employed with caution. For instance, we run out of bargaining power as soon as we run out of convicted terrorists, and what do the new terrorists do then? (And what if they up the ante very quickly – making the cost in innocent lives higher still?)

Extending the logic of this argument, there is the question whether the terrorist's friends, family, or close associates might not also be eligible for more risk than the general population in virtue of the terrorist's activities. I am not proposing that we descend to the terrorist's avowed view that there are no innocents. But suppose that we accept the terrorist's division of the world into two classes – His People and Our People – and his grisly implication that what he is at war with is Our People, *any* of whom are fair game. Very well, we may say: Then we shall make His People fair game as well, or at least fairer than we have hitherto been inclined to regard them. If his purpose is to protect and advance the welfare of those people, then we may make it a consequence of his activity that, instead, those people will be put at risk to a degree somewhat comparable to that which he exposes Our People to.

This last line of thought invites more straightforwardly the sort of moral outrage I have tried to dispel in reference to the policy of regarding terrorists as fair game or under conditional sentence of death. After all, we may ask, what has the sweetheart, brother, or friend of a terrorist done to deserve the evil he feels free to inflict on all and sundry among his supposed enemies? There is, in fact, a partial answer to this: Namely, they have harbored and shielded him, not only tolerated and exonerated but perhaps also actively supported his nefarious activities. This will not always be so, of course, and here again we have a policy that would have to be employed very cautiously indeed. But then, the primary impact of having such a policy would be its deterrent effect. Most terrorists do have some people they do not regard as pawns in a political game, and the possibility that their awful activities could have the consequence that people they love were treated just as they treat random members of our public would be likely, I surmise, to be an effective control on their tendencies.

Do we dirty our hands if we adopt such means? An important question, to be sure. But there is a partial answer whose logic I find difficult to resist. Consider the policy of, for example, nuclear deterrence, or indeed any kind of large-scale military deterrence. *Any* such policy carries with it the likelihood – "certainty" would be a better word, realistically speaking – that innocent persons will be slaughtered, butchered, burned, irradiated, and otherwise mistreated. Is a policy of countering terrorism with a response that is not, indeed, what the terrorist visits upon us, but admittedly more akin to it than we would like, any worse, morally, than those larger-scale deterrence policies? The terrorist lowers the price of human life; it is his fault if we engage in some trade on his terms.

Nevertheless, a plausible antidote to such thinking is that

one simply ought not to set an example of this sort, loosening as it does the fabric of civility in which we rightly take pride. The policy depends entirely on its deterrence effect, which is very hard to calculate in most cases. Its effects on social life generally are even harder to calculate, but can reasonably argued to outweigh most deterrence effects.

None of these policies, I hasten to agree, can be "the" answer to terrorism. There probably is no unique answer to it: There are only a range of responses of varying degrees of likely effectiveness. My argument here is that perhaps all of these may properly be considered, contrary to what many suppose.

THE HARD LINE

Whatever we might decide about the more morally worrisome responses we have just considered, one thing is very clear: Terrorism cannot be stopped if there is reason for those who would foment it to think that they can thereby succeed. The looming prisoner's dilemma here is stark. Give in to terrorists' demands, and you (perhaps) save the lives of current hostages. But terrorism is so easy to practice: Puny kids can do it, as well as adults with sophisticated weapons. Taking the easy way out in each case leads to a huge increase in the number of cases, and ultimately many more victims are endangered or killed. (It is precisely this in which much of the loosening of the fabric of civilization referred to in the previous section would consist.) It is essential that we do our best to see to it that the terrorist in each case does not succeed. If he proposes to harm hostages or other innocents, we must try to see to it that he is himself treated much worse than if he does not, but that in no case does he get what he has asked for. The choice for the terrorist must be the choice between getting out of here alive, though empty-handed, and getting out of here feet first – and empty-handed. We must do our best to ensure that terrorist methods are fruitless – not an easy thing to do, to be sure.

OTHER PARTIES: THE MEDIA

Most political terrorism is essentially aimed at publicity. This is so in different ways and at different levels. The Palestinians undertook their wave of terrorism in order to bring their cause to world attention, and in at least one major respect they succeeded. The public is aware of the Palestinians – though whether it is aware in a way that is really advantageous for them is quite another matter. (In North America at least, what they are widely known *as* is terrorists, rather than as possessors of a genuine and legitimate grievance.) Whatever the general upshot of that case, it is clear that, like it or not, the news media are closely and essentially involved in virtually all cases of terrorism. If A attacks B in order to influence C, C has to know about it; and where, as it often is, C is the public at large, the mass media are literally indispensable.[19] What to do about this is an extremely difficult problem. Schmid and de Graf point out that the media "are in an uncomfortable position. If they censor the terrorist news they are infringing on the public's right to know. If they give extensive coverage they might terrorize the public and become allies of the terrorists. If they follow the government line they might become a propaganda and police tool."[20]

There is much food for thought in the situation regarding the media. There is no mistaking the North American appetite for violence – probably shared by most humans. Life is dull, and violence represents a fascinating break with its routine. The media must cater to this appetite, or they lose their audience. Very well: But if the cost of attracting a large audience is the encouragement of terrorism, then what?

How would media be induced to manage their handling of this type of news in a responsible manner? One suggestion is that victims of terrorism could hold media companies liable whenever it proved possible to demonstrate that the terrorists' actions were motivated or assisted significantly by the media. This would have a deterrent effect, on the one hand, and on the other would allow media people to make a judgment about difficult cases, rather than having agencies of the public presume to make a better one on their behalf. But I hasten to add that the suggestion is embryonic.

THE BOTTOM LINE: TREATING PEOPLE RIGHT TO BEGIN WITH

One theme that recurs in this essay is also the one I shall end with: The first thing to do in any situation of terrorism is to find out whether there is anything legitimate among the grievances the terrorist is concerned about. If there were full employment at decent wages in Northern Ireland, would the IRA be so active? If the government of Israel even merely permitted freedom of commerce on equal terms with Palestinians, would the Palestinians be nearly as inclined toward terrorism? (It may seem a silly thing to say, but a high incidence of violence in the community really *is* bad for business, just as it is bad for life in general.) Terrorism may be wrong in virtually all circumstances, but there are too many in which it is understandable, perhaps even forgivable. We ought to do what we can to minimize "circumstances" of that kind.

Any kind of violent intervention in people's lives requires justification of a strong sort. Vague and amorphous complaints about the Establishment or "the system" are not enough. Nor, of course, are precise but abstract theories about ideal societies and the like. The evils visited upon us by terrorists are real and present; if the goods they promise are ill defined or, even if well defined, poorly defended as goods, or even just the wrong kind of goods, then that is no good either. Social change that is genuinely for the better ought to be attainable by voluntary cooperation, not by violence; and so strongly am I inclined to think this that I am tempted by the further suggestion that any change not so attainable is thereby shown not to be a social change for the better. This thesis, of course, casts into doubt not only terrorism but less overtly violent alterations of the social fabric: perhaps even most legislation. But that is a further story.

Jan Narveson

NOTES

1   Alex Schmid and Janny de Graf, *Violence as Communication* (London: SAGE, 1982).

2   A. James Gregor, "Fascism's Philosophy of Violence and the Concept of Terror," in *The Morality of Terrorism*, ed. D. Rapoport and Y. Alexander (New York: Pergamon, 1982), p. 159.

3   Alfred Louch, "Terrorism: The Immorality of Belief," in Rapoport and Alexander, eds., *The Morality of Terrorism*, p. 271.

4   George Quester, "Eliminating the Terrorist Opportunity," in Rapoport and Alexander, eds., *The Morality of Terrorism*, p. 346.

5   I develop this view in *The Libertarian Idea* (Philadelphia: Temple University Press, 1989); see pt. 2. See also David Gauthier, *Morals by Agreement* (New York: Oxford University Press, 1987), especially chap. 9, "The Liberal Individual."

6   See, in particular, my "Pacifism: A Philosophical Analysis," *Ethics* 75, no. 4 (July 1965): 259–71.

7   This is developed in my *Libertarian Idea*, pt. 1.

8   See David Braybrooke's *Meeting Needs* (Princeton, N.J.: Princeton University Press, 1987) for a number of interesting and sophisticated proposals about this issue. In my view, none of them solve the major problems. See my forthcoming critical notice of that book in *Nous*.

9   "After the British had announced their decision to withdraw from Palestine in the late 1940's, Zionist terrorists of the Stern gang and the Irgun . . . attacked an Arab village, Deir Yassin, and massacred 250 men, women and children" (Schmid and de Graf, *Violence as Communication*, p. 18).

10 I have argued thus in my "Equality vs. Liberty: Advantage, Liberty," *Social Philosophy and Policy* 2, no. 1 (Autumn 1984): 33–60; see also my "On Dworkinian Equality," with "Reply to Dworkin," *Social Philosophy and Policy* 1, no. 1 (Autumn 1983): 1–44. Two recent defenses of equality that try to reconcile it with liberty are Kai Nielsen, *Equality and Liberty* (Totowa, N.J.: Rowman and Allenheld, 1985); and Richard Norman, *Free and Equal* (New York: Oxford University Press, 1987).

11 I discuss the subject of violent revolution in my "On the Rationality of Revolutions," in *Revolution, Violence and Equality*, ed. Yeager Hudson and Creighton Peden (Lewiston, N.Y.: Edward Mellen, 1990), pp. 223–51.

12 Edward Hyams, in *Terrorists and Terrorism* (London: Dent,

1975), assembles the evidence that terrorism has been disconcertingly successful, notably in the cases of Ireland and Israel. But here the terrorists were in no need of "making friends": They were working for political goals that were highly popular with the populations on behalf of whom they worked.

13 John Taurek, "Should the Numbers Count?" *Philosophy and Public Affairs* 6, no. 4 (Summer 1977): 293–316.

14 Robert Nozick, *Anarchy, State and Utopia* (New York: Basic, 1974); see p. 30n. Charles Fried, *Right and Wrong* (Cambridge, Mass.: Harvard University Press, 1978); see p. 10 especially.

15 In "Pacifism," my earliest treatment of this subject, I set out to show that pacifism was outrightly contradictory. This is an overstatement in regard to the general theory. For my most nearly current view in detail, see "At Arms' Length: Violence and War," in *Matters of Life and Death*, ed. Tom Regan, 2d ed. (New York: Random House, 1986), pp. 137–42.

16 John Stuart Mill, *On Liberty*, in the Everyman ed. of *Utilitarianism, On Liberty, and Representative Government*, ed. A. D. Lindsay (London: Dent, 1926), p. 74.

17 Mill, *On Liberty*, p. 135.

18 I am considerably influenced here by Edward Said's *Question of Palestine* (New York: Times Books, 1979). See also that author's "Essential Terrorist," *Nation*, June 14, 1986.

19 "It is perhaps more than a coincidence that racial violence broke out massively in South Africa in 1976, the year television began to operate. The unrest in Iran that led to a successful revolution was, among other things, triggered off by the television pictures of the demonstrations against the Shah when he visited Washington in mid-November 1977. The outbreak of guerrilla warfare in the highlands of Peru in the early 1960s has also been attributed to the widespread appearance of the transistor radio in the region" (Schmid and de Graf, *Violence as Communication*, p. 108).

20 Ibid., p. 98.

Chapter 7

Which are the offers
you can't refuse?

ONORA O'NEILL

Coercion matters to almost everybody, and almost everybody thinks that it is often or always bad. Yet few agree on what counts as coercion. The theorists of coercion propose "analyses" of the concept of coercion, and are promptly refuted by rival theorists. In a recent essay with the implausible title "The Last Word on Coercive Offers . . . (?)" Daniel Lyons criticizes numerous complex and competing analyses of coercion proposed in recent philosophical discussions.[1] (His topic isn't only "offers" in a narrow sense that contrasts with "threats," but the whole gamut of proposals and demands that might be judged coercive.) He hopes to have the last word because, he claims, his own proposal of a few years earlier has stood up to trial by counterexample not perfectly but still rather well.

The debates that have led to this type of claim strike me as a reductio ad absurdum of certain procedures often used in ethical discussion. These procedures assume that "our" intuitions about possible examples and counterexamples can be treated as data, by which we may test and either refute or confirm proposed analyses of the necessary and sufficient conditions for the application of moral concepts. However, trial by counterexample cannot get going unless there is agreement on the classification of cases. It breaks down when examples and counterexamples cannot be reliably distinguished. In discussions of coercion there is no agreement about cases: Consider the long-running dispute between liberals and socialists about whether the wage bargain under capitalism coerces. The "intuitions" invoked by protagonists in this debate reflect no more than different assumptions about who "we" are: All that is on offer is the argument from (supposed) authority in contemporary dress. There isn't much prospect of resolving disputes about proposed analyses of coercion by appealing to contentious "intuitions" about cases. For this and other reasons I intend to bypass most recent philosophical and theoretical discussions of coercion. Instead I shall consult the experts.

EXPERT COERCION AND EXPERT VIOLENCE

The theoreticians may have reached an impasse, but there is plenty of expertise to be found. The real experts in this matter are, I take it, neither political or ethical theorists nor the victims of coercion, but the practitioners. They don't seem to find that theoretical uncertainty inhibits the practice of coercion. So we may be able to learn something from these experts. My title poses the questions the expert coercers address. They look for "offers" *you* can't refuse, not for "offers" *we* (some "we") can't refuse, or for "offers" that *nobody* (no unspecified other) can refuse. For coercers the victims are particular others, not necessarily one of "us" and not just anyone. Other sources of *practical* expertise include victims of coercion, who have to determine whether the proposals others make are genuine offers and so refusable, and what to do if they are not, as well as those who try avoid coercion in dealings with others.

Consulting the expert coercers is not easy. They are self-effacing, for the best of reasons. Since nearly all coercion is morally suspect and much of it punishable, successful coercers will not want to testify. They are not likely to come forward to tell us just what they have done, which options they considered and why they settled upon a particular strategy of coercion. So I shall rely on proxies for these experts by drawing on our common knowledge of journalistic, fictitious, and dramatized discussions of coercing. Even those of us who have not practiced significant coercion are familiar

with court reports, thrillers, spy stories, accounts of terrorism, and many other detailed descriptions of the business of
coercion. However, I shall not treat these case histories as
decisive or uncontentious instances of coercion: They figure
here not as *intuitions* but as *illustrations* of patterns of practical
reasoning that coercers might deploy.[2]

Experts in coercion are also often expert at inflicting violence. However, I shall try to keep these two sorts of expertise
distinct. The coercer's aim is specifically to get others to *do*
or to *desist* from acts that (supposedly) they would not do or
desist from but for the coercion. Coercion, to put it vaguely,
operates on the will and not essentially on the body. The
coercer's problem is not intrinsically a problem of working
out how to inflict violence, to maim, torture, or destroy others. Not all violent acts coerce, and not all coercive action
uses violence.

Some acts of violence aim only at another's body – for
example, acts done by those who have run amok, what we
call "mindless violence." Violence can be mute and brute. It
need not demand anything of its victims or of others; there
may be no implied conditions that the victims or others can
meet in order to avert the violence. Coercion, including violent coercion, is different: It has propositional content. Coercers communicate with those whom they coerce; they fail if
they merely destroy the agent whose compliance they seek.
This is hard to see because many discussions do not distinguish between victims of coercion and victims of the violence
coercers may inflict. These distinct roles are often combined
in acts of violent coercion. For example, if a coercer tortures
a child in order to get her to reveal where somebody else can
be found, the child is a victim both of coercion and of violence. The coercer aims both to get her compliance and to
inflict violence: The violence is the means of coercion. In
other cases the victims of coercion and of violence done to
coerce are distinct. For example, if a coercer tortures a child
in order to get her father to reveal somebody else's where-
abouts, of which the child knows nothing, then it is the father
who is the victim of coercion, although it is the child to whom

violence is done. It is the father who can comply, or refuse to comply. The child can do neither. In yet other cases coercers inflict no violence. They may rely on threat, menace, and gestures that point to varied harms to achieve their ends. Expert coercers concentrate on securing compliance; violence is important to them only because it often produces results.

RISK AND RETICENCE

The compliance coercers look for can often be achieved without coercing. For example, one can ask or pay another to do or desist in the desired way, or perhaps one can negotiate or manipulate. Since much may be risked by coercing, it will often be a strategy of last resort. Coercers turn to it when they have no other affordable way to secure compliance.

Because coercion is a potentially risky and costly strategy for securing action, those who use it will usually avoid describing what they do as coercion. They may go to great pains to present it as something quite different. This is evident in the famous Mafia description of protection rackets as "offers you can't refuse." On the surface this sounds innocent enough – on a par with all those irresistible bargains and once-in-a-lifetime opportunities that advertisers proclaim. In reality the reason why the mafioso's "offer" cannot be refused is that it has coercive backing. Those who don't comply will meet harm: perhaps only broken windows, possibly broken lives. Coercers' reticence about their activities and plans can pay off handsomely. If they are skillful their victims may not (fully) realize what is going on. Confused or unwitting victims may comply better and more quickly, and complain less or less effectively. (This suggests that coercion is also quite unlike revenge, which may not be adequate unless its victims realize fully what has happened. The Mafia demands varied expertise of its members.) A fuller description of the expertise that coercers need might be that they must work out how to secure compliance while minimizing others', and especially their victims', awareness that this is what they are doing.

Coercion is a skilled as well as a risky business. Coercers aim to control rather than to destroy their victims. To do this they must make their demands plain, so risking exposure. Ideally their communication must be simultaneously effective and opaque. They must both communicate with their victims and yet keep what they are doing obscure, so they have overwhelming reasons to be discreet about their activities, to disown what they do, to redescribe, and to refuse to acknowledge their actions.

Here the contrasts between coercion and mere violence are stark. The victims of coercion are to be got to *do* or *desist*. When victims are to be got to *do*, it is self-defeating to destroy them or to damage them in ways that disable compliance. Even when victims are to be got to *desist*, coercers often want them to remain alive and in action. If there are other respects in which coercers still want or rely on victims to act, it is once again self-defeating to reduce them to incapacity or inertia. Even when a coercer neither wants nor needs a victim who remains able to act – when the victim is first to comply and then to be "put out of action" – or when compliance is to be secured by damaging or destroying a third party, the coercer still has reason to use violence with care. Violence can be flamboyant even when its perpetrators are obscure; coercers need to communicate yet evade detection and minimize retribution, so must be reticent.

We can learn something about the difficulty of coercing by noting how attempts may misfire. Coercers fail unless their intended victim grasps *what* it is that is demanded, and *that it is demanded*. The intended victim who simply fails to realize what is demanded – who responds to the gun in the ribs as an invitation to play – may be a figure of fun, or tragic, but is insulated from coercion by failure to grasp the coercer's meaning. Such intended victims are exasperatingly uncoerceable, simpletons or saints who, whether they suffer at the hands of would-be coercers or elude their grasp, fail to comply because they do not understand what it is that they are to do. Like mute violence, deaf victims frustrate coercion.

The intended victim who grasps what is demanded but

sees the demand as mere request or proposal, which can be taken up or left, is equally awkward for the coercer's purposes. Faced with such a victim, a coercer may have to spell out the penalties of noncompliance or the gains of compliance more explicitly or to increase these penalties or gains, and so once again risk exposure.

These reminders of commonplace problems of coercion confirm that we are unlikely to get far in classifying acts decisively into the coercive and the noncoercive. Most coercive acts have other, more acceptable, faces as well as expert and interested parties who will insist that the more acceptable descriptions are the ones that should command our attention. This point alone provides sufficient reason for doubting that an analysis of the concept of coercion would have much practical use. (There are more general, and philosophically and historically deeper, reasons for doubting whether we can sensibly aim for or find definitive analyses of *any* concepts.)[3]

STRATEGIES OF COERCION

Typical examples can illustrate how the need for effective but opaque and relatively risk-free communication shapes the practice of would-be coercers. Suppose the potential coercers are residents of a presently all-white neighborhood, into which a black family plans to move. They want at all costs, and for whatever reasons, to prevent this move. Perhaps they fear that one move will spearhead the integration of a neighborhood, which will change greatly, leaving them feeling less at home and lowering the prices their houses command. In some places they need not coerce. For example, in South Africa under Apartheid they could rely on state power to secure residential segregation. In other places segregation may be illegal, but the residents might be able to rely on the "discretion" of local estate agents not to show or sell houses in "their" neighborhood to potential purchasers from the "wrong" background. In yet other areas, where discrimination in the sale of housing is monitored and penalized, coercers may have to act. They have to find other ways to deter the move they fear. They want to take action that can be "read" by their intended victims, yet for which they cannot easily be brought to book.

Many possible moves can be imagined. For example, they may intimidate those whom they want to keep out. They may put a brick through a window where the would-be movers now live. The damage to property will be slight, and there need be no violence done to any person. Yet the strategy may succeed because its victims interpret the thrown brick as a promise of further and worse harm if they persist with their plans. A drawback of this tactic is that throwing bricks through others' windows is illegal and readily detected: The communication is effective enough but rather too public. An alternative method of coercing may be preferred because it can less easily be brought to book. For example, one of the coercers may speak to a child from the family who plans to move, perhaps saying no more than, "Tell your Mummy and Daddy that if they love you they should not move here." What is said is open to multiple interpretations. It may, after all, be a friendly warning from somebody who observes but does not approve of the coercers' plan. The coercers' hope will be that the tone or gesture or circumstances will lead the child, and the family, to interpret these opaque words as threatening unspecified, perhaps terrible, harm to the child should the family move. Of course, even uttering the vaguest menaces may be risky, for the child may identify the coercer, and a court may conclude that they were indeed menaces. So other strategies may be judged safer. Perhaps the child's parents will find that a promotion or pay raise is made contingent on not moving. Perhaps this is an offer – a promotion only if you don't move – that they can refuse: But perhaps it is not. The would-be movers may grasp the apparent "offer" as a serious threat that tells them that if they move they will be blocked from any promotion or pay raise, or even as a guarded way of threatening dismissal and reminding them that their very livelihood is at stake. These ways of "reading" the "offer" may be entirely reasonable:

What the victims understand may be just what the coercers hope to convey.

Or take a quite different example, of attempted political coercion that uses terrorist tactics. A campaign of terror does not have to inflict exceptionally high levels of violence. For example, the use of terror by IRA and "loyalist" groups in Ulster, although extensive, has not raised the ratio of violent deaths to population as high as in many U.S. cities. However, the higher likelihood of violent death in U.S. cities is not a matter of terrorism or of more frequent coercion in the U.S. context. Some inner-city violence in the United States has no coercive aspects; some of it is coercive, but in the main it seeks compliance not with political but with more limited objectives. The coercers of the inner city often seek the compliance of a particular victim or a restricted range of victims, at most of a neighborhood or ethnic group. Gang warfare, murders of drug dealers, and the like differ from terrorism in conveying a demand for compliance with largely nonpolitical objectives to a generally limited range of agents.

The coercion terrorists attempt does not generally need exceptional levels of violence. It does need skilled judgment of the way in which the terrorists' message is to be conveyed to those for whom it is intended without so alienating or frightening them that they offer strong support to antiterrorist measures. The victims of terror are not just the (relatively) few on whom terrorists may inflict violence but the (often) numerous who are coerced or terrorized by these and other means.[4] Most of the victims of terror, like the victims of other forms of coercion, suffer no direct violence. Since terrorists aim at compliance, they must ensure that their victims (for the most part) remain able to comply. The victims must be given a message rather than be put out of action. Terrorists typically give many messages: Those who might normally either act against terrorism or at least refuse to aid or abet it are constantly reminded of the costs they may pay. They learn what it may cost them to testify against those charged with acts of terrorism, or to inform the police about crimes planned or committed, or to refuse to contribute to terrorist funds; simultaneously they may be reassured that the costs of tacit support for terrorism remain low. The ordinary dues-paying, passive supporters of terrorism are given to understand that this is not random violence, that their lives and livelihood are not endangered – unless they step out of line and oppose terrorism. Sophisticated terrorist groups like the IRA consciously convey different messages to different audiences on different occasions. The tandem policy of relying on "armalite and the ballot box" mixes the tactics of terror and political persuasion. When too much reliance on armalite provokes revulsion and opposition even among tacit supporters, the message of political grievance and martyrdom can be emphasized for a while.

If coercion succeeds by tactics such as these, its victims will have grasped what is demanded of them, and they will have a strong, if unclear, sense that it is demanded, not simply requested. The advantage to the coercers, if they have acted skillfully, is that their victims have little hard evidence that they were coerced and may be unable to identify their coercers. Sometimes everything will hinge on the interpretation of opaque messages, inexplicit communication, ambiguous gestures. On other occasions it will be a matter of grasping the implications of unattributable and scattered acts of violence and carnage. Even when coercion is laced with violence, as it is in campaigns of terror, much of the interpretation of the significance of any particular act of violence will be obscure. We have to work hard to decode the political messages conveyed by campaigns of terror aimed at other and unfamiliar audiences – for example, the messages given by hostage taking in the Middle East. We know how much of the fun of reading or watching well-crafted thrillers is that coercion can wear the most bland – or the most elegant – garb. We understand the thriller when we can follow a text or film at more than one level, and see the message implicit not only in grotesque tokens of violence (the severed horse's head, the dead cockerel delivered to the next victim, the tarred and feathered collaborator) but in the superficially innocuous small talk of the master coercers. We understand the politics when we can work out how and why terrorists' veiled messages can come to define the political possibilities for those who are terrorized. When we think about such political, criminal, and fictitious instances of coercion, we realize all too clearly why serious coercers veil their demands and the penalties of noncompliance, and why skilled coercion is a matter of communicating irresistible demands while appearing to do far less. It is typical of coercion that it can be presented as something else – as the business deal that nobody would turn down, as the warning that it would be foolish to neglect, as no more than a reminder to mind one's own business, or to pay one's dues by taking part in innocuous social practices.

REFUSABLE AND UNREFUSABLE OFFERS

These brief reminders of some of the strategies of coercion with which we are most familiar may suggest that nothing of general, let alone philosophical, interest can be said about coercion. If so, large stretches both of liberal and of socialist political philosophy need rethinking, since each tradition rejects certain types of social and political relations as unacceptable because coercive. Both liberals and socialists see slavery, serfdom, and certain uses of "private" violence as modes of coercion: They divide in their estimate of the coercive character of the wage bargain in a capitalist economy and of labor-allocation decisions in a socialist economy. Both traditions offer varying views of the status of coercion undertaken for political purposes. Anarchists of right and of left argue that state power itself is unjustifiable because coercive. Many other liberals and socialists think state monopoly of coercion justifiable, but condemn nonconstitutional political coercion by groups who dispute the legitimacy of established powers. Yet others in both traditions think that some political coercion is justifiable if undertaken *either* by legitimate states *or* by those (e.g., certain national liberation movements) who legitimately challenge unjust states. Neither tradition can do without an adequate understanding of coercion.

Are these disputes about coercion simply irresolvable, and futile if we cannot state necessary and sufficient conditions for applying the concept? This conclusion, it seems to me, would follow only if we took a wildly implausible – yet seemingly popular – view of the relation between political or ethical principles and judgments of cases. The disputes between those who have tried to analyze coercion are, after all, about the classification of cases, whereas those between liberals and socialists are, in the first instance, over very general principles. Only if we assume that principles are useless without complete instructions for their application, which enable us to classify cases definitively, should we take persistent disagreements over cases as evidence that it is futile to formulate or argue for principles for dealing with coercion. The assumption that principles without complete instructions for their application are pointless is belied both by theoretical considerations and by the daily practices of law, administration, and expert judgment. If we don't think that principles alone can determine cases, disagreement about cases where principles are agreed on merely confirms but does not condemn our lack of a definitive analysis of coercion. Principles such as "Do not coerce" or "Coerce only to prevent greater coercion" neither are nor require completion by an algorithm for disposing definitively of the cases that fall under them.

All that we need for a principle that forbids coercion to help guide action is, I suggest, a rough account of the types of considerations that will enable us to distinguish ways of getting others' agreement that coerce from ways that do not. However, this account cannot plausibly presuppose an antecedently established theory of rights. More probably a distinction between coercive and noncoercive ways of getting others' agreement would be an ingredient of an adequate account of rights. Even the most general rights – such as that to freedom or freedom of the person – presuppose rather than supply an understanding of the forms of action that would be wrongful interference. Any distinction between coercive and noncoercive ways of getting others' compliance would be circular if it presupposed an account of rights.

At a superficial level it is clear enough what coercers do. They make an "offer" that *imposes a certain choice* on their victims. Coercive "offers" limit agents' options in specific ways, and in so doing fail to respect their victims' agency and integrity. Coercers do not deny or damage victims' agency as completely as may be done by using force. A victim who is literally overpowered by *force majeure* is in no way an agent. The victim of coercion is "offered" certain options, so remains an agent. The victim can choose to comply with the coercer's demand – or to refuse to comply and accept what the coercer, disingenuously, calls "the consequences." However, the victim is denied the possibility of refusing the entire set of options that constitute the coercive "offer."

This can be seen very plainly in cases of overtly coercive "offers." When a coercer demands, "Your money or your life," there is still a choice to be made: either to stay alive or to keep the money but be killed. The victim can refuse either option, but cannot refuse both. The "offer" is unrefusable. A genuine offer, by contrast, can be refused: One of the options it includes is that of "no deal." This option is absent in coercive "offers": If the victim answers "Your money or your life" by saying, "Neither," the coercer will treat failure to hand over the money as if it were a choice to be killed. Often the coercive "offer" is more guarded, and it may be hard to see that the option of refusing the entire "offer" is missing. When racketeers suggest that a small trader either join the racket or move out of some line of business, a good deal more background must be filled in before it is clear whether this disjunction of options, and so the "offer," is refusable. It may be that the offer is unrefusable because the racketeers will inflict another, unacceptable option if the two manifest options are refused.

This account of the sense in which coercers make unrefusable "offers," thereby limiting their victims' agency, shows in more detail that coercion is not centrally a matter of producing hurt or harm, but rather of structuring the options available to another. Coercive offers are designed to produce compliance by making it the condition of avoiding unacceptable "consequences," so they always place severe restraints on victims' capacities to act.[5]

How much do we need to know if we are to avoid making others' unrefusable "offers"? Do we need to work out the necessary and sufficient conditions for making "offers" unrefusable? And would that require a complete account of what makes options unacceptable for any arbitrary agent? If so the theoretical difficulties that attempted analyses of coercion have encountered would be an urgent problem both for those who want to avoid coercing and for coercers. I shall argue that action does not need any general analysis of coercion, but rather a way of working out how to make, or avoid making, proposals that are unrefusable, and so coercive, for the particular others to whom they are addressed. This less ambitious task nevertheless raises some issues in the theory of action.

MOTIVATION AND ACTION

The preliminary account of coercion sketched in the last two sections suggests that "offers" are unrefusable when they exclude the option of refusal by linking refusal to unacceptable "consequences." It is often hard to see that an offer is unrefusable. Typically victims must infer from the options that are made explicit whether the offer is genuine or unrefusable, so coercive. How do they distinguish refusable offers from unrefusable "offers"?

On some accounts of human motivation it appears as if any *option* that is in fact accepted is unrefusable, hence that any proposal one of whose options is accepted is an unrefusable "offer." If, for example, we think that action is determined by desires and beliefs, and that desires are simply occurrent states over whose occurrence no agent has control, then options (not just offers) will be unrefusable when but only when the balance of an agent's occurrent desires happens (given the agent's beliefs) to constitute a stronger desire to accept than to refuse the option. On this view offers are all on a par: There is no distinction to be drawn between genuine offers and coercive "offers." This Hobbesian account of the relation of desire and action implies that agents cannot but act on whatever desires or aversions are strongest. If self-preservation is always the strongest desire, compliance with any powers that threaten survival will be unavoidable: A proposal is cogent and accepted precisely because it is literally unrefusable for that agent. Hobbes quite consistently views submission to the powers that be, including the infant's unrefusable "submission" to its mother, as legitimate, and rational.[6] In a Hobbesian state of nature all successful "offers" and no unsuccessful "offer" are judged compelling, so unrefusable; however, they are not thereby seen as unjust, but rather as lying outside the only framework that permits a distinction between just and unjust action. Within the Hobbesian civil state it is possible to distinguish between unjust coercion by lawless powers and just submission to lawful order. The vocabulary of morals can be constituted by the state, within which a certain distinction between "coercion" and "noncoercion" can be rehabilitated. But this revised distinction is superficial. On a Hobbesian (empiricist, determinist) account of motivation all accepted offers, whether "coercive" or "noncoercive," are literally unrefusable. A distinction between coercion and noncoercion can only be of fundamental moral importance within a different account of action and motivation.

If offers (or rather "offers") are to be judged coercive in a deeper sense, we must work within an account of action and motivation that allows that some options that are actually accepted may be refusable and others unrefusable. An account of action that allows for refusable proposals must accept that the balance of given desires does not always determine which act an agent will perform. (It is compatible with the view that agents always choose, or if rational would always choose, the most preferred available action, provided that preference is thought of as reflecting [as revealing] choices made rather than as antecedently given.)

Provided that there are some offers that an agent might in principle either refuse or accept, it makes sense to try to work out what it is about the options that compose particular proposals that make them unrefusable "offers." However, this task will have little point if we imagine that non-Hobbesian agents, if (sometimes) able to choose independently of given desires, are able to choose anything whatsoever. It is only for mythical agents – say, Kantian noumenal selves as commonly, if implausibly, conceived[7] – whose freedom is conceived as wholly unrestricted, that *all* options (hence all offers composed of disjunctions of options) would be refusable. Among such idealized agents with infinite capacities to choose or refuse, whatever their desires may be, any option and any offer that disjoins two or more options will be refusable, and nothing counts as coercion. Nothing that they do can be laid at another's door. Coercion, it seems, has no part in angelic politics: which may just show that angels can have no politics.

Any account of action and motivation that leaves room for a distinction between refusable and unrefusable offers must then allow both that action is not wholly determined by antecedently given desires and that there are limits to agents' capacities to override what they may desire. A distinction between coercion and noncoercion makes sense among agents who choose freely, but whose capacities to choose and to refuse are finite. It makes sense among human beings because we have reason to think that we are both free and finite, in this as in many other ways. Unless the experiences of choosing and of resisting temptation can be shown to be illusory, and all ethical and political principles nugatory, desires understood as antecedently given do not (even with given beliefs) wholly determine action. The material embodiment of human capacities to choose and refuse is finite and vulnerable in many respects, and can be further restricted by expert coercion. The expertise of coercers is a matter of preserving at least some freedom to act for their victims, while taking advantage of their victims' finite and vulnerable capacities in order to procure action that the victims would not otherwise undertake. (This suggests, among other things, that little can be learned by discussing the coercion of hypothetical agents with idealized cognitive and volitional powers.)

INTEGRITY AND REFUSABILITY

An account of motivation that leaves room for a distinction between refusable and unrefusable options and offers does not show us what it takes to make "offers" unrefusable. Yet this is what coercers must identify. They aim to present victims limited options and ensure compliance with one of them by embedding it in an "unrefusable offer." The victims are given to understand that they must comply with the coercers' plans or bear the "consequences" of noncompliance, and the coercers will aim to make sure that these "consequences" are unacceptable to the victims. An unrefusable "offer" is not one where refusal of a certain option is made logically or physically impossible for its victim. It is simply an "offer" by which coercers aim to prevent refusal of a certain option by making any other option unacceptable for their victim.

Victims vary in what they can accept. Martyrs, heroes, rebels, and men and women of honor often refuse options with which their would-be coercers aim to have them comply. Are we to take it that they refuse the unrefusable? In a colloquial sense this might well be said; but there is no paradox here. What exceptional people refuse when coerced is compliance with the *option* that coercers want. They do not refuse the *"offer"* of which that option is one disjunct. *The mark of coercion is the unrefusable "offer," not the unrefusable option.* An "offer" is not rendered uncoercive because some victims refuse to comply with the option coercers want and choose to take the "consequences." Such victims too have to stay within the framework of the "offer."

Heroes and martyrs refuse compliance because, harsh as the "consequences" of noncompliance may be, they cannot accept the option with which compliance is sought. They hold that compliance will destroy their integrity and sense

185

of self. Sometimes they will be able to accept the consequences that their coercer hoped to make unacceptable. Sometimes neither compliance nor "consequences" will be acceptable for them as they are, and their integrity and sense of self must break. In such cases noncompliance may cost them physical safety and integrity (as it might any victims of such an "offer"); but compliance may cost them their psychological or moral integrity.

Ordinary victims who comply may face the same double predicament. The harshest coercive "offers" are ones where *all* options cost the victims dire loss of integrity. Surrender to coercers may cost an individual, a group, or a nation integrity and sense of identity, yet nonsurrender may cost physical survival and consequently also integrity and identity. When invaded by the Nazis in 1939, the Poles could have complied with the Nazi ultimatum and accepted occupation; they chose to resist. The first option would have cost national and individual moral integrity; the second cost the physical integrity of the nation and the lives of many individuals.

The predicaments that coercers force on their victims are trivialized when placed within an empiricist theory of action, and thought of as a mere matter of adjusting the relative "costs" and "incentives" attached to different options among which victims are to choose in the light of their preferences. What is at stake is victims' survival and integrity. Unamuno put it with appropriate force when he noted that "neither a man nor a people (in a certain sense a people is also a man) can be asked to make a change that will break the unity or continuity of the person."[8] The coercer notes that such changes can be *asked* for, and can even be yielded: But in yielding, the victim's integrity is yielded. *An "offer" is made unrefusable when noncompliance is connected to "consequences" that cannot be accepted by that victim: "Consequences" are unacceptable by a victim if their acceptance destroys that victim's very integrity or sense of self.*

The worst coercive "offers" impose damage to integrity and sense of self both on those who comply and on those who do not. Heroic refusers as well as craven collaborators, and those whose capacities lie between, are coerced when they find that noncompliance, and at the limit both compliance and noncompliance, will destroy, damage, or transform who and what they are. Acceptance of benign, refusable offers achieves an outcome that one has a reason to suppose is acceptable. Compliance with coercive "offers" can cost their victims disintegration of the personality, dishonor, and the destruction of causes that are integral to their sense of self. Yet noncompliance may also destroy victims. Both those who bow to and those who resist coercers' demands may survive physically but be broken in other ways.

Coercers do not use or need any general formula for identifying unacceptable "consequences" and constructing unrefusable "offers." They need only identify some options that are unacceptable for their intended victims and "offer" a choice restricted to these and the option with which they seek compliance. The option with which they seek compliance is usually one the victim shuns, but might be a benign one that the victim in fact welcomes. In discreet, sophisticated coercion the unacceptable option that is linked to noncompliance may be kept in the background. Noncoercers have to make sure that they do not act in this way. Their offers must not link options either overtly or discreetly to the avoidance of unacceptable consequences. It follows that coercers and those who shun coercion both have to take account of *particular* vulnerabilities and the *actual* limits of others' capacities to choose. They have to estimate others' sense of self and integrity, and to note both their commitments and their weaknesses.

Both coercers and noncoercers may fail. Sometimes coercers fail to get compliance. A Socrates or a Sakharov may (at least partly) elude mighty institutions and experienced coercers. Of course. Socrates was killed, and Sakharov suffered greatly: But even the destruction of a victim does not secure the compliance that is the proper object of coercion. Equally, those who seek not to coerce may do so despite their aims: Particularly in dealing with others who are weaker or dependent a lack of imagination or restraint may lead would-be noncoercers to propose "offers" that, despite their benign intentions, are actually unrefusable by those others.

"Offers" that achieve ready compliance can show most about the tasks of coercing and of shunning coercion. Experienced coercers often achieve compliance by playing on the particular form of a victim's integrity and sense of identity. The unacceptable option that they disjoin with the option with which they seek compliance may be pain, death, or damage. These are obvious, if risky, strategies for securing compliance from most victims. More discreet approaches can be just as effective in many cases. Even the strongest may often be brought to compliance if coercers play on and menace the objects of attachments that constitute their very identity. The master coercers understand all too well that sheer courage is a slender defence against credible threats to those to whom victims are attached, where that attachment is in part constitutive of victims' integrity and sense of identity. Those whose sense of self is weaker and more vulnerable can be coerced by lesser strategies: The master coercers may use trivial humiliations, minor financial pressures, or specific phobias (Winston Smith and the rats). Often they make explicit only an innocuous-seeming proposal, and the coercive character of the "offer" becomes manifest only as victims refuse to comply. Those who succumb to mere gesture may seem to have yielded where there was no threat to safety, identity, or integrity – or they may have read the ostensibly mild warnings and trivial demands that were explicit correctly as foreboding disaster and destruction.

The expert coercer, whether of the weak or of the strong, is not, however, a technician who exploits some metric by which to decide how intense a pain, how severe a threat, or how potent a combination of "sticks" and "carrots" must be built into the options of an "offer" that will be unrefusable for all victims in all circumstances. Expertise is a matter of finding a particular sort of pain, menace, disorientation, insecurity, that will make an option unacceptable, and therefore an "offer" based on that option unrefusable, by a victim whose sense of self and integrity have a determinate configuration. Although it is true that an unrefusable "offer" shifts a victims's preference from compliance to noncompliance, this does not mean that it can be said in the abstract that incentives of greater magnitude are attached to compliance. Rather, the claim that greater incentives are attached to compliance is inferred from the fact that the agent complies. What makes the coercer's move sufficient to its purpose is not that it increases the magnitude of expected pain for noncompliance or of expected pleasure for compliance to a level where it outweighs all else: This metricized version of the story is derivative and its mathematical structure fictitious.

POWER AND WEAKNESS: THREATS OF HARM AND OFFERS OF BENEFIT

Would-be coercers must therefore have a keen eye for vulnerability. They don't merely assume that in general those whom they hope to coerce are agents who can choose, but whose choosing might be in part controlled by the construction of unrefusable "offers." They study the form. They look for the specific vulnerabilities around which they can structure an "offer" that is unrefusable, not indeed for any agent whatsoever, but for those victims. If they are fortunate these vulnerabilities will provide a ready-made "option" which that victim *cannot* accept. Rather than constructing an unacceptable option the coercers can seize an opportunity to formulate an "offer" whose options are compliance or catastrophe. For example, they can demand money of another in dire need: "You can use my phone to ring for an ambulance if . . . "

Only the most powerful, the boldest, or the least imaginative of coercers will rely on overt threats of physical damage or pain. Coercion that menaces only the body often has drawbacks. In making such threats coercers must expose themselves too much; in carrying them out they risk disabling victims' capacities to comply with their demands. If their power or willingness to deliver the violence they threaten is limited, they may find that many judge their "offers" quite refusable, and that some see them as reasons for retaliation. Even when coercers' power is not in question, they must reckon that some have the makings of martyrs and that they risk undermining their own power over others by making martyrs. In executing their threats they also risk revenge and the attentions of the law. Threatened violence is simply too blunt an instrument for many of the purposes coercers may have. Even state power to back laws with physical sanctions may fail in its purposes unless paralleled by other modes of discipline that secure legitimation. The risk of provoking rebellion or secession by merely repressive policies cannot be discounted.

These familiar points suggest more about coercers' penchants for opaque and deceptive "offers." Coercers cloak their "offers" not merely because they fear detection or resistance, but because the mask of persuasion is so valuable to them. It follows that attempts to define coercion by distinguishing systematically between "threats of harm" (to be condemned as coercion) and "offers of benefit" (to be condoned as noncoercive) can be seen in a new light. The threatened transformations of political, national, or personal integrity and sense of identity, which lead us to view certain offers as unrefusable, and which offer potent means of coercion, can often be described equally plausibly *either* as threatening harm *or* as offering benefit.[9] From the point of view of those on the receiving end of coercion, who are wedded to, indeed constituted by, their present sense of self, family, community, and nation, what is proposed is threat of harm indeed: the destruction of all that they hold dear and of their very selves. Those who propose the transformation may give a rosier account. They are offering others a chance to take on a new and grander identity, to be part of the empire rather than barbarian outsiders, to embrace progress and development, and to be uplifted by the *mission civilisatrice*. Or again, a threat to destroy the liberation movement may be an offer to pacify the countryside and to restore law and order. The proposal may be seen as benefit by those whose integrity and sense of identity hinge on mere survival: It can be seen as harm by those whose integrity and sense of identity hinge on commitment to the liberation movement. What appears in one perspective as threat of loss can often be depicted in another as promise of gain. Coercion cannot then be elucidated by invoking a supposedly sharp distinction between threats and offers.

Even a capitalist wage bargain might be either offer of benefit or threat of harm. Set in one context the worker has the option of pay with a certain independence in return for labor power, and this is often a much better option than slavery or serfdom in return for subsistence and less independence: It appears a refusable offer, and its acceptance a freely entered, so legitimate, contract. Set in another context the same wage bargain might be an option in a coercive "offer": If there is no welfare state, then those without other means must accept some proffered wage bargain or face destitution. Vulnerable workers may have to comply with a pitiful wage bargain. Yet the same terms of employment might be rejectable by workers with brighter prospects, fewer dependents, or a welfare state to fall back on. The two situations confront workers with distinct (though overlapping) sets of options. What makes one "offer" unrefusable is not the level of the wage, or its legal form, or the propositional content of the wage bargain, but that it is the sole alternative to an unacceptable residual option – the "consequences" of refusal – which are given by the vulnerable life situation of those to whom the proposal is made.

Put more generally, we can see that what makes "offers" unrefusable is the relative weakness of their intended victims. It is not their absolute lack of capacities and resources that constitutes vulnerablity to coercion. Rather it is the possession of fewer capacities, powers, or resources than are possessed by others with whom they have to interact. Agents become victims not just because they are poor, ignorant, unskilled, or physically or emotionally feeble, but because they are confronted by others who are richer, more knowledgeable, more skillful or physically or emotionally stronger, and prepared to exploit their advantage. Power depends on differentials. The prospects for making unrefusable "offers" will always be numerous and varied, and more numerous and more varied for the relatively powerful. The powerful can easily ensure that noncompliance with their favored option has "consequences" that are unacceptable by weaker victims.

This suggests that if we think that coercion is generally wrong, and to be prevented, two complementary approaches could be used. The first, and the more discussed, is to try to restrict the ways in which the relatively powerful exploit their advantage. A system of laws before which all are equal is a potent restraint on the ways in which the relatively powerful can use that power to make others unrefusable "offers." Such a system may itself require a coercive backing of enforcement, and this coercive backing may in many circumstances inflict less coercion than it prevents. So at least we are told by long traditions of political theory, which I shall not discuss here. The second strategy is to try to reduce not the misuse but the differentials of power by reducing the relative weakness of those who would be otherwise most vulnerable, and so most open to coercion. No doubt it is impossible to eliminate all differentials in vulnerability; but many glaring differences have been eliminated. The abolition of slavery eliminated a set of social roles that ensured acute vulnerability for some and ease of coercion for others. The gradual reduction of the subjection of women in many parts of the world promises an even wider reduction of differentials of power and vulnerability and the elimination of many contexts of easy coercion. Like the use of state power to enforce laws, the use of state and other powers to eliminate differentials of power may itself have coercive aspects. Nevertheless, here too we may find good reasons to judge that (on balance) such transformations reduce coercion by eliminating or circumscribing the contexts of vulnerability that provide coercers with the opportunities they exploit.

NOTES

After presentation at the Bowling Green conference, a typescript of this paper was published abroad in a volume of working papers entitled *Family, Gender, and Body in Law and Society Today*, ed. Jacek Kurzewski and Andrzej Artur Czynczyk (Warsaw: IPSIR, University of Warsaw), pp. 325–49.

1   See Daniel Lyons, "The Last Word on Coercive Offers . . . (?)" *Philosophy Research Archives* 8 (1982): 393–414. The analyses of coercion that Lyons criticizes are to be found in J. P. Day, "Threats, Offers, Law, Opinion and Liberty," *American Philosophical Quarterly* 14 (1977): 257–72; Don Vandeveer, "Coercion, Seduction and Rights," *Personalist* 58, no. 4 (1977): 374–81; Cheyney C. Ryan, "The Normative Concept of Coercion," *Mind* 89 (1980): 387–8; David Zimmerman, "Coercive Wage Offers," *Philosophy and Public Affairs* 10 (1981): 121–42. His own earlier article was "Welcome Threats and Coercive Offers," *Philosophy* 50 (1975): 425–35. The approach to analyzing coercion was used earlier by Robert Nozick in an influential essay titled "Coercion," reprinted in *Philosophy, Politics and Society*, ed. Peter Laslett, W. G. Runciman, and Quentin Skinner, 4th ser. (Oxford: Blackwell, 1972), pp. 101–35. More recently Alan Wertheimer has criticized proposals to "analyze" coercion and claimed that "the truth of a coercion claim is largely the *result* of a moral inquiry rather than the *ground* for a moral conclusion," in his *Coercion* (Princeton, N.J.: Princeton University Press, 1987), p. 309.

2   My reasons for treating examples as illustrative rather than as intuitions that form part of the basis for ethical reasoning are set out in Onora O'Neill, *Constructions of Reason: Explorations of Kant's Practical Philosophy* (Cambridge: Cambridge University Press, 1989), pp. 165–86.

3   For the philosophical reasons one might look to Wittgenstein and to Quine; for the implications of such views for the history of ideas to Quentin Skinner, especially to "Meaning and Understanding in the History of Ideas," *History and Theory* 8 (1969):

3–53, reprinted in *Meaning and Context: Quentin Skinner and His Critics*, ed. James Tully (Cambridge: Polity Press, 1988), pp. 231–88.

4   This crucial point is often missed in journalistic treatments of terrorism, and sometimes in theoretical discussions. Those who are attacked by terrorists are classified as their victims, but those whom they intimidate, who are their real targets, are not.

5   This suggests a line of argument that is compatible with the theory of action implied here and that offers reasons for thinking coercion wrong. Coercers act on principles that could not be universally adopted: Victims' capacities to act are so circumscribed by coercion that they cannot act on a principle of coercion. Of course, the journalistic and fictional accounts of coercion that most interest us often depict cases of attempted coercion, whose victims turn the tables and coerce their erstwhile coercers. However, dramatic reversals don't show that coercion can be universally undertaken. Since coercion always requires victims, it is an activity that is open only to some in any group. If we think that we should act on principles that can be universally held, we must commit ourselves not to make others unrefusable "offers." In various essays in *Constructions of Reason*, I have tried to present arguments for a principle of noncoercion without presupposing any theory of rights.

6   Cf. Carole Pateman's discussion of Hobbes's imputation of a contract between the infant and its mother in *The Sexual Contract* (Cambridge: Polity Press, 1987).

7   For contrasting interpretations of Kant's conception of freedom see Iris Murdoch, *The Sovereignty of the Good* (London: Routledge and Kegan Paul, 1970), p. 80; Allen Wood, "Kant's Compatibilism," in *Self and Nature in Kant's Philosophy*, ed. A. Wood (Ithaca, N.Y: Cornell University Press, 1984), pp. 73–101; and O'Neill, *Constructions of Reason*. The view that human freedom is unlimited is more Cartesian than Kantian. Contrast Descartes's assertion (in his fourth *Meditation*) that the human will is unlimited and the human intellect very limited with Kant's identification of reason and autonomy, and with his insistence that we are finite rational beings who can make only "negative" use of the concept of a noumenon.

8   Miguel Unamuno, *The Tragic Sense of Life in Men and Nations*,

trans. Anthony Kerrigan (Princeton, N.J.: Princeton University Press, 1972), p. 13.

9 Cf. Virginia Held's "Coercion and Coercive Offers," in *Coercion*, ed. J. R. Pennock and J. W. Chapman (New York: Aldine-Atherton, 1972), pp. 49–62. She writes: "There seems to be a way in which threats and offers can be translated into one another: the law that threatens punishment may offer liberty" (p. 55).

Chapter 8

Making exceptions without abandoning the principle: or how a Kantian might think about terrorism

THOMAS E. HILL, JR.

THE PROBLEM FOR KANTIANS AND THE LARGER ISSUE

Terrorism poses a practical problem that is urgent and difficult. How, within the bounds of conscience, can we respond effectively to violent terrorist activities and threats, especially given the ideological fanaticism and nonnegotiable demands that typically accompany them? The problem is partly instrumental and partly moral. The instrumental task is to find, among the morally permissible means, the best way to minimize terrorist violence, taking into account our other goals and values. The moral task is to determine what means of response are morally permissible. I shall focus here on this second problem, or rather on one way of thinking about it.

Terrorists, of course, often claim that their ends are morally worthy and that their means are morally justified in the context. Some of these claims deserve a serious hearing, and even the more outrageous claims can pose challenges that moral philosophers should not ignore. For present purposes, however, I shall simply assume that terrorism is morally indefensible, at least in the cases to be considered; and I will not be discussing why this is so. My inquiry, instead, is about what *responses* are permissible when terrorists *immorally* threaten the lives of innocent hostages.

Even this somewhat more limited question is too large to undertake here. To give an adequate answer would require

196

us not only to resolve deep issues in moral theory but also to investigate relevant matters of fact, make careful distinctions among cases, review our moral judgments regarding similar problems, and so on. Thus my remarks will address only one theoretical aspect of the larger moral issue: namely, how can a Kantian ethics, suitably interpreted and qualified, handle the life-or-death choices posed by terrorist threats? For example, can it ever permit the use of deadly force against terrorists even at the severe risk of killing innocent hostages? Can one refuse to negotiate for the lives of a few hostages in hope that a tough policy will in the long run save more people?

Although I shall explain the Kantian point of view I have in mind, my aim here is not to defend it either as a moral perspective or as an interpretation of Kant. Rather than presupposing the correctness of the Kantian perspective, I see my project here as preliminary to any final assessment of the relative merits of Kantian versus alternative perspectives: That is, it is simply an attempt to work out how a Kantian approach might direct us to think about some of the terrible choices forced upon us by terrorists. More specifically, can a person (rather like me) who is sympathetic to some main features of Kant's ethics make (intuitively) reasonable judgments about terrorism without, in effect, abandoning the fundamental Kantian principles? And if one admits that terrorism calls for "exceptions" to the straightforward applications of Kant's basic principles for normal circumstances, can one acknowledge these exceptions coherently, and not in an ad hoc manner, from a moral perspective that preserves much of the spirit of Kant's ethics?

My project, I should stress, is not to use Kantian principles to draw a precise line between permissible and impermissible responses to terrorism but rather to see whether a basically Kantian ethics has any reasonable and coherent way to approach the troublesome cases. Many of these cases leave me morally perplexed. I am not confident about what would be right to do. But even this uncertainty is enough to raise the problem, for it seems at first that basic Kantian principles leave no room for what generates the uncertainty. What pulls us even to consider, say, sacrificing a few to save many seems to be a kind of reasoning that makes sense only within a moral perspective radically opposed to Kant's. Even to acknowledge the reasoning in favor of the exceptions, it seems, is to abandon the Kantian perspective.

The issue here is an instance of a more general problem faced by many people who have never heard of Kant but who believe in taking a "principled stand" on moral questions. The problem is posed sharply by an old dialogue that could take many forms.[1] One person, A, asks another, B, whether for a million dollars B would do something against B's principles (e.g., go to bed with a stranger, tell a racist joke, or take hotel towels without paying for them). B responds, "Yes, I suppose I would." Then A asks, "How about five dollars?" B retorts indignantly, "What do you take me for!" "We have already established that", says A. "Now we are dickering over the price."

To those who take pride in standing on principle, the story poses a dilemma: Either you hold rigidly to your principles for all circumstances or else you are prepared to suspend them, or open gaps in them, for special cases. In extreme abnormal circumstances the first course may begin to appear foolish, contrary to both common sense and reflective judgment; but taking the second option raises the suspicion that one's principle is just a rule of thumb and that one is open to persuasion by considerations that have nothing to do with the rationale for the alleged principle.

The sort of dialogue just illustrated was not meant to pose a serious moral dilemma, but more dramatic cases are not hard to imagine. Suppose, as in John Fowles's *Magus*, one were forced to choose between beating two Nazi resisters to death and having the vicious Nazi commandant shoot down a dozen or more resisters. Suppose one had to torture a terrorist in order to learn the location of a bomb set to blow up New York City? If we admit exceptions to familiar moral principles in these cases, then critics can start to push us down the slippery slope. How about if the bomb would blow up only the Bronx? Or a half of that? Or a dozen people? Or two? If we take a hard stand on principle, refusing to make the exception, then the critics' move will be to "up the ante," asking, for example, whether we would kill the two resisters or torture the terrorist in order to save the whole world? The critics' objective here is to open a hole in the absolutist dike, leaving only consequentialist resources to hold back the flow of exceptions. They may even admit that it is almost always right to do as the principle prescribes, for the main issue is not how frequent the exceptions are. Rather, the critics want to raise a suspicion that there is no good reason to maintain the principle *as a principle*, as opposed to a flexible rule of thumb.[2]

One who insisted on standing by ordinary principles in all circumstances, despite the critics' challenge, could of course take a leaf from the consequentialist's book, denying the relevance of merely fictional cases and arguing that we do not actually face such stark alternatives. But though options in the real world are rarely as clear-cut and certain as those in philosophers' examples, to insist repeatedly that each tough case is merely fictional seems a lame defense, one that appeals more to faith than to experience. Besides, since defenders of principle have so often used fictional counterexamples against utilitarianism, they should be more than a little embarrassed to resort to the wholesale rejection of hypothetical examples when trying to uphold their own position.

The history of ethics is full of subtle attempts to meet our imaginary critics' challenge to those who hold familiar moral principles as principles. I shall not review these attempts here, but one common strategy deserves special mention. This is the tendency to append a "catastrophe clause" to familiar principles whenever the consequences of adhering to the principles are so repugnant that it seems morally perverse to refuse the exception – for example, "Do not even threaten to kill innocent people, unless doing so helps to avert a nuclear war" or "Let justice be done, unless (thereby) the heavens should fall." This strategy of adding catastrophe clauses formally maintains the principle as nearly inflexible and yet allows us to side with common sense on extreme counterexamples. The problem with the strategy, however, is that it leaves our critics' main challenge unanswered: If the balance of consequences determines what to do in the extreme case, why not in the case slightly less extreme, and so on? If one may sacrifice a life to save a million and one lives, then why not to save a million, or a million minus one, or a million minus two, or . . . three, or four . . . ? Isn't it basically a matter of calculation, after all? This remains a serious challenge unless one can give a coherent common ground both for maintaining the familiar principle as nearly inflexible and for making exceptions for extreme cases.

Although my discussion will be somewhat abstract and theoretical, the sort of problem raised here is not merely a philosopher's puzzle but a crisis of conscience for many people. Try to imagine, if you can, one of my typical undergraduate students whose talents and ambitions lead her into the inner circles of Washington facing decisions and a world view more akin to those of Oliver North than to those of the local minister. Raised in a small peaceful community with shared values and limited global outlook, she has come to take for granted certain absolute prohibitions as the framework of any tolerable social life and of any decent person's conscience. Unreflective religious beliefs tend to reinforce her principles, but one suspects that it is not so much that her principles are derived from religion as that her theological beliefs are reinforced by the way they wrap an aura of authority around those principles. In the local world the hard cases did not force themselves upon her thinking. Removed to the tougher world of international conflict, power politics, terrorism, and constant compromise, however, she must live with the widespread opinion that her initial principles are foolishly rigid and face choices where sticking to those principles seems unbearably costly. Making an exception here and there, perhaps with a bad conscience, may not at first force her to rethink her position; but after a while she may well wonder how she can continue to make what seem at each time justifiable exceptions without having, in effect, abandoned her principles. Ships with too many holes sink, and principles with too many gaps no longer function as principles.

KANTIAN PRINCIPLES AND THE PRESUMPTION AGAINST KILLING

For the would-be Kantian the challenge takes two forms: First, can the Categorical Imperative, in some form, be sensibly maintained as an inflexible principle in the face of extreme cases? Second, if one admits intuitively reasonable exceptions to the more specific principles about killing (lying, promise keeping, etc.) commonly associated with Kantian morality, in what sense can these still be maintained as principles without abandoning the basic Kantian point of view? For example, can the exceptions themselves be justified by appeal to the Categorical Imperative, or are they, after all, partial concessions to a radically different moral point of view? My main focus will be on the first question, but what I say will also be relevant to the second.

Unlike many who are sympathetic to Kant's moral philosophy, I have little confidence that Kant's famous "universal law" formulations of the Categorical Imperative can function adequately as guides to moral decision making. More promising, I think, is Kant's principle that humanity in each person must always be treated as an end in itself, never simply as a means. This principle, Kant says, is unconditionally binding on all human beings, whatever their circumstances and regardless of what (contingent) ends must be sacrificed to satisfy it. It is, supposedly, not merely one "perfect" duty among others but an articulation of the comprehensive ground of all duties, "perfect" and "imperfect." As a foundation of a rational system of moral principles, it is not supposed to generate or allow any genuine conflict of duties or (what are often called) "moral dilemmas." If unresolvable conflicts of duty are derivable from it, then it cannot have the status Kant claimed for it.

Now despite the warm reception Kant's principle receives from nonconsequentialists everywhere, its interpretation remains controversial. For our purposes, however, I shall simply take as given the following reconstruction.[3]

First, the "humanity in persons" that we are urged to respect is the "rational nature" of human beings, or human beings insofar as they are considered as rational agents with autonomy. The rationality and autonomy in question here are capacities and dispositions that virtually all sane adult human beings are presumed to have, not the full manifestation of these in actual conduct. Thus people who act foolishly and immorally are, in the relevant sense, rational agents with autonomy, and their "humanity" too must be treated as an "end in itself."

The status of infants and the mentally incompetent remains problematic under the principle, and the principle does not address the value of nonhuman animals. But we can set aside these special problems if we limit our examples to mentally competent, adult human beings and do not presume that the humanity principle alone is adequate to settle all moral issues.

Second, the injunction not to treat humanity merely as a means is incomplete and inapplicable without the contrasting phrase "always as an end in itself"; for without knowing what it is to treat humanity as an end in itself we cannot judge what would be, in the intended sense, treating it *merely* as a means. In contrast, if we succeed in treating humanity always as an end in itself, we automatically satisfy the prohibition against treating it merely as a means. Further, as Kant makes clear in his later writings, treating a person's humanity as an end in itself requires more than refraining from acts that would exploit the person as a mere means. Indifference to a person is also forbidden, and positive assistance may be required.[4]

Third, the term "end" here, as Kant acknowledges, is a potentially misleading technical term, meaning roughly something giving a reason or "ground for determining the will." An "end in itself," or "objective end," is a ground of choice that would determine the will of a fully rational agent and should determine ours. In the ordinary sense, of course, neither persons nor the rational nature of persons is an "end."

Fourth, in saying that rational agents with autonomy are ends in themselves, I take it, Kant is saying that they have "dignity," which he defines as an "unconditional and incomparable worth" that, unlike "price," "admits of no equivalent." As an unconditional value, dignity does not depend on the contingent fact that something is useful, desired, or even liked. By contrast, things with mere "price," or conditional value, have a value that is dependent upon utility ("market value") or at least upon individual sentiments ("fancy value"). Anything with mere price has a value that "admits of equivalents" and so is subject to calculated trade-offs; however great its value, there can in principle be something else that could compensate for its loss and justify its sacrifice. Material goods, reputation, and pleasures as such have mere price, and so even great amounts of these things may at times be reasonably sacrificed for other things with the same sort of value. By contrast, dignity is "above all price" and so one can never act contrary to the dignity of someone for the sake of things with mere price, no matter how great the price.[5]

Fifth, Kant's fundamental principle is directly concerned, not with "external actions," but with the attitudes, or value priorities, that lie behind the ways we treat ourselves and others. Acts, for example suicide and murder, and institutions, for example slavery, are condemned not merely as kinds of intentional behavior with undesirable consequences but as manifestations of value priorities that are intolerable. The example of suicide is instructive here. In the *Groundwork*, for example, the suicide Kant condemns is terminating one's life because a hedonistic calculus predicts that one's future will contain more pain than pleasure.[6] Kant later says that to avoid suicide is a "perfect" or exceptionless duty, but he admits that it is an open question for casuistry whether we should *count as suicide* deliberate self-sacrifice for one's country or killing oneself to avoid an unjust death sentence or terminal madness from the bite of rabid dog.[7] The operative principle here is obviously not that intentional killing of a human being is always wrong but rather that (with a few conceivable exceptions) the reasons people have for killing themselves have only a conditional value ("price") that is not to be compared with human dignity.

This understanding of Kant's dignity principle fits well with Kant's other uses of the idea of humanity as an end in itself in the second part of *The Metaphysics of Morals*, which is concerned with ethics beyond questions of law, justice, and rights. For example, the principle is used to condemn drunkenness and gluttony (which interfere with rational functioning), mockery (which treats people as worthless), and servility (which expresses the attitude that one's human worth is measured by one's utility to others).[8] The duty to respect others is grounded in the value of their humanity, not in their achievements or their moral conduct; and significantly, the duty to promote the happiness of others is not grounded explicitly in the dignity principle.[9] In summary, these principles say that one must seek to preserve, develop, exercise, and "honor" rational agency in oneself and to respect it in other human beings, no matter how immorally and irrationally they may behave. To preserve human life per se is not among the principles.

Now though these applications illustrate the dignity principle, they are not concerned with the sort of life-or-death choices that terrorism can force us to confront. Regarding these cases, what Kant says about law and justice, in the first part of *The Metaphysics of Morals*, is more relevant. But before we turn to that, we need to face a further question about the interpretation of the dignity principle.

In brief, the problem is this: Granted that dignity cannot be exchanged for price, can dignity be exchanged for more dignity? To put the question less cryptically: Assuming, as already decided, that dignity is "above all price" and so cannot be sacrificed for things of merely conditional value, does the principle imply, further, that dignity itself is a nonquantitative value that does not admit comparisons like "the dignity of this (person) is greater than the dignity of that (person)" or "two things of dignity are worth twice as much as one"? Does dignity merely "admit of no equivalent" among the things of conditional value or are there no equivalents even among things of dignity? Since dignity is the value attributed to human beings, these questions obviously have a bearing on the question when, if ever, the dignity principle permits the sacrifice of one human being for the sake of one or more other human beings.

Now when we read that Kant approved of capital punishment, and sometimes killing in war, it is tempting to jump to the conclusion that Kant himself understood the dignity principle in the more permissive way, allowing us to justify some killing of human beings on the ground that the dignity of many persons outweighs the dignity of a few. However, for textual reasons I shall pass over here, I do not think that this interpretation is correct. More important for our purposes, the permissive interpretation would undermine what seems to be the strikingly special character of Kantian ethics, namely, its refusal to reduce moral decisions to the weighing and balancing of commensurate values.[10] On the permissive interpretation, the theory would become just another version of an all-too-familiar type: namely, a theory that first assigns a quantity of intrinsic value to various possible outcomes and then treats the right decision as a function of these value assignments. Kant's theory, to be sure, would have the unique feature of having two scales of value (dignity and price), with any amount of value on one scale always "trumping" any amount on the other; and it would place the higher value on living as a rational agent as opposed to hedonistic values. But nonetheless, like sophisticated forms of utilitarianism that place a higher priority on human life than on animal pleasures, such a theory would hold "the good prior to the right" and make moral choices fundamentally matters of calculation.

Thus, to further discussion, let us work with the alternative, nonpermissive interpretation. On this account, dignity is still "above all price" in the previous sense: Dignity must never be violated in exchange for things of mere price. But now dignity is not to be construed as a quantitative notion.

Dignity is "without equivalent" even among other things with dignity in the sense that one cannot justify a violation of dignity by claiming it as a necessary sacrifice to promote "more" dignity elsewhere. Thus the destruction of something with dignity, if ever justifiable, cannot be justified simply by weighing quantities of intrinsic value, even value of the highest order. The assignment of dignity to each rational agent, then, functions not to introduce a new kind of value calculation, but rather to block our tendency to treat rational agents as interchangeable commodities. Moreover, "the right" remains "prior to the good" in that the attribution of dignity to rational agents stems from a rational/moral command to adopt and act consistently with a certain attitude toward rational agents, not from a metaphysical claim about intrinsic values or from an empirical claim about preferences fixed by human nature.

Though the analogy is not perfect, we may say that the Kantian attitude toward preserving the lives of rational agents is rather like the attitude that some pious persons take toward an object they regard as "sacred" or "holy." They revere and treasure the object and seek diligently to preserve it. Even the thought that they might have to destroy the object is abhorrent, and so they make every effort to avoid situations where that would be necessary. They view any such object as "irreplaceable," not merely in the sense that they would not trade it for an exact copy but in the sense that they would not view even its replacement by many other things revered in the same way as commensurate values compensating for the loss. Nonetheless, if certain deplorable circumstances arose, they might grant that they must destroy the object, for example, to keep it from being defiled by enemies. The attitude that such objects are "without equivalent" does not translate simply into an action principle that they must never be destroyed but is more complex. It is also concerned with how one should view their loss, how one must work to prevent situations where losses will inevitably result from one's choices, and how one should think about what to do when such tragic situations occur.

The attitude in question is perhaps more intuitively recognizable when one reflects how a loving parent would view the horrible situation of being able to save one of her children from drowning or to save two others, but not all. Surely she is justified in saving the two, but it is hard to conceive that she would accept that the rationale was that two are worth twice as much as one. The problem, of course, is to say what other rationale there can be.

It is the more radical, nonpermissive reading of the dignity principle, I believe, that accounts for its wide appeal; but this is also what raises most acutely the consequentialist's challenge. The principle does not absolutely prohibit killing human beings, nor does it necessarily forbid us, when faced with no other option, to make the hard choice that results in the death of a few and the preservation of many. But if such choices are morally defensible, they cannot be rationalized simply by the thought that "the lives of many people are worth more than the lives of few people" or even "many innocent lives are worth more than fewer." Even more obviously, the dignity principle does not permit the choices to be justified by the thought that by preserving the lives of more happy people we will bring about the most "intrinsically valuable" experiences.

The problem, then, is how, despite this severe restriction on consequentialist thinking, can the Kantian ever justify making the hard life-or-death choices that seem intuitively compelling, particularly in cases where at some level of deliberation the numbers do seem to matter? The problem is far easier to state than to answer, but some clues toward an answer, I think, can be found in Kant's views on state coercion and punishment, to which I now turn.

DIGNITY, PUNISHMENT, AND DEADLY FORCE AGAINST TERRORISM

Kant held that justice not only permits but even requires capital punishment for murder. I disagree, but I think that what Kant says in support of his view at least suggests how the dignity principle can be reconciled with the use of deadly force against terrorists in some cases. It also opens up a way of thinking about cases where a response to terrorists would endanger the lives of innocent persons. Once again I shall reconstruct Kant's views liberally, without argument, but the purpose here is to focus attention on the possible reconciliation, not on questions of textual interpretation.[11]

The background assumption is that we are dealing with agents who are rational though not necessarily moral or ideally rational. They know what they are doing, are capable of self-control, and know well enough the difference between right and wrong. Moreover, they are disposed, even when they act immorally, to acknowledge moral requirements as rational and not merely imposed by others. When conscience and moral argument fail to dissuade them from their immoral projects, they are at least rational enough, as a rule, to be deterred by clear and credible threats to their own welfare. These assumptions, of course, are not always satisfied in the real world; and to the extent that they are not, the Kantian rationale may be vitiated.

Next, let us grant that, for various reasons, human beings need to join together into communities with common laws that assign to each rights and responsibilities. In a state of nature (or anarchy) individual reason and conscience would not in fact suffice to create and preserve the conditions necessary for people in close proximity to have lives appropriate to rational agents. So states are needed to define and secure to each person a reasonable opportunity for life and liberty as a rational autonomous agent. Thus there are moral as well as prudential reasons to form and support civil authorities with coercive powers.

This being so, the dignity principle must be applied not merely to relations between individuals isolated from others but, first and crucially, to the construction of a system of laws that can provide the framework for moral relations among individuals.[12] In working out the implications of the dignity principle for laws, one should take the point of view of legislators in the "kingdom of ends," that is, fully rational and autonomous persons, each with "private ends" but "abstracting from personal differences," and making only universal laws.[13] From this point of view, Kant and Rawls agree, the first principle of justice adopted would be that the system of laws should try to ensure to each person, viewed in advance of particular contingencies, an equal and full opportunity to live out his or her life as rational agent within the constraints of those laws. This is essentially what Kant calls "the universal principle of justice," and, of course, it is more or less Rawls's first principle of justice.[14]

Unfortunately, human nature being what it is, merely articulating laws that coordinate activities and define fair shares of liberty to each will not suffice to ensure compliance. Many would overstep the bounds and encroach on others' liberty. Thus coercion is needed as a "hindrance to hindrance of freedom."[15] The coercive power of the state must provide incentives so that even without conscience everyone will have clear and sufficient reason not to violate the liberty of others (as defined by just laws). The aim of the coercive legal system is not to maximize welfare or to give the morally vicious their just deserts but rather to create the conditions in which each has, so far as possible, a fair chance to live out a life as a rational autonomous agent.

State officials cannot, of course, be present at each moment a person begins to invade someone else's freedom contrary to just laws, and so a system of punishment is needed. Though applicable only after a crime has been committed, it can serve to "hinder hindrances to freedom" by credible threats that provide rational incentives, apart from conscience, for each to stay within the bounds of the freedom he or she has been fairly allotted. The threats must be genuine, enforceable, and public in order to be credible, and they must be carried out as legally prescribed for the sake of both fairness and efficacy.

The system of punishment, however, must not only be a rational deterrent; it must also honor the dignity of each rational agent. This means that criminals must be treated with respect as human beings, not humiliated or manipulated like animals. It also means that the criminal, like every other citizen, must have had a fair chance to avoid the penalty. Thus ex post facto laws, strict liability, and unpredictable penalties must be avoided; the criminal law must be public, easily understood, uniformly enforced, and concerned with provable "external actions" rather than inner moral qualities. Ideally, the penalties would be just severe enough so that, given effective enforcement, reasonable self-interested persons could see that each crime is unlikely to be profitable and yet standards of proportionality of penalty to offense are maintained. The system must be defensible even to the criminal insofar as he or she is willing to look at the matter from the perspective of one rational agent, with dignity, among many.

Kant thought that the system that best satisfies these criteria relied on the *jus talionis,* or "an eye for an eye," as the rule for determining the degree and kind of punishment that should be attached to each offense.[16] Thus execution should be the punishment for murder. As I have argued elsewhere, this is not because the "inner viciousness" of the murderer deserves the death penalty, still less because the murderer has forfeited all consideration under justice and as a human being. Nor, I think, is Kant's main argument the implausible claim that in choosing the crime with a known penalty the criminal has actually willed his or her own punishment. The rationale implicit in the central features of Kant's theory of law is that capital punishment is a necessary part of a fair system needed to secure to each citizen, so far as possible, the opportunity to live out a life as a rational and autonomous agent.

We may doubt various assumptions, for example, that only the death penalty can provide adequate (nonmoral) disincentives to murder and that fairness requires inflexible application of the penalty. But let us grant these points for now. How does the reconstructed rationale for judicial killing of human beings square with the dignity principle? That principle, applied to legal systems, clearly implies that criminals should be treated with respect, that the death penalty should be imposed reluctantly, and that the systems should contain other features designed to prevent the crimes that call for capital punishment. The dignity principle also implies that capital punishment cannot be justified by the argument that it saves money, reduces fear, or promotes the happiness of most people. Nor can the rationale be simply "we will save more people than we kill" or "the people we save are worth more than those we kill."

But the justification I sketched was not of these kinds. It used the dignity principle to set standards for a general system of laws, concluding that a legal system expresses its respect for the incomparable worth of each rational agent by seeking to secure for each, in advance of particular contingencies, a full fair opportunity to live as a rational agent. A general system of laws acknowledges the worth of citizens, not as defined at a given time by character traits, social roles, achievements, and records of conduct, but as conceived more generally as rational agents extending over time, capable of choosing any number of roles and courses of action. In carrying out just punishment, one can argue that the system did, so far as possible, secure for even the criminal, in advance of the criminal's particular choices, a full life with as much liberty as possible in an impartial system of laws. Though the criminal does not wish for the courts to apply the punishment in his or her case, the system respects as far as possible what he or she wills, or would will, as a system of laws when looking at the matter just as a rational agent apart from a particular history and circumstance. If, as Kant thought, capital punishment for murder is a necessary part of that system, criminals should have no legitimate complaint that the law failed to respect their human dignity.[17]

This line of thinking, if cogent, can readily be extended to justify laws authorizing the police in some extreme cases to kill a terrorist who is immediately threatening the lives of law-abiding citizens. By my initial assumption, our terrorist, like the murderer, is a rationally competent agent who flagrantly and immorally crashes across the boundaries of freedom that a just system of law tries to ensure for each, including him- or herself.[18] By authorizing police to use necessary force, even deadly force, against terrorists actively engaged in life-threatening activities, the system serves to "hinder hindrances to freedom" without violating anyone's dignity. In fact, the case here for deadly force against terrorists in action seems stronger than the case for capital punishment for murder because in the latter case prevention efforts have already failed and it remains controversial whether capital punishment is necessary as a deterrent.

DIGNITY AND ENDANGERING INNOCENT HOSTAGES

So far I have considered only how the dignity principle might be reconciled with policies that involve taking the lives of the terrorists themselves, given some strong assumptions about what the terrorists are like. This suggests that a Kantian may admit legitimate exceptions to the rule "Do not kill human beings," even though there remains a strong presumption in favor of that rule in most circumstances. More controversial questions arise, however, when we consider responses to terrorism that endanger the lives of innocent people. In these cases we could not argue to the persons whose lives we endanger that they have knowingly overstepped the bounds of liberty allotted to them under a fair system of law. Moreover, in at least some of these cases common sense tells us that the numbers matter, that (for example) risking the life of one hostage to save hundreds is not unreasonable.

The issues here are complex. Many variables may be relevant. For example, do we have an option to negotiate without endangering anyone? If not, will the deaths result from our violent attack on the terrorists or from the terrorists themselves when we refuse to negotiate or attack? Are the persons we put in jeopardy already in danger from the terrorists? Is there a chance of rescuing the very persons we put in danger? How do we estimate the odds of our killing the hostages, of the terrorists' killing the hostages, of our rescuing the hostages, and of the terrorists' killing other people? And how certain are we of these estimates? How many survivors and how many dead do we expect in each scenario? How pure are our intentions in imposing the risks? Is there publicly known and accepted policy concerning these situations?

We cannot review all variations, but let us begin with one of the easier cases. Suppose that negotiation to free the hostages is not an option, and so we must attack or stand by and accept the consequences. Suppose, further, that it is nearly certain that all the hostages will be killed if we do not make a rescue attempt. If we do make the attempt, there is a rather good chance that we can save all the hostages, but there is also a nonnegligible chance that we may kill some hostages in the effort. For simplicity, suppose that the danger to the attackers and other innocent people is minimal.

Most people, I suppose, would say that we should make the rescue attempt and that if, despite our precautions, we kill innocent hostages in the effort we were still justified in doing what resulted in their deaths. After all, they might say, it is a question of some being killed or all being killed. So, it seems, the intuitive judgment is that the numbers matter here. Since the lives of nonthreatening, law-abiding persons are at stake, the Kantian cannot accommodate the intuitive judgment by the same argument we considered for capital punishment and for using deadly force against the terrorists themselves. The Kantian must refuse to permit the attack, contrary to common sense, or else find a new argument.

The case is made easier by the fact that we stipulated that hostages who may be killed in the attack would be killed by the terrorists if we do not attack. We do not need to endanger one person in order to save others. We need only to justify risking our killing that person in an effort to prevent that person's nearly certain death at the hands of others.

Could the Kantian ever justify this? Again, the dignity principle implies a reluctance to kill or even risk killing human beings, and it implies that we should make every effort not to be forced into situations where these actions might be required. But as the dignity principle does not absolutely prohibit killing human beings, it cannot absolutely forbid taking a serious risk that we may kill human beings. The question is, can we risk killing innocent persons in the sort of situation at hand?

Taking a clue from the argument for state coercion and capital punishment, the Kantian should consider the question not in the isolated instance but as it falls under general laws and policies applicable to everyone over time. Here the issue is: What public policies would it be morally legitimate for a community to adopt in authorizing official responses to terrorism? As before, the appropriate Kantian point of view for deliberating about this is presumably that of a rational legislator in the "kingdom of ends."

The legislators' commitment to the dignity principle means that they have a strong concern to preserve each person's opportunity to function as rational autonomous agent. So they have an initial interest in saving lives. But the dignity principle also imposes constraints on how they can justifiably do this. For example, the legislators cannot simply assign a quantity of value to each life and then try to find the value-maximizing policy. Moreover, they must find policies that are justifiable even to those who will suffer under them (insofar as they adopt the same legislative point of view). Further, since human dignity means more than merely preserving life, the legislators must consider other ways that policies can affirm that central value. They would, for instance, tend to favor policies that strongly express and encourage mutual respect, and oppose the opposite, independently of the policies' effects on survival rates.

Considerations of dignity alone are not always sufficient to resolve an issue. But nonetheless there may be a reasonable way of thinking about the problem from the Kantian legislative point of view. Each legislator not only values human dignity but also has a set of "private ends" that he or she can pursue only while living. (I set aside here beliefs about immortality.) Valuing each other person as an end, the legislator also has reason (Kant implies) to give some weight to the ends of others. From the legislative point of view lawmakers must "abstract from the content of private ends" and so cannot concern themselves with the details of who wants what. But that each has a general concern for his or her own survival seems to follow from the idea that members have private ends (and know so). To be sure, legislators are committed to seeking policies promoting their own survival only on the condition that each policy is equally acceptable to others. But others have a similar concern for their own survival. Thus, one might argue, all would favor any policy that promised to prolong the survival of representative persons as rational autonomous persons, other things being equal and provided the policy is otherwise consistent with the dignity principle. Each legislator would favor the policy when looking at it from his or her own perspective (abstractly conceived) and also when reviewing it from the perspective of each other person.

Now if suitably hedged with restrictions, some policy that permitted authorized agents to endanger the life of a hostage in an attempt to save that hostage and others from almost certain death would be seen, in advance of particular contingencies, as enhancing each representative law-abiding citizen's chances for surviving terrorist situations. If so, the policy would be reasonable and, it seems, not inherently contrary to the dignity principle. If, in addition, the policy was decided upon in a legitimate political process, was known to all, and was carried out by authorized individuals, then (absent further objections) the dignity principle would seem to permit its execution, even at the serious risk of innocent lives.

This argument is too sketchy to draw any precise line between permissible and impermissible cases, but it suggests at least that the Kantian is not forced to choose between treating dignity as a measurable quantity and condemning all avoidable killing of innocent persons. The reasoning allows us to consider "chances of survival" and so (indirectly) the numbers of lives at stake, but this consideration enters the deliberation not as a basic principle ("many lives have greater value than few") but as pertinent information at a later stage. "Try to save the most lives" may become a highly qualified derivative principle for specified circumstances, but this is compatible with the dignity principle. And of course, to deny that the chances of survival under different policies should ever in any way be a relevant moral consideration would be sheer madness.[19]

A more difficult question arises when the persons endangered by our efforts to free the hostages are not the hostages already at risk but others. Even if the attack will save many lives, it cannot be defended as giving a better chance of survival to the very people endangered by the terrorists. To attack, it seems, would be to treat the fewer persons as exchangeable for a greater number of persons, contrary to the dignity principle.

Although I think there are strong reasons not to endorse a general permission to attack in such cases, the Kantian line of thinking we have been considering need not lead to an absolute prohibition. It might allow the attack in certain carefully circumscribed extreme cases but, of course, not on the ground that "more lives are worth more than fewer." The reasoning in favor of the attack, as before, would have to be that the policy of attack in exceptional cases of this kind could be defended from the general legislative point of view even to those who turned out to be the victims under the policy. The argument from that point of view would be that the policy, all things considered, enhanced each representative (law-abiding) citizen's chances of survival, without violating any of the essential constraints of the Kantian legislative perspective. To show this we might need to establish that the chances of each citizen's falling into the unfortunate hostage role, independently of his or her choice to take special risks, is more or less the same. We would also need to take into account the likelihood that the policy would undermine respect for life, would lead to foolish risk taking, and would be abused by callous, trigger-happy officials. A legal system or moral code that said, without careful qualification, "Authorities may risk killing one person whenever they think that they can thereby save more than one" would invite abuse and probably cost more lives in the long run. Moreover, prolonging human life is not the only value implicit in the dignity principle. Any policy must also be evaluated according to the way it expresses and encourages mutual respect, honors prior commitments, upholds just institutions, and so on.[20]

Nonetheless, a more circumscribed policy of this sort could conceivably give each representative citizen a better prospect for living out a full life as a rational agent than would an absolute prohibition on endangering innocent lives in such cases. Though the stakes may be higher, the argument for the policy would in principle be like the case for current laws that permit police to speed when actively pursuing armed robbers even though this imposes risks on law-abiding motorists. If all other constraints were satisfied, such policies might be approved by all from the appropriate point of view.

In this way of thinking, our calculation of each representative person's chances of survival under different general policies would be information relevant in the overall justification, but the fundamental principle regarding official responses to terrorism would remain "Public policies must conform to principles acceptable to all from the abstract legislative point of view that, among other things, regards each person as of incalculable worth." One way of respecting the dignity of all is to authorize police to impose grave risks only as permitted under public policies that they themselves, as rational agents, would approve.

INTENTIONAL SACRIFICE OF INNOCENT PERSONS

My aim in reviewing this series of cases has been to suggest a (more or less) Kantian way of thinking that might reconcile the dignity principle with the common opinion that in some circumstances it is morally permissible to kill terrorists and to endanger innocent hostages. The scenarios we reviewed posed questions only about taking risks that we will kill innocent persons, unintentionally, as we try to save others.

Reasonable people may differ about the degree of risk that is warranted, but almost everyone agrees that some such risks are worth taking. Unfortunately, we can imagine situations where terrorism confronts us with choices more horrible than those we have considered, and about these cases philosophers will disagree more sharply. For example, suppose that the only way to prevent a terrorist from blowing up a building with many hostages in it is to shoot the terrorist through another innocent hostage who is held as a shield. Or, still worse, suppose that we could save the many hostages only by deliberately killing an innocent victim of his choice.

Here traditional morality draws the line, refusing to authorize the intentional sacrifice of an innocent person even to save others.[21] Kant too would be horrified at the thought, and no doubt many consequentialists would feel the same way. But the question here is whether the theories in question could permit the killing, and how they could justify their conclusions.

These more extreme cases pose a challenge to the Kantian quite different from the one that has been my main concern. The worry now is not that the Kantian cannot permit *enough* of what reasonable persons would allow; it is that the Kantian *as construed here* will permit *too much* to be morally tolerable, authentically Kantian, or significantly different from the consequentialist.[22]

These are important concerns, deserving a fuller treatment than I can attempt here.[23] A thorough response would require a more detailed characterization of the Kantian legislative perspective than what has been sketched here. But even without that, it seems clear that our Kantian legislators have strong reasons for refusing to authorize the intentional killing of innocent persons in response to terrorism.

Most obviously, all the considerations making the Kantian legislators reluctant to *endanger* innocent hostages will be even stronger reasons not to authorize *intentional* killing of innocents. To legitimize any such killing as public policy would be a dangerous invitation to abuse by corrupt, self-deceiving, and bungling officials. The policy would likely lower everyone's sense of security and trust. Those in authority could not honestly say even to a loved one, "I would never kill you or turn you over to killers." Worse yet, official readiness to kill innocent persons in response to terrorists' threats not only would encourage such blackmail but also would enhance the terrorists' power. By making convincing threats to do a greater evil, terrorists could easily manipulate the authorities into doing a lesser one. The lawless could thus enlist the aid of law enforcement to get their dirty work done for them.

Few would deny that the general policy of killing innocents to placate terrorists would have these bad consequences, and more; but some may try to press an objection often posed to consequentialists. That is, they may argue that, in some extraordinary situation, a one-time, secret, unauthorized sacrifice of an innocent person might save lives without incurring all the problems of openly admitting a policy of negotiating with terrorists. Here, the objection continues, the killing would still be wrong but not for the reasons given above.

Now this counterexample may pose a problem for consequentialism of some kinds but is irrelevant to the Kantian legislative thinking proposed here. This idea was introduced not as a comprehensive moral decision procedure but as a thought experiment to guide and constrain attempts to justify public policies with regard to issues, such as murder and terrorism, where not having enforceable public policy would be disastrous. A crucial background assumption was that the procedure justifies policies only *as openly acknowledged and scrupulously administered*.[24] If any "exceptions" are to be justified by the legislative procedure, then, they must be justified as overt aspects of a general public policy, not as secret, one-time deviations.

A Kantian ethics must also take into account the following. The dignity principle requires that we *always* regard each person as having incomparable worth, and so not as a mere means even to worthy ends. This is an attitude to be maintained in daily living as well as a stipulated constraint on thinking from the abstract legislative standpoint. Thus, to be justified in a deliberate killing, a person would need to be able to face the victim and say, *sincerely* and *truthfully*, "I choose to kill you (when I have an option not to); but still I regard you as more than a mere means, in fact, as a person with a worth that is incalculable."[25] Now it is not easy to imagine that a human being could *maintain* this attitude while deliberately killing another, even though apparently Kant thought that public executioners could and many think that doctors administering euthanasia can.[26] It seems even more unlikely that human beings in general could authorize, approve, and carry out public policies of deliberate sacrifice of innocent persons while continuing honestly to affirm an untarnished respect for human dignity. As Kantian legislators they could not approve of any policy that they could not carry out consistently with the dignity principle. Thus it seems implausible that they could accept any policy involving deliberate sacrifice of innocent persons even if they predicted that it would save more lives.

RESPONSIBILITY AND "CLEAN HANDS"

A final issue that calls for fuller discussion but can only be briefly mentioned here is how we should determine responsibility for the deaths in our terrorist situations. The worry is that our abstract deliberations about the numbers of lives saved and lost have not taken into account *who* will be responsible for the deaths. Mustn't we consider not only how many will die but also whether the deaths result directly from our acts (or omissions) or from another's immoral response to what we do (or refuse to do)?

Traditional morality does not impute to me, as the "consequence" of my action or inaction, every event to which my action or inaction was a causally contributing factor, even if that event would not have occurred but for my action or inaction. We are "responsible" for some of the effects of what we do but not for others. If, for example, prior to President

Bush's inauguration someone had threatened to kill himself if Bush took up the presidency and Bush, knowing this, did so anyway and the threat was carried out, common sense does not impute the death to Bush but to the person who foolishly made and carried out the threat. Kant seems to agree, for he argues (in a far less convincing case) that even if one's refusal to lie to a murderer causally contributes to the murderer's finding one's friend and killing him, the death of the friend is imputed entirely to the killer, not to oneself for refusing to tell a lie. This suggests that, in a Kantian ethics, one must at least take into account whether deaths are a direct result of one's own actions (or inactions) or whether they result from someone else's immoral responses to what one does (or refuses to do). Judgments of responsibility after a death has been caused often take this factor into account, and so it seems also relevant as we deliberate before acting about what would be the right thing to do.

To expand our previous case, suppose that we have three options: Submit to terrorist demands, attack the terrorists, or refuse their demands and do nothing further. If we submit, let us suppose, we will save the hostages but almost certainly encourage further terrorism that will cost even more lives. If we attack, we will kill some hostages but will save more hostages. If we refuse to negotiate and do nothing else, the terrorists will probably kill all the hostages. In the first and third cases the deaths that occur will result through the agency of the terrorists themselves, even though our choice is a causal condition. In the second case (attack), the deaths will be a direct result of our actions (though we are responding to a problem posed by the terrorists). Prior to trying to figure out which course, all things considered, is morally best, we need to assess, in addition to our intentions and the estimates of lives expected to be lost and saved, whether it is also relevant whether the deaths are directly caused by us or by the terrorists.

Extending our previous line of thought, we could also address this question from the abstract point of view of Kantian legislators. The dignity principle itself should make us extremely reluctant to risk killing human beings, but it should also make us very hesitant to do something when we are confident that others will respond by killing human beings. Perhaps the refusal to take action that may kill others, other thing being equal, is more directly expressive of the way we value human lives; but other things are rarely equal, and refusal to take extraordinary steps to save lives can also express inadequate concern. We cannot be certain, of course, that the terrorists will carry out their threats if we do nothing; but then we are also uncertain how other options would turn out, and our question now is whether anything but these estimates of probabilities and numbers should make a difference. If it is generally worse to risk killing someone than to do what has the same probability of someone else doing a killing, then there must be reasons for this policy that are cogent from the Kantian legislative point of view. But what could they be?

The policy in question is a fairly specific application of a more general principle that is often maintained, namely, that it is generally better to "keep one's own hands clean" than to do what would normally be wrong in an effort to prevent wrongs that one anticipates that others will commit. This says, vaguely, that one's primary responsibility is to worry about the direct consequences of what one does or fails to do, without excessive regard to whether others will take the occasion to respond immorally.

Now I can imagine four considerations that might be offered in support of this principle for a world in which most are conscientious and even those who are prone to crime are often amenable to reason. First, a public policy that gives you greater responsibility for what you cause independently of the immoral responses of others might work to minimize the damage so often caused by well-meaning people in their efforts to prevent the wrongdoing of others. If most people are conscientious and many are bunglers, we would perhaps all do better if we do not encourage people to anticipate and act violently to prevent the crimes of others. Second, the policy would curb lawbreakers' power to get their way through blackmail. If authorities were prepared to harm innocent persons whenever someone made a convincing threat to inflict more harm, then by using manipulative threats criminals could in effect make the authorities their accomplices. Third, the policy might promote the opportunity for most people to live out their own lives as rational agents because it places a higher priority on "keeping one's own house in order" than on intervening in the lives of those that we expect will act badly. By contrast, a policy that required everyone to be a moral busybody, always ready to do a lesser evil to prevent others from doing a slightly greater evil, would leave less room for planning and living out one's own preferred life. Fourth, the policy that makes each person primarily responsible for his or her own actions expresses a hope or faith that others will, after all, listen to reason despite their threats and past records; and so affirming that policy is a way of expressing respect for them as rational agents.

Though relevant, these policy considerations do not decisively support an inflexible "clean hands" principle, even in good conditions; and they are even less persuasive when violent crimes become more frequent and criminals more oblivious to reason. Moreover, the reasons that favor a "clean hands" policy for ordinary citizens do not apply equally well to law enforcement authorities. There are fewer risks and interferences with rational life plans when responsibility to prevent crimes is restricted to selected officials who voluntarily take up the task.

Furthermore, I suspect that the "clean hands" principle gains much of its popular support from a confusion. Suppose it is assumed that a certain act, say, telling a lie, is always wrong. Then if someone is tempted to lie to prevent another person from doing something worse, it might be appropriate to admonish the would-be liar by saying, "No, forget what others may do; your responsibility is for what you do." Similarly, if we assume that any intentional killing of a human being is wrong in itself, then even when killing one person would prevent others from killing many, we may say, "Keep your own hands clean; what others do is not your responsibility." But the assumption in both cases is crucial. Unless we take as given that what we propose to do is wrong in itself, it remains an open question whether "what others do" affects our responsibility. And from the Kantian legislative point of view, what specific acts, if any, are always wrong and the degree to which we should take responsibility for preventing the consequences of others' crimes are matters about which we need to reason, not principles we can assume from the start.

CONCLUSION

My conclusions are limited and tentative. First, it seems that we can maintain the dignity principle without insisting that it is always wrong to kill human beings and to risk killing innocent human beings in response to terrorism. Second, there is a Kantian way of thinking about hard choices that admits, without abandoning the dignity principle, that at some level one must take into account the relative numbers of people whose lives can be prolonged by different policies. Third, though further discussion is needed, the objection that Kantian legislators would authorize some deliberate sacrifices of innocent persons seems dubious. Finally, although this Kantian perspective may give some support to a limited "clean hands" policy for most people under good conditions, it does not endorse the absolute principle "Regardless of what others threaten to do, your only responsibility is to ensure that you don't kill any innocent person."

Can the substantive principles "Don't kill human beings" and "Avoid endangering the lives of innocent persons" be maintained as principles in a Kantian morality even though they admittedly have exceptions? This depends on what "maintaining them as principles" means. Clearly not, if it means trying to keep the majority of people thinking of them as exceptionless rules while privately admitting that there are justified exceptions. But there may still be a sense in which the principles, with exceptions implicitly understood, might be held as quite fundamental principles, more so than others (like "Don't commit incest") that have far fewer justified exceptions. That is, though qualified, the principles are partial expressions, in action terms, of the very attitude that the dignity principle itself demands, and the exceptions they contain are not concessions to a radically different moral point of view but rather refinements consistent with the basic Kantian viewpoint.

NOTES

This essay was written for the conference on violence and terrorism sponsored by the philosophy department at Bowling Green State University in November 1988, and subsequently discussed with faculty and students at the U.S. Airforce Academy, the College of Charleston, the College of William and Mary, UCLA, and the North Carolina Triangle Ethics Group. I want to thank the participants at these meetings for their many helpful comments.

1 Here I rephrase an often-repeated dialogue, sometimes attributed to G. B. Shaw, because the original version exploits sexist stereotypes and the differences are irrelevant to my point.

2 For simplicity I am imagining that my "critics" here are "act-consequentialists" and not "rule-consequentialists," for the latter might urge us in practice to treat certain rules as inflexible principles and yet defend this at a "higher level" of deliberation by appeal to consequences. The Kantian alternative to be considered, however, is opposed to both forms of consequentialism because of the constraints it places on the role of consequences in justifying principles.

3 Some of these points are spelled out in more detail in my "Humanity as an End in Itself," *Ethics* 91 (October 1980): 84–90, and (in slightly modified form) in my "Kantian Constructivism in Ethics," *Ethics* 99 (July 1989): 752–70. Many of Kant's works are relevant, but especially his *Groundwork of the Metaphysics of Morals*, trans. H. J. Paton (New York: Harper and Row, 1964), pp. 89, 97.

4 See Kant's *Metaphysical Principles of Virtue: Part II of the Metaphysics of Morals*, trans. James Ellington (Indianapolis: Bobbs-Merrill, 1964), p. 54.

5 Because of the centrality of the idea of "dignity," I shall here-

after refer to my reconstruction of Kant's principle that we
should always treat humanity as an end in itself simply as "the
dignity principle."

6   Kant, *Groundwork*, pp. 89, 97.

7   See Kant, *The Metaphysical Principles of Virtue*, p. 84.

8   Ibid., pp. 88–90, 96–100, 132–3.

9   Ibid., pp. 112–19.

10 Refusal to *reduce* moral decisions to weighing of costs and
benefits does not, of course, imply that such weighing never
has a legitimate role in moral thinking, even if some of Kant's
more extreme remarks might suggest that he thought so.

11 Kant mentions punishment in several works but primarily in
the first part of *The Metaphysics of Morals*, translated as *The
Metaphysical Elements of Justice* by John Ladd (Indianapolis:
Bobbs-Merrill, 1965). My view of Kant's position is presented
briefly in "Kant's Anti-Moralistic Strain," *Theoria* 44 (1978):
131–51. For another view see Edmund L. Pincoffs, *The Rationale
of Legal Punishment* (New York: Humanities, 1966), chap. 1.

12 This is a crucial move in the Kantian line of argument I am
suggesting. It is similar to Rawls's procedural commitment to
first fixing the moral constraints on the basic structure of society and only then working out principles for interactions
between individuals. The idea is to take the dignity principle,
as initially presented, to be inflexible but abstract, with its
mode of application not yet specified. The examples in the
Groundwork illustrate its application to interpersonal relations
in a presupposed background of an ongoing society with a
legitimate legal order. *The Metaphysical Elements of Justice* raises
prior questions about the moral justification and limits of any
system of public laws, with the assumption that day-to-day
relations among individuals must conform to whatever justice
demands regarding this necessary background. Thus the suggestion under consideration is that the dignity principle applies
first to decisions about the basic system of public laws and
only then to individual decisions remaining undetermined by
this system. Though the priority implicit here may be doubted,
it is not the inconsistent view that the absolute dignity principle
applies independently to laws and to individual conduct and
that when these applications conflict we should make exceptions in the individual sphere.

13 I draw here on a reconstruction of the Kantian legislative per-

spective that I sketch more fully in "The Kingdom of Ends," *Proceedings of the Third International Kant Congress*, ed. Lewis White Beck (Dordrecht: Reidel, 1972), pp. 307–15. This view is expanded (and modified slightly) in my "Kantian Constructivism in Ethics." The basic idea is similar, of course, to the idea of the "original position" in John Rawls's theory of justice, but there are important differences.

14 See Kant's *Metaphysical Elements of Justice*, p. 35; and John Rawls's *Theory of Justice* (Cambridge, Mass.: Harvard University Press, 1971), chap. 1.

15 Kant, *The Metaphysical Elements of Justice*, pp. 35–6.

16 See ibid., p. 101.

17 It is worth reemphasizing here that the dignity principle does not say that prolonging the life of a rational agent is the supremely overriding value, though Kant's strong stand against suicide (with absence of cases of justified killing) in the *Groundwork* often suggests this conclusion to readers. The most obvious way to show that one treasures a physical object, say a "priceless" vase, is to do all one can to prevent its destruction, (almost) no matter what. But "rational agents" are not things like vases, and what it means to treasure them for what they are is accordingly more complex. Placing a supreme value on rational agents as such requires us not only to seek to preserve them but also to abide by the structures that they, as rational agents, endorse.

18 These assumptions, of course, may not be satisfied in actual cases. Terrorists often claim high-minded motives and deny the justice of the legal systems they attack. Because of cultural differences we often cannot assume that the terrorists knowingly violate a shared moral framework, and in some cases they may not satisfy even the minimal rationality condition. To the extent that the assumptions fail, the line of justification we have been considering does not apply in any straightforward way.

19 Because of his rigorist stand on certain issues (e.g., lying), contemporary discussions often simply label Kant an "absolutist" while treating any theory that allows that "the numbers count" as "consequentialist"; but this is misleading. It matters how, for what reasons, and under what constraints a theory allows the numbers to count. An interpretation (or extension) of Kant's theory that admits that sometimes one should take

into account, at some level of deliberation, whether one or a thousand will be killed does not thereby "reduce" to consequentialism.

20   These other constraints are potentially important. My argument is not that any policy is acceptable if it would be approved by rational impartial legislators focused exclusively on survival. There is more involved in valuing human dignity than caring about prolonging the lives of rational agents. The point is that, unless circumstances reveal ways that a life-maximizing policy violates or undermines some other value implicit in human dignity, the dignity principle will allow and even encourage us to take into account whether the policy is likely to save the most lives.

21   To focus discussion, assume that the victim in question is either unable or unwilling to volunteer and that he or she is law-abiding and is not among those at serious risk of being killed by the terrorist. Further, from now on I shall concentrate on cases where the sacrificial killing in question would be intended, not merely a "foreseen unintended consequence." (Killing a chosen victim to placate the terrorist is a clear example; shooting the terrorist *through* the hostage is more controversial.). Also, as before, I am restricting my remarks to official (e.g., police) responses to terrorism and assuming the victims are "innocent" in an intuitive, but still undefined, sense. In a fuller discussion, of course, other variations would need to be considered.

22   These worries have been often and well expressed at the meetings where I have presented this essay and by an anonymous reader for the press. To these I owe not only thanks but, in time, a more fully developed response.

23   It is worth keeping in mind here, as Larry Becker has reminded me, that any theory that attempts to resolve these dilemmas will leave conscientious persons unhappy because, despite the best of will, some things about which good people care deeply will be lost and our choices affect which these will be.

24   The aim of the legislative thinking is to find public policies that officials should scrupulously carry out. This does not mean, of course, that in their deliberations the Kantian legislators should foolishly assume that in fact there will never be abuse and corruption by public officials.

25   Treating someone as more than a "mere means," in the or-

dinary sense, does not suffice to show that one regards that person as an "end" in Kant's sense. One might, for example, regard a cherished old car as more than a "mere means" without attributing to it an "unconditional and incomparable worth."

26 This was suggested to me by Andrews Reath. The point here is not that it is logically impossible to attribute an incomparable or incalculable worth to a person while one deliberately kills that person. Perhaps some community of superhuman beings, with complete self-control and purity of motive, could mutually agree on a policy of deliberate sacrifice when it would save more lives and then carry out the policy from pure devotion to duty, never once seeing this as an exchange of less value for more. But we are not like that. So, given human nature, it seems unlikely that we would, or even could, agree on and implement the policy "Deliberately kill innocent persons when it will save more" without coming to regard persons as things with a value subject to exchange.

Chapter 9

State and private; Red and White

ALAN RYAN

PHILOSOPHY AND VIOLENCE: SOME ANXIETIES

This essay asks some quintessentially philosophical questions about violence and terrorism – is violence "special," demanding a particular kind of moral treatment; can a state properly be called "terrorist"; is there anything worthwhile in the old radical distinction between "Red" and "White" terror? It begins with a prior question, whether philosophy has anything to contribute to the discussion of violence in the first place. The *philosophical* treatment of violence, and particularly of terrorist violence, suffers more than most political philosophy from a disproportion between the inevitable and proper impracticality of philosophical inquiry and the all-too-urgent practicality of the problems addressed. Every time the IRA blows an innocent family to pieces, and each time an Israeli reprisal raid on a Palestinian camp reduces a child to bloody rags, the life of reason is mocked, and the hope recedes of a politics based on debate and conciliation, a politics based, if you like, on "reflective equilibrium" rather than partisan passion. It is all too easy to see why an ordinary citizen, not otherwise ill disposed to intellectual activity, might question the point of a *philosophical* account of violence and terrorism. He or she would surely think a political sociology of terrorism was worth having; if it was soundly based, we might understand what drove the warring factions into violent conflict, and that might enable us to see the terms of a peace treaty, and how we might deflate their readiness to act violently. By the same token, the ordinary citizen would think a psychopathology of violence worth having as offering some hope of identifying, and then isolating and controlling, those who are too readily attracted to political violence. What comparable promise can philosophy make?

On one view, gallantly defended over many years by Richard Hare, philosophical clarification can contribute something useful, though nothing very exciting. By attending carefully to the logic of moral discourse, we can separate factual disputes from differences of moral outlook. Sometimes people will see that their disputes are merely factual disputes, and *moral* passion will evaporate. Sometimes they will see that their views are not moral views at all, and they will see them as mere expressions of taste, or of simple self-interest. If they really want to be governed by morality rather than self-interest or the passions of the moment, they will rethink the morally proper path of action. Whether rethinking will lead to agreement – or enough agreement to reduce the amount of violence in the world – does not depend on the logic of moral discourse. The character whom Hare nicknames the "fanatic" will pursue his moral goals even if the result is destruction for himself, and with him there is no arguing. The only hope must be that there are few, or no, reflective fanatics. If the old empiricist view is warranted, and human nature is sufficiently uniform for few ultimate moral differences to survive genuine factual agreement, then we may hope that if we become clear about what separates us we shall find that little does.[1]

Hare's critics have observed that the real difficulty lies in getting even the unfanatical to engage in such reflection in the first place, and have doubted whether this is a task for philosophers at all. Most writers gloomily accept that a readiness to engage in such reflection postdates the attainment of peace, and cannot be expected ahead of that event. Hobbes can speak for many. Whether or not he meant to say that even coherent speech depends upon the existence of a sovereign power sufficient to "overawe them all," he was sure that the theorems of his philosophy had authoritatively to be dinned into people's skulls before they would do any good.[2] Once there was peace, people would see the point of peace and would listen to the arguments; until there was peace, they would be carried away by self-love, pride, and religious frenzy. Securing the peace could not be left to philosophers.

The example of Hobbes, indeed, shows how few philosophers have said anything both useful and interesting about violence. Hobbes himself aimed to be useful, but not to say anything philosophically interesting about violence. Although he explores the philosophical complexities of basing political obligation on natural insecurity and the fear of sudden and violent death, he does not offer a "philosophy of violence." He was an original theorist of the problems of deterrence; he was theologically unconventional in his insistence that God had obtained his kingdom "by violence." Still, it was not a *philosophically* interesting fact that men feared violent death above all else. It was important, for it provided the essential motivation for peace, but the treatment of the fear of violent death is rhetorically rather than intellectually central to the plot of *Leviathan*. Hobbes's rhetoric performed the task that Richard Hare brackets away – it got people to think morally. Hobbes rubbed people's faces in their fear of violent death because the philosophical demonstration of the laws of nature would have an impact only on people who had been put in the right frame of mind by that earlier psychological move.[3] One might say the discussion of violence was intended to be useful rather than philosophically illuminating.

Conversely, philosophers who have thought that violence was a central part of politics and a subject for philosophy have not intended to be *useful*. Hegel's "Owl of Minerva" flying at dusk reminds us what politics and law are, not what they ought to be[4] and it is no part of Hegel's philosophy of history to deny that history has been a slaughter bench or to encourage us to lament the fact.[5] Nietzsche's political reflections have been domesticated by writers who think that he *should* have had the aim of teaching us how to be less violent because less repressed, but it is hard to see such humanitarian concerns in the text.[6] He was no friend to political violence in its modern form because he was no friend to the modern state or to modern political concerns in general. Nonetheless, even if the modern hero is an artist, a poet, or a philosopher, he must also be a *hero*, and the impulse behind the demand that he stake his life on his quest for a meaning to his life comes directly from archaic heroes whose lives were literally staked on the outcome of violent personal encounters. The last thing Nietzsche hoped to be in appealing to this image was *useful*. Sorel has often been softened in the same fashion because he emphasized that frustrated liberal rationalists were more bloodthirsty in their disappointment with their fellows than "pessimists" who never expected to create utopia in the first place.[7] There, too, it is hard to accept that Sorel's hard-boiled insistence that he preached no messages disguised a humanitarian soul. His pessimists accept violence as natural and proper; their ethic is the ethic of a good fight, not of the avoidance of the fight. It is proper to observe that Sorel is no friend to terror, murder, or torture; but he is not interested in "violence minimization."

RECENT ARGUMENTS: MORE ANXIETIES

The list could be prolonged, but it is long enough. In the past two or three decades, there have been three kinds of "philosophies of violence," two of which have operated in the same metaphysical mode, and have therefore taken in each other's washing, while the third has defended a toughly utilitarian stance, and provides much of the substance of this essay. On the one side, there have been the existentialist or Sartrean reflections of Franz Fanon, emphasizing the purgative and creative role of violence.[8] On this view, violence is indeed at the heart of politics and the fact is to be understood, and embraced when understood. This line of thought is indebted to Nietzsche, but even more to the idea that social subordination, especially the racial subordination of colonized blacks, exists because the oppressed sees himself through the eyes of his oppressor. Kill the oppressor, and you not only reduce the enemies' ranks, you add a brand-new individual to the ranks of the revolted. This positive enthusiasm for violence need not rest on a Nietschean or Sartrean foundation, of course. Sartre's own reflections on violence occur in a work which claimed that twentieth-century philosophy is essentially Marxist, and the New Left was quick to embrace Marx's suggestion that the proletariat discovers itself only in the process of insurrection, and that the need for revolution is apparent only to those who engage in it.[9] Whether or not power flows from the barrel of a gun, self-understanding does. The supports for such a view are many; sometimes, as with Fanon, the emphasis lies on the psychological transfiguration of the actor; sometimes, as with Baader-Meinhof, the thought is that a social order that relies on a disguised (but real) terrorism to secure itself against its victims will be forced to unmask itself, and provoke the retaliation from below that Marxists have awaited since 1848; sometimes, as with Marx himself, the thought is that combat welds us into a fighting force and makes clearer what the conflict is about.[10] What holds these disparate ideas together is the thought that the hierarchical order of all political systems, and the unequal distribution of the costs and benefits of all economic systems, are in the last resort sustained by violence; whether countersystem violence clarifies our minds, strengthens our resolve, or replaces repressive violence by creative and progressive violence, everything rests on a sociological assumption about the way order is sustained.

It would be tiresome to dwell on what often accompanies such thoughts, the attempt to reconceptualize "violence" and "terrorism" in such a way that inequality just is a form of violence, or in such a way that the gaudy consumer society of the middle 1960s appears as a society of psychological terrorism by its very nature. It is worth noting such brazen reconceptualizations, however, since one way in which the costs of violence and the evils of terrorism may be played down is by insisting that violence and terrorism "are always with us," and so suggesting that revolt, murder, assassination, and hijacking are pretty much on a level with the continued prosperity of Macy's and Bloomingdale's.[11] Skepticism about such claims is no obstacle to agreeing that prosperous societies may harbor a lot of violence in their bosoms, as the United States plainly does, or impose a great deal of it outside their own boundaries, either through the deliberate actions of their rulers or by unwittingly causing upheavals elsewhere that lead to indigenous violence. Nineteenth-century Britain was domestically tranquil, but frequently engaged in violent, if usually small-scale, conflict abroad; and all developed countries have inadvertently brought the sort of social and economic disruption to simpler societies that has led to domestic violence there.[12]

The antithesis to this thesis, so to speak, is represented in Hannah Arendt's *On Violence*. It addresses the Sorelian or Fanonesque enthusiasm for violence, but its primary purpose is to contradict the New Left thought that power flows from the barrel of a gun. Power is quite another phenomenon from violence, and entirely at odds with violence. "Politically speaking, it is insufficient to say that power and violence are not the same. Power and violence are opposites; where the one rules absolutely, the other is absent. Violence appears where power is in jeopardy, but left to its own course it ends in power's disappearance. . . . Violence can destroy power; it is utterly incapable of creating it."[13] Her account of what power is and how it relates to the characteristic means employed by governments and their opponents is enigmatic, but it suffices to pick on two thoughts. The first is that violence represents "one against all"; the solitary man with the rifle tries to overawe numbers of other people. Power represents "all against one"; the community opposes its will to the will of the single individual. It is thus a failure of social will that creates the shortage of power and leaves people only the recourse to the *techniques* of violence.[14] The second, which follows, is that power rests on agreement; it is because the many constitute themselves a political body that they have a single will that they can oppose to that of any single individual. Although Arendt's formulation of these points reflects concerns familiar in *The Human Condition* and elsewhere, such as her distaste for the human sciences, and her insistence that politics is profoundly non-"natural," the contrast between the deliberative and willed nature of politics and the suddenness and reactiveness of violence is not unfamiliar in other writers. The enigmatic formulation of her views sets her at a greater distance from everyday sociological views than does their substance.

Talcott Parsons's view of power as essentially residing in the hands of an organized community, and consisting in a capacity to set and achieve societal goals, may not be terribly persuasive as a general definition of power, but it picks up one concern of those who want to distinguish private violence from public power, and it does it in much the same way as does Arendt's view.[15] In this Parsonian view, power is creative, whereas violence is essentially destructive; and although he makes nothing of it, it is also important that power is public. Nobody need be ashamed of exercising power; violence belongs with the surreptitious and the antisocial. *Ceteris paribus*, employing violent means is a source of shame.[16] Once again, violence is special, but this time deplorably so.

The third strain of thought is tough-mindedly utilitarian, and strives for matter of factness. It has many exemplars. If romantic Marxists hanker after Götterdämmerung, the ranks of the toughly utilitarian are swelled by unromantic Marxists ready to calculate the costs and benefits of insurrectionary politics and the revolutionary overthrow of whatever social and political order is under their gaze. To avoid clogging this account with excursions into the distinctively Marxian aspects of the case, however, we may here concentrate our attention on Ted Honderich's *Violence for Equality* – an expanded version of his earlier *Three Essays on Political Violence.*[17] Honderich does not need to insist that much of the inequality he is concerned with is instituted and maintained by force. It plainly is, particularly in dependent colonized or neocolonial societies, or in nominally independent states that in fact are dictatorships sustained at arm's length by American or Soviet pressure. There is no need here to balance Honderich's emphases by pointing to the conjunction of economic *equality* and political subordination that was characteristic of the satellite states of Eastern Europe, where it was *equality* rather than *inequality* that was forcibly instituted and sustained.[18] All this can be put to one side to isolate the one argument at stake, which is that liberal political theorists are prone to suggest that violence is never a legitimate means to secure egalitarian social goals, whereas from a utilitarian standpoint it is clear that *some* equalizing of economic outcomes would increase general well-being, and that the question whether egalitarian violence is justified reduces essentially to a calculation of the costs of that improvement. On this view, either it is presumed that violence is not *peculiarly* evil, or it is presumed that even if it is, the ills to which it is addressed are themselves so awful that the evil of violence is not different in kind from the evils it may put a stop to – one must presume this to see the issue as amenable to utilitarian decision making at all.[19] Violence, on this view, is the use of a lot of force; terrorism is the use of particularly frightening kinds of force and threatened force. That both states and individuals can resort to violence and terror is obvious. The utilitarian radical's preference for "Red" terror is simple enough. Red terror is simply terror employed in the interests of justice and equality, White terror simply terror employed in the interests of an inegalitarian status quo. Since there is nothing morally peculiar about violence, all interesting questions can be translated into issues of the high social and psychological costs of achieving or resisting social change. Again, the one thing to notice is that anyone trying to lessen our discomfort at the thought of violent measures will, even if he or she is of an unromantic and utilitarian turn of mind, want to remind us of "the violence of normal times," the quantity of unacknowledged, removable, but systematically applied damage done to individuals without *overt* or visible violence, but possible only because real violence lurks in the background.[20]

This position is unexceptionable in its own terms, although insofar as it is a classically utilitarian argument it must suffer from the difficulties that beset all utilitarian arguments. However, the remainder of this essay comes back to this point a long way round, by first tackling two issues that obstruct our adopting so simple a position. The first issue is whether it is right to treat all violence as essentially alike, or whether we must distinguish between state violence and individual violence; and in asking that question, terrorism is a paradigm case. If states employ violence to get their own way, and if states can be terrorist states in just the same way as individuals can be individual terrorists, then terrorism is discussable in simple utilitarian terms, for violent means are simply violent means, and their drawbacks can be set against the ends they serve.[21] It is clear why we can expect this result; utilitarianism has no special place for such notions as legitimacy, and is intrinsically hostile to trying to give a special moral status to the distinction between de jure – that is, official and licensed – exercises of legitimate *force* and de facto – that is, unofficial and unlicensed – *violence*. The question we face is how far we can go in carving out room for such notions in a generally utilitarian framework. The second issue, tackled very briefly, is whether there is any distinction between Red and White terror. On the face of it, anyone of a utilitarian disposition will think the distinction farfetched or an awkward way of making a tautological point: Whether terror is employed for supposedly "progressive" purposes – Red terror – or for supposedly "reactionary" purposes – White terror – is neither here nor there, since the only question worth asking is whether the costs of either promoting or resisting change are outweighed by the gains of so doing. Again, our problem is whether we can find some room for the distinction, either to discredit or, more guardedly, simply to complicate a utilitarian perspective.

CAN THERE BE A TERRORIST STATE?

Arendt claims that violence is an individual or antipolitical use of force, whereas what a state employs is strictly speaking power.[22] The first reaction of many of her readers is to throw up their hands and insist that violence is a matter of the kind of force employed, and the amount of force employed and the degree of resistance that has to be overcome, rather than a matter of who employs it or whether they are licensed to employ it, or whether they have the majority of the people with them. The British army in Northern Ireland meets IRA violence with official violence; certainly, it relies on its own legitimacy to secure the uncoerced support of the bulk of the population in its fight against IRA terrorists, but what it employs against the terrorists when it has to is violence. Yet there is a certain awkwardness about saying simply that the IRA's campaign of unofficial violence is being met with a campaign of official violence. Or, better, anyone who said that would mean it as a criticism rather than as a neutral description of the facts. So the reader who throws up his or her hands at Arendt's sharp distinction between power and violence may need a more elaborate response.

A fortiori, if we flinch at the idea that what is leveled against the IRA is just "official violence," then the thought that the state meets IRA terror with legitimate, or official, terror will seem even more awkward. The neatest route to good sense is not wholly clear, however. It is not enough merely to stare at such terms as "force," "violence," and "terror," as if we might divine their essences; we have to come to terms with the reasons why we are pulled in two directions, recognizing on the one hand that states secure obedience by coercing the recalcitrant and threatening violently inflicted harm to anyone tempted to rebellion, and on the other that states regard such sanctions as something to

239

be relied on only when appeals to *authority* have failed. In spite of Max Weber and Jeremy Bentham both, we are not tempted to *define* a state's authority in terms of its ability to command a monopoly of legitimate violence, though we may well be willing to concede that a state cannot be expected to exercise the authority it claims unless it can also command a (near)-monopoly of violence.[23] It appears on inspection that there are some quite strong reasons behind our sense of the awkwardness of certain ways of talking, even if they do not license categorical claims of the kind that Arendt makes.

In thinking about the state's use of *terror*, one writer takes a position extreme enough to anchor one end of our argument. This is Joseph de Maistre, whose *St. Petersburg Dialogues* contain a long and rather revolting description of a man being broken on the wheel for blasphemy or parricide. The point of the passage is the ambiguous status of the hangman. The hangman cannot be thought of as a member of society, though he prays in God's church and is evidently one of our species. For he lacks crucial human qualities, and what he does cannot be made sense of in ordinary human terms. Nonetheless, he is the key to social order: "And yet all grandeur, all power and all subordination rests on the executioner: he is the horror and the bond of human association. Remove this incomprehensible agent from the world, and at that very moment, order gives way to chaos, thrones topple, and society disappears."[24] That is, in de Maistre's scheme of things, states secure themselves by terrorist methods. To call them terrorist methods needs a little explanation, and in giving it, we can see what is peculiar about terrorism in the usual sense and why it is worth distinguishing it from legitimate force.

The point is this: The activities of terrorists are marked by two characteristics. The first is a willingness to employ methods that deprive their victims or targets of the power of a graduated, rational response. This is what de Maistre thought authority required. It is certainly what most people think is intolerable about terrorism. There is a disproportion between the goals aimed at and the sanctions threatened that takes terrorist "bargaining" out of the realms of bargaining as usually understood, and turns it into the simple imposition of the will of one party. Consider the IRA. The goal of a united Ireland is not a simple goal – it is exceedingly hard to say what arrangements would be needed to stabilize a united Irish state, because so much would depend on the frame of mind of the citizenry at the point where a united state was instituted. Even if there is less "pure" mutual detestation between the two communities, North and South, than there appears to be, there is a great deal of mutual apprehension; a combination of high apprehension and a belief that it might be possible to unscramble any union would surely be likely to replace IRA terrorism with Ulster Volunteer Force terrorism in an attempt to take the Six Counties out of a United Ireland. The resolution of the difficulties facing union, or rather reunion, would be a complicated matter to bargain one's way through, assuming we had two governments and a good many community representatives at the bargaining table. If IRA terrorism is seen as a way of getting a united Ireland that anyone wants to live in, it must look absurd. Its only purpose must be to so intimidate and alienate the army, Ulster Protestants, and the ordinary civil authorities that they acquiesce in some *simple* demand – such as "Brits Out." Similar tactics got the British out of Palestine, even if the subsequent forty years are a bad advertisement for securing nationhood in such a way. As Arendt remarks, though apropos of nowhere in particular, the main thing that violence is good at bringing about is more violence.[25] Governments that refuse to negotiate with terrorists almost perpetrate a pleonasm inasmuch as it is not the terrorists' intention to negotiate over anything save the question "What will you give me to stop?" This question, the blackmailer's or the terrorist's question, suggests that the terrorist's demands are, as they commonly say, "nonnegotiable," and that the terrorist is interested only in applying whatever pressure is necessary to get his or her own way in something simple and immediate.[26]

In so doing, the terrorist reveals the other aspect of terrorism that sets it apart from ordinary politics. The terrorist operates essentially by being willing to do what others would not knowingly and in full consciousness do. To be a terrorist is to notify everyone else that there are literally no limits to one's willingness to behave badly. The terrorist in effect declares that in his or her moral universe, the categories of innocence and guilt have been abandoned; children may be taken hostage, old women thrown out of airplanes – anything goes, so long as it terrifies one's opponents. The two things go hand in hand; the element of shock involved in declaring one's willingness to behave atrociously is both a natural and a predictable social response to the atrocious behavior itself, and the *felt* atrociousness of the behavior is partly a consequence of our sense that the terrorist really will stick at nothing. The degree of shock may also reflect baffled outrage at something that is a consequence of these two things, and that is the sense that the terrorist is inviting us and defying us to break all our own rules; the Irish Free State put down the IRA in the 1920s by executing hostages, and part of the horror of terrorism is just that it incites such wickedness in those whom it threatens. The glee of ordinarily decent Americans at the bombing of Tripoli in the spring of 1986 is perhaps a commentary on such tensions.

This may be the key to the urge to draw a categorical or conceptual distinction between – however one puts it – legitimate force and mere violence, between the state's threat of punishment and the terrorist's threat of "punishment," the urge to say that power is one thing and violence another, the urge to deny that power can flow from the barrel of a gun, to deny that authority is accepted and effective threatening. For a state to trade in the currency of authority, and to claim the *right* to have its demands taken seriously, the state must work within a rough moral consensus; not only must its demands on the citizenry be demands that the citizenry think it reasonable to make of one another – the repression of violence, the security of contract, and so on – but their sanctions must also fall within that consensus.

This is not a precise claim. Little of the empirical literature on political ideology and citizen loyalty is precise even where it is considerably bolstered by statistical data, and I know of no empirical literature on just this point. Still, it explains two things that are obvious enough but readily overlooked. The first is the extent to which governments secure obedience without drawing attention to the sanctions that underlie their demands for it; individuals do what they are asked because they think they ought to do it whether asked or not, and their interest in their government's capacity to wield sanctions is confined to the question whether the government can prevent others' taking advantage of their own compliance.[27] Taxpayers pay their *fair* share willingly enough, so long as they believe that others who are tempted to cheat can be prevented from doing so; rational people put away their guns, so long as they believe that the government can disarm others who might be tempted to take advantage of their unarmed state. We do not ask whether the state can terrify *us* into obedience. The other is the informal convention about the limits of punishment under which most societies appear to operate. Capital punishment for parking offences would make vastly more difference to the number of parking offenders than it would to the murder rate. It would, however, be quite mad to hang someone for meter feeding or overstaying the allotted time, or for being ten feet nearer a hydrant than allowed. Herbert Hart refers to the idea of a "tariff" that guides judges and legislators in their view of what punishments to impose, and how far to go in making use of the penalties provided for. Only serious outrages justify severe penalties. What seems at first glance to be the utilitarian view, that a very, very few judicial executions would have a disutility overwhelmingly offset by the increased utility of all those millions of occasions on which it was easier to park somewhere, is at odds with this "tariff" conception according to which each crime can only draw down a penalty that is a good match on the same scale.[28]

This is confessedly an imprecise claim. It makes tolerably good sense nonetheless. In the first place, there are penalties and judicial practices, that we – twentieth-century, liberal-democratic we – regard as dreadful, and yet understand as not all that dreadful in context. Treason, for instance, was punished in classical Roman law and in medieval English law not only by hideous physical ill-treatment of the actual traitor but by what amounted to perpetual disinheritance of the traitor's family. It so to speak "tainted the blood" of the perpetrator. This strikes us as unjust and superstitious, and it was ruled out by the U.S. Bill of Rights, by the revolutionary constitutions of France, and by modern practice; but we do not feel inclined to hold that against the Romans and the medieval English. They held curious views about the divinity of authority, they were more inclined to merge individual and collective responsibility, and they lived in shakier societies than ours, where unusual deterrents seemed more reasonable.

A second thing that is illuminated by the thought that governments must generally stick within the accepted moral boundaries in making and enforcing law is the Bill of Rights prohibition of "cruel and unusual" punishment. One might think it sufficient to prohibit punishment of "excessive" cruelty, or some such thing; but the idea that we want to prohibit unusualness has a certain logic to it. Terrorists ply a trade to which ingenuity and surprise are all too relevant; a terrorist organization whose tactics and methods were predictable would be out of business in a week. Equally, they have to beware of inducing a resigned acceptance of their activities among the population they attack. The IRA suffers to a degree from the fact that it tries to behave somewhat like an army, and therefore murders a predictable group of people; since it kills fewer people than do everyday murderers in an average American city of the same population as the province, its activities can be put up with if not exactly shrugged off.[29] Yet a campaign to create "pure" terror would put it at odds with its claims to be the army of a future republican government. The Baader-Meinhof gang caused more alarm in Germany than the IRA causes in Britain, not just because German society is more readily alarmed than British – though it may be – but because its activities and targets were so much less predictable. Since its aim was to force the state to reveal its own terroristic aspect, its tactics were to unsettle and panic the government by opportunistic violence against targets it selected as peculiarly representative of capitalist oppression – judges and businessmen prominent among them – but without much apparent logic about who out of a large group was likely to be attacked.[30] There lies another crucial difference from the behavior of governments; predictability and regularity are of the essence of government. Governments do not wish to leave their citizens in the dark about what is going to happen next. Indeed, there is something like a conceptual connection between purporting to be a *government* and attaching fixed sanctions to known demands. Hence, the thought that a government might resort to unusual penalties is not just disturbing as a matter of inducing anxiety among the citizenry; it is also disturbing as a blow to the idea that the government really means to govern.

TWO OBVIOUS COUNTEREXAMPLES

To any claim about such a conceptual or near-conceptual connection between being a government and eschewing terror or violence, there are obvious counterexamples – certainly Nazi Germany, and probably both Nazi Germany and Stalin's Russia. The government's reliance on terror as a standard tool of government features prominently in most definitions of a totalitarian state.[31] Such states display no sense that cruel and unusual punishment is somehow at odds with being a government at all. Anyone who finds this obvious will certainly think that I have absurdly underestimated the number of counterexamples. All too many governments have gone down the same track; Pinochet's government in Chile and the military regime in Argentina connived at, sponsored, and perhaps deliberately organized the abduction, torture, and murder of women and children, as well as of suspected terrorists; the Indonesian government behaves quite as badly in Timor. Indeed, governments that engage in such activities may well outnumber those that do not.

There is no point in trying to maintain that the governments of Nazi Germany and Stalinist Russia were not governments – Aristotle might well have thought that whatever they were they were not political regimes, and Augustine would have had no qualms about describing them as mere "armed bands of robbers," but that is not much help here.[32] General Pinochet's government was for better or worse the government of Chile; the Argentinian junta was manifestly the government of Argentina. If we think that there is all the same a large distinction between these and nonterrorist regimes, and wish to illuminate their relations with their subjects, and the odd combination of terrorist and legalistic behavior these involved, there is more mileage in the thought that such regimes have declared war on some segment of the population. That means that the government stands in a slightly odd relationship to its victims, treating them both as subjects and as enemies. Often such governments have themselves faced domestic terrorism, and claim that their behavior is a reaction to it. This is consilient with one liberal argument against terrorism, that the great defect of terrorism is that it cannot undermine a determined government but does lead to the destruction of civil liberties. A government that behaves atrociously in the Argentine fashion accepts the declaration of war from below and fights with as few legal restraints as there would be on the field of battle. Since its opponents are not in fact enemy soldiers but all too often unprotected and innocent civilians, we have the horrors of civil war compounded.[33]

Of course cases vary. In Chile, there was no justification for Pinochet's savagery; but in Argentina there had been enough urban terrorism to give some color to the government's claim that it was already fighting a virtual civil war, though the revolting behavior of its agents exceeded anything done by Pinochet's forces. No such argument applies to Nazi Germany or Stalin's Russia. One of the many madnesses of Hitler's Germany and the Russia of the purges lay in the way they fought a crusade against their own subjects, none of whom had taken up arms against the regime, and few of whom had much idea wherein their offense lay. At the other end of the spectrum, British civil and political liberties have perhaps not been much more eroded by the campaign against the IRA than they would anyway have been under a prime minister of Mrs. Thatcher's temperament. Still, the campaign has seen some nasty innovations in reducing the defendants' rights in criminal trials and has involved a good deal of passing brutality, some cases of what amounts to murder by the police, and the erosion of the rights of free travel and free speech.[34]

The rather feeble conclusion toward which this points is thus that the bold conceptual claims of writers such as Arendt pick up something important even if they misstate what it is. There is every reason in morality to wish governments to observe a distinction between force and (mere) violence, between legitimate punishment and attempts to terrorize their subjects, and there are plenty of empirical grounds for supposing that a stable and productive society is possible only if such distinctions are built into the legal practice of the society. But no conceptual argument could show that a government cannot maintain itself by terror, or that it would cease to be a government if it did; certainly it sacrifices consent to brute force, but plenty of regimes have been happy enough to do that. One can see why so many writers have wanted to say that what exists in such conditions is not law, or is not government, or is not politics; but it seems better to admit that it is politics of a particularly disgusting kind than to get embroiled in conceptual squabbles. The point, after all, is less to find a label for it than to try to stop it.

RED AND WHITE: A REDUNDANT DISTINCTION

This discussion has been tied almost entirely to the question whether a government can be accused of behaving like a terrorist toward its own subjects. It has taken for granted that no useful distinction is to be drawn between Red and

White terror, since it has taken for granted that terrorism is no way to secure either justice – which is characteristically the goal of Red terror – or order – which is the goal of White terror. To subvert that conclusion one would have to demonstrate that there was some essential connection between the aspirations of the progressive and conservative forces and the brutalities they resort to. It is not impossible to make a start on such an argument. Jeane Kirkpatrick's much-mocked defense of the United States' authoritarian allies in Central America relies on the thought that totalitarian regimes have no logical stopping place in the infliction of violence; they wish to remodel human nature, and this is an endless task. The less horrible kind of authoritarian regime merely wishes to frighten a finite number of enemies so that the status quo can be maintained.[35] Still, one might wonder what this implies about Hitler's Germany, which was by most lights conservative or reactionary, and showed no signs of such self-restraint, and in any scale of horror General Galtieri's Argentina does as badly as any regime of the left. The truth seems to be rather that regimes that live by brute force have every reason to go on using it, seeing that they must create enemies as fast as they kill them, and may well create imagined enemies a great deal faster than that. To find the distinction between Red and White terror useful we have to swallow a great deal of contentious sociological theory, which is at the least outside the scope of this essay.

TERRORIST STATES

It is time to conclude by listing fairly briefly some ways in which governments can straightforwardly be accused of engaging in terrorism and a few ways in which they may contentiously be said to be so engaging. The first two cases are simply those in which a government hires, or employs, or sponsors terrorists to attack either its own citizens or those of other countries. The status of the death squads of Central American countries such as Guatemala and El Salvador is for

for obvious reasons veiled in obscurity; but in each case they were probably hired, and certainly protected, by the regime of the day, and that by anyone's reckoning made it a terrorist regime. If Syria paid for, protected, equipped, and assisted hijackers and would-be bombers of El Al aircraft, that makes the Syrian regime a terrorist regime. In neither case does it make the regime *merely* a terrorist regime, any more than the fact that governments of liberal democracies rely on armed force and possess large standing armies makes them merely military governments. But just as relations between government and the military in many democracies suggest that the continuum between military and nonmilitary regimes really is a continuum (even though the distinction between *gaining* power by military force and gaining it by other means remains a difference in kind), so the distinction between terrorist and nonterrorist regimes lies on a continuum, where some hands are dirtier than others (though the distinction between states where the rulers *acquired* power by murder and violence and those where the rulers acquired power through the ballot box also remains a difference in kind).

There is, however, a rhetorical force to "terrorist regime" that goes beyond observing that regimes exist which hire assassins, hijackers, kidnappers, and bombers. There is at least a suggestion that these are regimes that are happy to do so, and would rather get their way in this fashion than in any other; they are regimes that have been seduced by the allure of the gunman. Now, when one comes to decide which countries belong in this category, contentiousness is the order of the day; visiting Martians might well think that several Middle Eastern countries are in that condition – not *official* Iran, perhaps (if such an entity exists), and certainly not Egypt, but unofficial Iran, Libya, and Iraq quite plausibly. It is not a description these countries would themselves accept; and it is one that has been overused in American and Israeli rhetoric. On the other hand, visiting Martians might think that the Israeli government showed some of the symptoms, and that the actions of Mossad were not far enough removed from those of the Hezbollah to sustain the moral weight the Israeli government would like to place on the difference.

Martians might be persuaded either way by further argument; they might think that Mossad was fastidiously controlled as a result of its official status, that it was careful in its choice of targets and sufficiently accurate in its operations to sustain the moral difference between a covert war against noninnocent enemies and a mere campaign of terror designed to shut up political dissent. They might, however, find themselves thinking that what was going on in the Middle East was a total war in which there were no innocent parties, and that Hezbollah was fighting as legitimate a war as anybody else. This essay is not committed to siding with one claim or the other, but to making some sense of the rhetoric in which arguments in this area are dressed.

If one accepts the suggestion that succumbing to the allure of the gunman is part of what makes a government a terrorist government, the moral mess into which governments can get themselves is not always far from home; the British government's readiness to hero-worship the SAS is unlovely enough, and a taste for, and a belief in the possibilities of, covert violence has marked the behavior of the United States ever since the end of World War II. It is a vice that is likely to infect any regime that gained its nationhood by force of arms in the not-too-distant past; one of Israel's difficulties in sustaining its own moral principles is just that Irgun and the Stern Gang were successful. It is doubtful whether the visiting Martians would think any government absolutely immune from at least the temptation.[36]

WAR AND ''OFFICIAL TERRORISM''

Finally, there is "ordinary" warfare. This is commonly taken to be a paradigm of what terrorism is not; it is violent, but it is overt, legitimate, directed against combatants, started and finished by legally recognizable acts, and so on. However, this all supposes that governments do in fact manage to sustain all these crucial differences, and in the twentieth century there is no evidence that they do or that they have seriously intended to "Total war" is, on the face of it, terrorism under the aspect of war; the British fire bombings of Hamburg and Dresden were deliberate attempts to break civilian morale by killing as many noncombatants as possible. It was not a matter of arguing that munitions workers in Hamburg were as important to the war effort as soldiers on the Russian front and therefore legitimate targets, though it is sometimes passed off in that way. It was a deliberate attempt to erase a whole city, and that is to say that it was a deliberate attempt to massacre a large civilian population. President Truman's justification of the destruction of Hiroshima and Nagasaki, like the British defenses of the fire bombing of Hamburg and Dresden, relied on the consequentialist argument that fewer people got killed that way than would have got killed if the war had been allowed to go on. Nonetheless, this was a defense of a massacre of the innocent, and thus a defense of essentially terrorist methods. It does not follow – save in some interpretations of just war theory – that the defense is unacceptable.[37]

Couching things in those terms is, of course, rhetorically impossible to square with the repeated insistence of current Western governments that it is illicit to meet terrorism with terrorism, and that the resort to terrorist methods is absolutely wrong. So used are we to the picture of the terrorist as *essentially* private, engaged in some revolutionary cause on the Red end of the spectrum, that we find it a wrench to contemplate the idea that terrorism can also be massive in scale, officially organized, delivered by people in uniform, subject to legally certified orders, and so on. But all the usual features of terrorism apply to total war; it is waged without distinction between the innocent and the guilty, and although we have got used to the idea that nuclear war is the ultimate horror of our time, we ought not to forget that its horrors are only those of Hamburg and Dresden magnified a good deal. Burning women and children to death as an instrument of policy is the same act whether the means chosen include incendiaries and high explosives or nuclear weapons.

Total war resembles terrorism in its contempt for negotiation, too. The demand for unconditional surrender may once, on the battlefield, have simply been a way of making the point that the opposing, losing army was in no condition to carry on.[38] In the two world wars of this century, it became the decision that the Allies would stop at nothing to win, and that winning was a matter not of inducing the other side to return to the negotiating table from the battlefield, but of annihilating its capacity to sustain the war. Aside from the tactics – it may well be that a better postwar settlement could have been achieved if the Allies had from the very beginning and certainly after 1943 offered a negotiated peace to anyone who could remove Hitler and open negotiations – the morality of "unconditional surrender" is open to question. In its absolutism, it too much resembles the "nonnegotiability" of the terrorist's demands.

We must now end by coming back to our utilitarian starting point. Does this bring us all the way back to the highly plausible view that violence is violence, whoever perpetrates it, and that whether it is public or private, we can ask only the question we began with – is it morally justified by its results? Not quite. If it is true that twentieth-century warfare has turned into officially practiced terrorism, not as a definitional or conceptual matter, but morally speaking, we may still want to hang onto some of the moral and conceptual claims made in the just war tradition, not, so to speak, seeing them as deliverances of pure reason or natural law, nor seeing them as somehow built into the fabric of the world, but seeing them rather as distinctions and calls to self-restraint that we may be able to enshrine in international law and international organization if we work at it.

One powerful domestic argument for maintaining regular, legal government is that it replaces the feud, private vengeance, and other forms of self-help, which not only are frequently ineffective, but readily degenerate into uncontrolled brutality and cruelty. Once one sees that the international system of self-help that is what war amounts to can operate in a controlled way but generally does not, one can begin to see how states can use force to get their own way without behaving too hideously, but also how perilous this process is, and how likely it is that they will be faced with the choice between behaving as terrorists and making a humiliating retreat – or, as in the case of the United States in Vietnam – stumbling into doing both. If there is anything to be said for the philosophical investigation of such issues, it is that it can help us make our way more steadily through this moral minefield.

NOTES

1 R. M. Hare, *Applications of Moral Philosophy* (London: Macmillan, 1972), pp. 1–3.
2 Thomas Hobbes, *Leviathan* (Harmondsworth: Penguin, 1968), pp. 188, 727–8.
3 Ibid., chap. 13.
4 G. W. F. Hegel, introduction to *The Philosophy of Right* (Oxford: Clarendon, 1941),
5 G. W. F. Hegel, *The Philosophy of History* (New York: Dover, 1954).
6 Walter Kaufmann, *Nietzsche: Philosopher, Psychologist, Anti-Christ* (Princeton, N.J.: Princeton University Press, 1950), seems to me to plead too hard for such an interpretation.
7 Georges Sorel, *Reflections on Violence* (New York: Collier, 1961), app. 2, "Apology for Violence."
8 Franz Fanon, *The Wretched of the Earth* (New York: Grove, 1965); J.-P. Sartre, *Critique de la raison dialectique* (Paris: Gallimard, 1960).
9 As was argued by Regis Debray, *Revolution within the Revolution* (Cambridge, Mass.: MIT Press, 1967).
10 Karl Marx, "The Civil War in France," in *Karl Marx: Selected Writings*, ed. David McLellan (Oxford: Oxford University Press, 1977), pp. 539–58.
11 John Harris, *Violence and Responsibility* (London: Routledge and Kegan Paul, 1980), chap. 2, " 'Non-Violent' Violence."
12 John Dunn, *Modern Revolutions*, 2d ed. (Cambridge: Cambridge University Press, 1989), pp. 204ff.

13 Hannah Arendt, *On Violence* (New York: Harcourt Brace, 1970), p. 56.

14 Ibid., pp. 84–7.

15 Anthony Giddens, "Power in the Writings of Talcott Parsons," in Giddens, *Studies in Social and Political Theory* (London: Hutchinson, 1977), chap. 10.

16 George Kateb's *Hannah Arendt: Politics, Conscience and Evil* (Totowa, N.J.: Rowman and Allanheld, 1983), pp. 38–40, stresses the extent to which political action in Arendt's sense of the term(s) is a violent business that often eventuates in harm to a good many people. This is a proper emphasis; not the least of one's difficulties in understanding *On Violence* is that of squaring its account of politics with the enthusiasm for Machiavelli expressed in *The Human Condition*. This paragraph is only about *On Violence* and does not pretend to be an adequate account of Arendt's views more generally considered.

17 Ted Honderich, *Violence for Equality* (New York: Routledge, 1989). See also C. A. J. Coady, "The Morality of Terrorism," *Philosophy* 60 (January 1985): 47–69.

18 As argued some years ago in Frank Parkin, *Inequality and Political Order* (London: McGibbon and Kee, 1971).

19 Honderich, *Violence for Equality*, pp. 187–210; Harris, *Violence and Responsibility*, chap. 2; Barrington Moore, Jr., *Social Origins of Dictatorship and Democracy* (Boston: Beacon, 1967), p. 103.

20 Harris, *Violence and Responsibility*, pp. 21–3.

21 The force of this varies a good deal according to whether writers think that there is something *especially* evil about violent methods; Honderich and Coady plainly represent different views of this issue.

22 Arendt, *On Violence*, pp. 45–8.

23 This is plainly the proper interpretation of Hobbes's account of political obligation; see Brian Barry, "Warrender and His Critics," in *Hobbes and Rousseau*, ed. M. Cranston and R. S. Peters (London: Macmillan, 1972), pp. 36–8.

24 Joseph de Maistre, *Works*, trans. and ed. J. Lively (New York: Macmillan, 1965), p. 192.

25 Arendt, *On Violence*, p. 80.

26 Though Honderich, *Violence for Equality*, pp. 198–9, takes the simplicity of the IRA's aims much more for granted than I would.

27 R. M. Hare, "The Lawful Government," in Hare, *Applications of Moral Philosophy*, pp. 84ff.

28 H. L. A. Hart, "Prolegomenon to the Principles of Punishment," in Hart, *Punishment and Responsibility: Essay in the Philosophy of Law* (Oxford: Clarendon, 1968), pp. 1–27.

29 In 1986, there were 61 sectarian killings in Ulster, in 1987 there were 91, but in 1988 there were 332 murders in Washington, D.C., whose population is less than a third of the province's.

30 Jillian Becker, *Hitler's Children* (Philadelphia: Lippincott, 1977), pp. 227–40, is the best account I know of of the Baader-Meinhof gang.

31 Carl Friedrich, ed., *Totalitarianism* (New York: Grosset and Dunlap, 1954); Hannah Arendt, *The Origins of Totalitarianism* (New York: Meridian, 1958).

32 St. Augustine, *The City of God* (Harmondsworth: Penguin, 1984), p. 139: "absit justitia, quod est civitas nisi magna latrocinia?"

33 John Simpson and Jana Bennett, *The Disappeared* (New York: St. Martin's, 1985).

34 Hugo Young, *One of Us* (London: Macmillan, 1989).

35 Jeane Kirkpatrick, *Dictatorships and Double Standards: Rationalism and Reason in Politics* (New York: Simon and Schuster, 1982).

36 Bob Woodward, *Veil: The Secret Wars of the CIA, 1981–87* (New York: Simon and Schuster, 1988).

37 But see Paul Fussell, *Thank God for the Atomic Bomb and Other Essays* (New York: Summit, 1988).

38 Bruce Catton, *The Terrible Swift Sword* (New York: Doubleday, 1963).

Chapter 10

State terrorism

Jonathan Glover

PART ONE: TERRORISM

"Our" cause is usually supported by the resistance, by the underground, or by freedom fighters, while "their" cause is often supported by terrorists. The use of the word "terrorism" is often so loose and so loaded that it is tempting to abandon it. Perhaps we would do better with more fine-grained concepts, distinguishing types of political violence on the basis of different aims, victims, methods, and use by different groups. But there are some common patterns, and perhaps they make the category of terrorism, if carefully used, worth retaining for some purposes.

It may be Procrustean to start with a very detailed account of the boundaries of terrorism. There is a case for starting with a rough-and-ready account, bearing in mind that it may need tightening up or modifying as we see which activities seem to cluster together.

The central feature of terrorism is political violence. Murders or armed robberies without political motive are not terrorism. The terrorist aims to further a political cause by using or threatening violence. And the violence is not directed merely against property. People are killed, or subjected to kidnapping, hijacking, wounding, or other severe ill-treatment. Or there is an attempt to coerce people by the threat of these things. The violence or the threats have to be of the kind that can strike *terror* into people.

This account leaves various loose ends. For instance, it

leaves open whether threats by states to use nuclear weapons count as terrorism. And it leaves open the question of a boundary between terrorism and war, civil war, or revolution. Conventionally these other things are not thought of as terrorism. To include them would be to expand the concept in a perhaps perverse way. But to exclude them may be to sustain a conventional blindness to important similarities to the standard cases of terrorism. Here these matters will be left open. The focus is on another possibly deviant case: state terrorism.

Two types of terrorism

The "standard" cases of terrorism, those which most commonly come to mind, are carried out not by governments but by their opponents. The PLO, the IRA, the Basque organization ETA, the Baader-Meinhof group in Germany, the Red Brigades in Italy, the ANC in South Africa, the Stern Gang in Palestine, the French Resistance, the FLN in Algeria, and EOKA in Cyprus are among present and past groups to use the kinds of political violence that usually qualify as terrorism. There are morally important differences among them. The ANC was a nonviolent organization until means of peaceful campaigning were shut off. The French Resistance was opposing occupation of its country by the Nazis. And so on. To say that these groups use or used terrorist methods creates a strong presumption against their activities, while not totally excluding the possibility of justification. But these groups have in common the violent pursuit of their nationalist or other political causes in opposition to the government in power.

In other cases, those who use violence for political purposes are those in power or their agents. The extreme cases of this state terrorism are among the great twentieth-century horrors: Hitler's extermination camps, Stalin's terror and the Gulag, the rule of Pol Pot in Cambodia. But on a smaller scale, state terrorism is quite widespread.

Sometimes it takes the form of the political use of torture.

Examples include its use by the French army in Algeria, by the British army in Cyprus, and by the South African police, and its still widespread use by the authorities in numerous Latin American and other Third World countries.

It can include responding to an uprising, as in the Israeli-occupied territories, with brutal beatings of civilians by soldiers.

It may involve responding to political dissent, as in Cuba and many other countries, with executions or long prison sentences or, as in the Soviet Union, with "psychiatric" treatment.

It may take the form of large-scale abduction and murder, with torture sometimes included. The activities of the police death squad in Brazil are an example. Another is the treatment of the thousands of the "disappeared" in Argentina. Most of them, after torture, and sometimes after the theft of their babies, ended in mass graves or were thrown, dead or alive, from aircraft into the sea.[1] To varying degrees the Brazilian and Argentinian cases have been paralleled in – at least – Bolivia, Chile, El Salvador, Guatemala, Haiti, Paraguay, and Uruguay. These are only a few examples in each category of state terrorism. The lists can go on and on.

These cases are not all the same, and certainly differ in degree of moral wickedness. But they have in common the use for political causes of what would normally be considered unacceptably deadly, violent, or brutal methods. And being used by the authorities, these policies are deprived of one possible defense of terrorist activities by unofficial groups: that they have no other way of furthering their cause. That defense does not apply to "unofficial" terrorists in all cases. Some operate in countries where democratic means of persuasion are available. And the absence of other means does not without further argument justify policies of abducting, killing, or maiming people. The point is not to justify "unofficial" terrorism, but to suggest that state terrorism is in this respect even harder to justify.

State terrorism: some distinctions

State terrorist violence is not a single phenomenon. Sometimes it is unprovoked, and sometimes it is a "counterterrorist" response to violence, as in the assassination (probably by the Israeli Mossad) of the PLO leader Abu Jihad. Sometimes state violence is directed against external enemies (perhaps using local intermediaries, as in the CIA intervention against Allende in Chile) rather than used for internal repression. Here attention is on the internal version.

Another distinction concerns legality. Perhaps examples, including some that have been given, should be excluded where no illegality is involved. If a Cuban is sentenced to death by a court for his critical comments about the government, or a Soviet dissident reaches a psychiatric unit after proper legal formalities have been observed, perhaps they are not victims of state terrorism. It depends on how the boundaries of the concept are drawn. Perhaps nothing important hangs on the definitional question, provided we remember two things. There *is* a difference between the rule of law and arbitrary terror. And yet legality is not the only thing that matters. I do not know whether the policy of shooting people trying to leave East Germany over the Berlin Wall had legal authority. But even legality would not give it great appeal.

Another distinction is in the scale of the violence. In many countries, the police are not entirely under control, and some people are brutally interrogated by them. I do not wish in any way to defend this practice, and on the account given here it qualifies as state terorism. But clearly there is a great difference between rare cases of this sort and a state of affairs like that in Guatemala, where out of a population of 8 million people, "conservative estimates put the number of killings and disappearances since the 1960s at 100,000 and 40,000 respectively."[2] There is a case for confining the term "state terrorism" to the major episodes. Once again, nothing much hangs on the definitional question. Minor and major episodes are on the same continuum, but at extreme poles of it. These two points both have to be remembered, on whichever side of the minor episodes we draw the definitional boundary.

Another distinction of degree concerns the inclusion of the Nazi extermination camps in the category of state terrorism. I have a lot of sympathy with the view that the Nazi atrocities should be kept quite separate, in a class of evil all their own. The last thing I want to do is provide some kind of retrospective whitewash by suggesting that the Nazis were just like lots of other governments now. (This is one reason for disliking the casual application of the word "fascist" to political opponents.) But in trying to analyze state terrorism, it is hard to overlook strong traces of the psychology that led to the Nazi atrocities. (Some of the architects of the apartheid system now protected by state terrorism came from the pro-Nazi *Ossewabrandwag*. Some Argentinian interrogators were particularly vicious toward Jews, and openly identified with Nazism. The regime of General Stroessner in Paraguay was an example both of state terrorism and of Nazi links. But the point here is independent of such explicit Nazi sympathies. It concerns more general aspects of the psychology of atrocities.)

The suggestion here is that the Nazi crimes were in certain ways continuous with some other wrongs still with us. To ignore this continuity is to miss important aspects of the present forms of state terrorism. But there is no need retrospectively to minimize what the Nazis did. That still retains a particular evil all its own.

PART TWO: PSYCHOLOGY

The psychology of state terrorism: hot and cold violence

There is a case for studying state terrorism by looking at some aspects of its psychology. When people do appalling things, there is the question how they could bring themselves to act in such way. Trying to answer this question is part of understanding state terrorism. No doubt it is *only* part of it. The social and economic conditions in which state terrorism flourishes are important. So are the responses of neighboring countries or of the international community. The emphasis here is on the psychology, but no claim is made that this is the whole story.

And the story that is told here perhaps contains few surprises. In a way we are all familiar with the phenomena of state terrorism. We have all heard about mass murder and about horrendous interrogations, and if we make the effort, it may not be too difficult to guess the psychological states lying behind a particular episode. But perhaps it is worth trying to bring a few different examples together, and looking for common patterns in the psychology. The aim is to work toward a more systematic psychological typology. No doubt what is set out here will need many modifications. But the hope is that a systematic view of the psychology may make us more aware of which tendencies are dangerous, and so need watching, whether they appear in ourselves or in others.

To be found sometimes among the background psychological conditions of state terrorism are the familiar human defects that contribute to war and many other evils: tribalism and Belief. Tribalism made it easier for the Nazis to do what they did to Jews, Poles, and others, and perhaps for the South African police interrogators to murder Steve Biko. Centuries ago Belief made things easier for those running the Inquisition. In this century, Belief has perhaps made things easier for those running the Gulag, and for those running the Islamic reign of terror in Iran, and for those in Latin America who believe that their prisoners are Communists. (The Believer's religous-style commitment to an ideological system is marked off by the capital letter from more tentative kinds of belief.)

But tribalism is not always present. Those terrorized by the Argentinian kidnapping squads were not from a different ethnic group, nor were the victims of the Iranian clampdown. And Belief is not essential either. The junior officers who roamed the streets in Argentina looking for girls to torture, rape, and kill probably did not inquire into their politics. Tribalism and Belief are perhaps dispositions helpful to state terrorism, but as well as not necessary for it, they are clearly not sufficient. The world is full of those with tribal loyalties and Beliefs who live harmless or benevolent lives.

The emphasis here is on other psychological conditions. They are aspects of the psychology of violence. This approach starts from the point that terrorism involves the use or threat of violence. This other cluster of conditions is neither necessary nor sufficient for the occurrence of state terrorism. But members of the cluster can plausibly be said to be among the immediate causes of its manifestations.

Violence can be hot or cold. Hot violence either gives pleasure to its perpetrators or else arises out of their being in a heightened emotional state in which it is exhilarating. Cold violence is emotionally detached, though it may be backed up by fear. It is often more calculating and bureaucratic: A clear case case is Eichmann methodically planning the deportation of European Jews to the death camps. Often there is division of labor, with coldly detached senior people drawing up policies to be implemented by aggressive or sadistic juniors.

Hot violence

Men who have been in battle sometimes describe it as the most euphoric experience of their lives. Their exhilarated emotional state can transform acts that they might otherwise find appalling into things done with exultation.

Perhaps sometimes the state functionaries who kill and torture have something of the psychology of combat. And sometimes they kill in anger. But more often, their hot violence is more controlled.

It may involve taking pleasure in power. In Argentina, General Galtieri visited a center where prisoners were held. To one woman, who had been blindfolded and tortured for months, he said: "If I say you live, you live, and if I say you die, you die. As it happens, you have the same Christian name as my daughter, and so you live."[3]

It may involve the excitement, sexual or otherwise, of watching and controlling another's pain or degradation. One example, taken from an account by Breyten Breytenbach, will stand for many.

> F., an ex-sergeant in the South African Police, now a prisoner, told me of how he assisted one Sunday afternoon at the torturing of a Black detainee. Not because they wanted information from him, but because the men on duty were bored, because they wanted some amusement, maybe also because the *kaffir* had to be kept in his place. They had the prisoner undress completely; they then emptied his cell of everything except a blanket; the cell was hosed down, the blanket soaked in water too. The naked prisoner was then locked in the wet cell and the blanket, through the bars of the door, connected to an electric current. The fun was to see the man trying to climb up the electrified walls.[4]

I have little to say about hot violence. We all know that there is this side of people. There are some questions about how widespread it is. Are some people specially inclined toward these horrors, or would any of us do these things if in the appropriate circumstances? Is it a feature of human beings in general, or only of men? Women have done a lot less of this kind of thing than men have. Is this because of a difference of genetic disposition, or just because of a traditional difference of upbringing and of social roles?

At our present stage of understanding, the only thing we know for certain about these questions is that the capacity for hot violence is at least fairly widely distributed among men. When we understand the psychology better, we may be able to devise kinds of upbringing that weaken these dispositions. But at present political approaches seem more promising: What matters is to prevent the existence of the kinds of regime in which hot violence has a role.

Cold violence

There is more to say about cold violence. A provisional classification of its psychological roots is

1. The attempt to coerce by terror
2. Fear, conformity, and obedience
3. Distance and dehumanization
4. Blurring, denial, and evasion.

Coercion by terror. Breyten Breytenbach says that a calculated atmosphere of terror is the "basic thrust of the repressive interrogation system" in South Africa: "Not only are these acts not disavowed in practice – the 'anti-terrorist strategists' *want* their opponents to know that, when captured, they will be brutalized. The clearly signalled intention is itself part of the strategy."[5]

Again, to take one example among many, it was surely not an accident that some of those in Argentina who brought habeas corpus cases on behalf of people who had disappeared started to disappear themselves.[6]

It is clear that those running state terrorist systems use violence and its threat to defend their own power. There is a deliberate policy of intimidation of those who might support their opponents or critics.

Fear, conformity, and obedience. Some of those who carry out state terrorist policies are intimidated as well as intimidators. Greek military policemen described the role of fear when they had carried out torture during the regime of the colonels. One said, "There were always two servicemen torturing a prisoner so that one would spy on the other and the officers spied on both, through the hole in the door of the cell." Another said, "An officer used to tell us that if a warder helps a prisoner, he will take the prisoner's place and the whole platoon will flog him. We always lived with that threat over our heads."[7]

It is not only in the agents of terror that fear plays a role. The acquiescence of the larger population is often needed for the policy to be carried out. Conformity, together with a reluctance to face what is happening, contributes to a lack of civil courage. Inge Deutschkron, who spent the Second

World War in hiding in Berlin, describes this process:

> I remember the day when they made Berlin *Judenrein*. The people hastened in the streets; no-one wanted to be in the streets; you could see the streets were absolutely empty. They didn't want to look, you know. They hastened to buy what they had to buy – they had to buy something for the Sunday, you see. So they went shopping and hastened back into their houses. And I remember this day very vividly because we saw police cars rushing through the streets of Berlin taking people out of the houses.[8]

Those of us who have been lucky in when and where we live sometimes wonder what we would have done faced with such a test as Nazism. The view is sometimes put forward that any of us could have been a torturer. It is hard to be sure that this view is false, but there are cases of heroic refusal, and we may hope that we should have been among them. But even if we would have refused to perform atrocities, it is another thing again to show civil courage by stepping, unasked, out of ordinary life to protest. Perhaps many of us, disconcertingly easily, can see ourselves hurrying home as the Berliners did.

When people acquiesce in state terrorism or contribute to it, they do so sometimes out of obedience or deference to authority. There are reasons for thinking that this attitude is psychologically separate from fear or from lack of civil courage. In Stanley Milgram's well-known experiments on obedience, people thought they were helping with a psychology experiment on the effect of punishment on learning. In obedience to the orders of the "experimenter," many people pressed switches that they believed would give the "subject" severe electric shocks.[9] Those who obeyed these orders had nothing to fear from the "experimenter." The explanation of their obedience seems to have more to do with the authority he appeared to have as a scientist in charge of an experiment than with fear of him.

Armies often first use bullying techniques to create fear in and impose conformity on new recruits, but in time the soldiers usually see higher-ranking figures as having legitimate authority over them. It is, or should be, a bit disturbing that the magic of authority used by respectable armies of democratic states is put to the same use by the forces of state terrorism. The military police under the Greek junta again provide an example:

> After an initiation beating inside the cars taking the recruits to the camp and upon entering the camp, they were asked to swear allegiance to the totemic-like symbol of authority used by the junta, promising on their knees faith to their commander in chief and to the revolution. Thereafter, the general ideas that they belonged to their commanding officers and that the junta officials were gods to be obeyed, were continuously pressed upon them. A closing ceremony at the end of the three months, in which the recruit was presented with his cap was the ritual ending the whole process.[10]

Ritual ceremony and indoctrination generate a respect for authority that, independent of fear, gives a motive for obedience.

Distance and dehumanization. A striking feature of Milgram's experiments on obedience was the way people were less likely to obey the orders to give electric shocks when the victims were made more vivid to them. In the first version, the victim could be seen through glass. In later versions the sound of the victim's voice was added, then the victim was brought into the same room, and then the subject of the experiment had to force the victim's hand onto a plate for the shock. Each of these changes reduced the percentage of subjects who obeyed the order to give the shock.[11]

This fits with other psychological phenomena. In war, it is harder to use bayonets to massacre a group of people than to kill the same number of people by dropping bombs from an aircraft. The bayonet massacre is also more shocking to others. There is a kind of moral distance, which makes acts seem less bad when the victim is less salient.

When we are close enough to respond to each other as human beings, there seem to be psychological mechanisms that inhibit the worst of our violence. George Orwell describes how he did not shoot a Fascist soldier in the Spanish civil war:

> He was half dressed and was holding up his trousers with both hands as he ran. I refrained from shooting at him. It is true that I am a poor shot and unlikely to hit a running man at a hundred yards, and also that I was thinking chiefly about getting back to our trench while the Fascists had their attention fixed on the aeroplanes. Still, I did not shoot partly because of that detail about the trousers. I had come here to shoot at "Fascists"; but a man who is holding up his trousers isn't a "Fascist", he is visibly a fellow creature, similar to yourself, and you don't feel like shooting at him.[12]

Hot violence has its own motivation, but cold violence often depends on these inhibiting mechanisms' being weakened or overridden. One device is physical distance: The cold bureaucrat plans a policy of torture or killing, to be carried out by hotly violent subordinates somewhere else. Another is to create moral distance by dehumanizing the victims.

There is some evidence that within an institution like a prison the role played by prison guards changes the way they see prisoners in a direction that weakens their inhibitions against cruelty. In one study, in which students were randomly assigned to play the roles of prisoners and guards in a mock prison, the "guards" increasingly seemed to see the "prisoners" as inferior and to derive pleasure from ill-treating them.[13] If this happens in a mere role-playing experiment, where at some level both groups know that they are really similar, it is likely to happen at least as much in a real prison context.

Where the victims are of a different ethnic group, either from those carrying out the policy or from the public who might be stirred to protest, the dehumanization has sometimes already partly occurred. Abraham Bomba described the view through the cracks of the railway wagon going to the concentration camp: "Most of the people, not only the majority, but ninety-nine percent of the Polish people when they saw the train going through – we looked really like animals in that wagon, just our eyes looked outside – they were laughing, they had a joy, because they took the Jewish people away."[14]

In war, language is used to dehumanize enemies: Vietnamese become "Gooks," or Argentinians become "Argies." In state terrorism the classification is sometimes ideological. According to where you are, it may be easier to ill-treat someone seen as an imperialist or as a Communist than someone seen just as a person. Those who tortured for the Greek junta were given orders about the prisoners by their officers: "to crush them because they are communists, they are enemies of the country, they are worms."[15]

Blurring, denial, and evasion. People can slide by degrees into doing things they would not do if given a clear choice at the beginning. (This is a psychological truth underlying the perhaps overused "slippery slope" arguments in ethics.) Each of the early steps may seem too small to count, but later anxiety about the moral boundary may suggest only the uncomfortable thought that it has already been passed.

The prisoners abducted under Argentinian state terror would sometimes be given improved conditions in exchange for cooperation, which would start with small cleaning jobs. A few went by degrees to taking part in interrogation and even torture. Police in Greece being trained as torturers took food to the prisoners and were occasionally told to hit them at the same time. Then they would act as guards watching others torturing prisoners. Then they would take part in group floggings. Then they would take part in the "standing ordeal," having to beat the prisoner on the legs when he moved. Then they would be told they were full torturers. After the first blow, there were only blurred boundaries on the way to full torture.

These slippery slopes go on all the way to mass extermination. Franz Stangl, the commandant of Treblinka, was later asked, "If they were going to kill them anyway, what was the point of all the humiliation, why the cruelty?" He replied, "To condition those who actually had to carry out the policies. To make it possible for them to do what they did."[16]

Taking part in atrocities can also be eased by various ways of denying or obscuring the reality of what is being done. Sometimes reality is obscured by bureaucratic euphemisms ("final solution," etc.). Sometimes it is obscured by an evasive jokiness. The Greek military police used nicknames for different kinds of torture: "the tea party," "the tea party with toast," and so on. The South African interrogators do the same thing: "telephoning," "playing the radio," "the submarine," "the aeroplane ride," and so forth. Some of these same terms crop up in the Argentinian accounts, showing that there is a revolting international language in which to be amusing about torture.

The evasions of responsibility are very familiar. There is what Robert Jay Lifton in his study of Nazi doctors has called "doubling": a split into two selves, where the kindly family man at home feels he has nothing to do with the "Auschwitz self" who carries out appalling medical experiments.[17] Then there is the exploitation of different roles in the chain of command. If all pleas were accepted, it would seem that no one was to blame. State terrorists seem to divide into those so senior that they did not have any contact with the way their highly general policies were implemented, and those junior cogs in the machine who plead that they were only obeying orders. These pleas are probably not only attempts to escape punishment. They probably also function at the time of the acts as ways of escaping guilt, and so of more comfortably participating in the terror.

269

Jonathan Glover

PART THREE: THE RESPONSE TO STATE TERRORISM AND TO OTHER TERRORISM

Long-term psychological change

Some of the psychological components of terrorism are dispositions that, in other contexts, have their beneficial uses. Fear no doubt has its evolutionary value. Conformity and obedience make many social enterprises easier. And even the ability to distance yourself from the suffering of people you are harming may sometimes be essential to the success of a morally necessary project. Anyone who is neither a pacifist nor ignorant of what war is like has to accept this. For instance, I am glad that there were armies willing to fight Nazism, and this might not have been possible if those participating had kept all their decent human responses intact. (Here I do not want to be misunderstood as saying that in a justifiable war anything goes: I am not defending the bombing of Dresden, nor the use of the atomic bombs on Japan.)

Although some of these psychological dispositions have their uses, it should also be clear that they have great dangers. State terrorism is sufficiently widespread to show how easy it is, under fairly common political conditions, for these dispositions to combine together to produce horrors.

At this point, an incompleteness in the argument is apparent. If war can sometimes be justifiable in defense of certain values, is it clear that state terrorism cannot be justified on the same grounds? This is a possibility. Perhaps it would have been a good thing if the authorities in the Weimar Republic had arranged for the few thousand leading Nazis to "disappear." And, more realistically, there is the question of "shoot to kill" policies used by states against leaders of terrorist organizations that themselves kill many people. A few comments on this kind of case will end the essay. But even if there is no absolute principle ruling out the use of terrorist methods by states in all circumstances, any possibly justified use is surely the rare exception rather than the rule. The cases given here have been assumed to be evils the world would be well rid of. This has not been argued in detail. It has just been assumed that state terrorism is not justified in defense, for instance, of rule by a military junta or of apartheid.

If state terrorism is recognized as a major evil, and seen as in part the product of these psychological dispositions, this may make us more alert to their dangers. We cannot simply decide to change ourselves in such a way as to eliminate them. But their harmfulness in part depends on their operating by stealth. If we are aware of the dangers of obedience, or of the way group stereotypes can dehumanize people, or of the effects of moral distance, this very awareness can weaken their power. Part of the long, slow evolution of human consciousness may be to absorb these lessons about ourselves from the horrors of our century. The additional self-consciousness may give some basis for greater self-control.

Political responses

But people are being tortured and killed now. For our present problems, these long-term psychological changes are *too* long-term. Political responses seem more immediately hopeful. There is no political policy that gives a certain way of eliminating these evils, but there are ways of making it harder for them to flourish.

There is a case for promoting a common international legal response to state terrorism. When a regime practicing state terrorism collapses, prosecutions should be brought. Obedience to orders should not be recognized as an adequate defense to charges of atrocities. Amnesties granted by governments to those involved in their state terrorism should not be recognized. (The Alfonsin government in Argentina in these respects set an admirable precedent.) Those accused of state terrorism should be denied political asylum in other countries unless it is clear that they would not be given a fair trial. None of this is enough to defeat state terrorism, but it would at least make the odds less weighted in its favor.

There should be international courts to which human rights complaints could be brought against states (by, or on behalf of, individuals as well as governments). The European Court of Human Rights is a possible model. Acceptance of the jurisdiction of such courts, and the provision of access to their investigators, could be regarded as a test of a country's fitness to participate in the international community. It could perhaps be a condition of membership of various international bodies (in the way that Spain, Portugal, and Greece would not have been able to join the European Community while under dictatorships). It might also be made a condition of such things as eligibility for loans from the World Bank or the International Monetary Fund.

The existence of the nation-state contributes to many evils. Enlightened people in the eighteenth century hoped it would wither away. But this hope now seems unrealistic. Much terrorism is itself a testament to the power of nationalism. The self-governing nation-state has deep roots in people's sense of their own identity, and this will not easily change. But some of the evils of the nation-state could be reduced by weakening its absolute nature. Giving international bodies some authority to limit human rights violations by states against their subjects would be one of the most acceptable limitations on the nation-state. A good thing for the protection it might provide, it might also make a small contribution to the slow growth of a human rather than a national consciousness.

Another helpful political response would be to cultivate the habit of objectivity, caring as much about state terrorism in "friendly" countries as in countries thought to be opponents. I do not want to say anything at all against the concern in North America and Western Europe with human rights abuses in Eastern Europe during the Communist period. But perhaps we should be troubled by the much smaller attention given to abuses on a horrendous scale in Latin America.

The response to nonstate terrorism

Terrorism by unofficial groups is often much more dramatic than state terrorism. Unofficial groups engage in dramatic hijackings and bombings, partly because they need "the oxygen of publicity." State terrorism often flourishes in secrecy. Most of us are much more aware of the hijackings and bombings than of disappearances and torture organized by governments. Yet even a casual study of state terrorism shows that it totally dwarfs unofficial terrorism in its contribution to human misery.

It is of course right to be concerned with unofficial terrorism. It too has caused many deaths and much grief. But there is a question of the kinds of responses to it that are justified. In particular, could it be right to use small doses of state terrorism to counter it? This question has come up, for instance, in the context of the British response to IRA terrorism. Interrogation techniques in Northern Ireland (until stopped by the then prime minister, Edward Heath) included putting the person's head in a black bag, continuous loud noise, sleep deprivation, and continuous standing in an uncomfortable position. And more recently, there have been (controversial) allegations of a "shoot to kill" policy by the security forces. Some people argue that either of these policies would be justified if it helped to defeat the terrorists who have themselves killed many innocent people.

Those of us who are not absolute pacifists have difficulty in ruling out the killing of terrorists in principle. (A government could, for instance, declare war on a terrorist organization. Such a war would have to be judged by the moral criteria appropriate to judging any other war.) The use of a small dose of state terrorism might have short-term gains that outweighed the losses. It might cripple a terrorist organization, and save many more lives than it took.

But thinking more generally about state terrorism puts the issue in a new light. Two central claims are relevant here. One is that full-blooded state terrorism is normally a *much* worse evil than unofficial terrorism. The other is that the psychological roots of state terrorism are very widespread and very deep. This means that, if it gets established at all, there is more danger of it growing than is often realized. Not all "slippery slope" arguments are good. But the combination of the power of the psychological factors with the lack of control over what state functionaries do in secret make this one more impressive than many. And it is perhaps quite a bit more impressive than the arguments in support of the claim that "it could not happen."

NOTES

1 *Nunca Más: A Report of the Argentine National Commission on the Disappeared,* English trans. (London: Farrar, Straus and Giroux, 1986).

2 Catholic Institute for International Relations, *A Thousand Times Heroic* (London: Catholic Institute for International Relations, 1988).

3 Quoted in Ronald Dworkin, "Report from Hell," *New York Review of Books,* July 17, 1986, pp. 14–15.

4 Breyten Breytenbach, *The True Confessions of an Albino Terrorist* (London: Faber and Faber, 1984), p. 350.

5 Ibid., p. 351.

6 *Nunca Más,* pp. 418–25.

7 Mika Haritos-Fatouros, "The Official Torturer: Learning Mechanisms Involved in the Process; Relevance to Democratic and Totalitarian Regimes Today" (1985), typescript (Athens).

8 Quoted in Claude Lanzmann, *Shoah: An Oral History of the Holocaust* (New York: Harper and Row, 1985), pp. 50–1.

9 Stanley Milgram, *Obedience to Authority* (New York: Harper and Row, 1974).

10 Haritos-Fatouros, "The Official Torturer."

11 Milgram, *Obedience to Authority,* chap. 4.

12 George Orwell, "Looking Back on the Spanish War," in *The*

    Collected Essays, Journalism and Letters of George Orwell, vol. 2 (London: Penguin, 1968).

13 C. Haney, C. Banks, and P. Zimbardo, "Interpersonal Dynamics in a Simulated Prison," *International Journal of Criminology and Penology* 1 (1973): 69–97.

14 Lanzmann, *Shoah*, p. 310.

15 P. Rodakis: *The Trials of the Junta Criminals: Full Records*, vol. 2 (Athens, 1976), trans. and quoted in Haritos-Fatouros, "The Official Torturer."

16 Quoted in Gitta Sereny, *Into that Darkness* (London: Pan Books, 1974), p. 101.

17 Robert J. Lifton, *The Nazi Doctors: A Study in the Psychology of Evil* (New York: Macmillan, 1986).

Chapter 11

Nuclear hostages

GREGORY S. KAVKA

Most of us believe that terrorists act wrongly when they seize civilian hostages to enforce political demands or otherwise advance their political programs. At the same time, many of us believe that nuclear deterrence is morally permissible, or at least would be if that policy were carried out in the right way.[1] There is an apparent inconsistency lurking here. For as has been frequently pointed out since early in the nuclear age, when nation A practices nuclear deterrence against nation B, A – in effect – holds a large fraction of B's civilian population hostage to the good behavior of B's government. As Thomas Schelling aptly puts it, "The 'balance of terror' . . . is simply a massive and modern version of an ancient institution: the exchange of hostages."[2]

This view of the balance of terror immediately suggests an argument against the moral permissibility of any form of nuclear deterrence that threatens retaliation against civilians. This argument – the nuclear hostages argument – is a deontological argument; that is, it condemns nuclear deterrence not because of its consequences, but on the basis of morally objectionable features inherent in the policy itself (or the acts required to implement it). More specifically, the nuclear hostages argument says nuclear deterrence is wrong because, as a form of political hostage taking, it shares the features that make terrorist hostage taking morally wrong.[3]

My aims in this essay are two. First, I argue that there is no genuine inconsistency in our beliefs about nuclear deterrence and terrorists' holding people hostage. The nuclear hostage argument fails and we may condemn terrorist hostage taking without similarly condemning nuclear deterrence. And second, I use the hostage matter as an entry point into one aspect of the perplexing issue of how to combine deontological and consequentialist considerations into an overall moral evaluation of nuclear deterrence.

HOSTAGES IN PLACE

Nuclear hostages – civilians held hostage to the good behavior of their governments under threatened penalty of nuclear annihilation – are hostages *in place*.[4] This means that, unlike those held by terrorists, they can go on with their normal lives while they are hostages, save for any psychological effects they may suffer as a result of the threat of nuclear destruction. Hence, of the two main kinds of wrongs suffered by terrorists' hostages – increased risk of death, and loss of liberty – only the former is borne by nuclear hostages. And of the two major kinds of apparent wrongs done by terrorist hostage takers – imposing increased risks of death, and limiting liberty – only the former is done by nuclear hostage takers. The implication is strong that ordinary hostage taking is morally worse than nuclear hostaging.

Consider an analogy. Would it be worse to dump toxins secretly in a neighborhood, thus endangering its citizens, or to dump the toxins *and* unjustly imprison those citizens in the neighborhood jail (where they would still be exposed to the toxins' effects)? Obviously the latter. As in the two hostage cases, imposing risk plus unjustified loss of liberty is worse than imposing risk alone.[5]

This analogy goes a considerable way toward showing that the deontological case against terrorist kidnapping of civilians is stronger than the deontological case against nuclear deterrence, insofar as the latter is based on considerations related to the practice of holding hostages. It does not go all the way, however, for the strength of obligations not to impose risk may depend upon the degree of risk. If the risks of death imposed on nuclear hostages were much greater than the risks to ordinary hostages, this might outweigh the fact that the latter risks (but not the former) are accompanied by loss of liberty.

Is this the case? It partly depends upon what we mean by degree of risk. If we mean the *probability* of an individual hostage being killed, this probability seems low, though hardly negligible, in the case of ordinary hostages. (In the average airplane hijacking, for example, only a few hostages – if any – out of hundreds end up dead.) But the probability of nuclear deterrence failing so as to produce the death of a given superpower citizen is also low. Or at least this is what defenders of nuclear deterrence are likely to believe. Otherwise, they would have to reject deterrence on straightforward utilitarian or prudential grounds.

What if degree of risk is interpreted to take account of the number of people affected, as well as the probability of each suffering death? Then it is clear that nuclear hostage taking imposes greater risks than ordinary hostage taking simply because it threatens millions rather than scores of people.

There is a danger, however, in relying on this notion of degree of risk to prop up the nuclear hostage argument. Doing so rests the core of the argument on essentially consequentialist considerations. Deterrence is bad, we now say, because it puts so *many* people at risk. This position not only abandons the initial deontological intuition that hostage taking is wrong because it treats (or mistreats) individuals in particular ways, it also invites the obvious reply that nuclear deterrence may be good because it protects so many people.

These considerations are not conclusive. It may be possible to formulate plausible deontological theories concerning these matters that can accommodate both (1) the primacy of the protection of individuals against misuse and mistreatment and (2) the importance of the number of people wrongly used or mistreated. Indeed, traditional just war theory, which is briefly addressed in the next section, may be seen as an attempt to formulate a theory of precisely this sort. But until the theoretical underpinnings of such theories are made clearer, we do not know how protections from being misused by others are to be sensibly integrated with appropriate concern for numbers of persons affected.[6]

So far, we have observed that the nuclear hostages argument may not be able to answer the "no loss of liberty" objection without abandoning its distinctly deontological character. But actually, matters are worse than that for the argument, once we note that each of the main wrongs suffered by terrorists' hostages – risk of death and loss of liberty – has two dimensions: opportunity costs and psychological costs. If one ends up being a dead hostage, one loses all the goods of the life one would otherwise have lived. Thus, being taken hostage imposes a risk of these heavy opportunity costs. Also, awareness of the increased likelihood of an early death will tend to make one anxious and unhappy now (and independent of whether early death actually eventuates). These psychological costs may carry over into the post-hostage period, if the fear of death traumatizes one or leaves permanent scars on one's psyche. Similarly, if held hostage, one misses out on the things one would have otherwise chosen to do in that period of time. In addition to this opportunity cost with regard to liberty, one suffers the psychic pain and frustration of knowing one is missing out on the activities of a normal life, of missing one's friends and loved ones, and so on.

It is important to treat psychological losses separately, because such losses owing to restraint on liberty and fear of death are often interactive. That is, one tends to dwell on the prospect of death more, and hence be more miserable, if one is prevented from carrying on with life's normal activities. This is especially so if the restrictions and the threat to life have the same cause, or are otherwise linked in the agent's mind, as they inevitably are in an ordinary hostage situation. By contrast, since a nuclear hostage is able to carry on with her normal life, the salience of the risk she is under is likely to be small as she directs her attention to more mundane matters. She is thus much less likely to suffer from severe fear of death than a hostage held by terrorists facing an equal objective probability of death.

There is a factor on the other side: Nuclear hostages are under risk for longer periods of time than ordinary hostages (who may be held for only hours or days). Indeed, many of us may live our entire lives as nuclear hostages. Thus, nuclear hostages undergo *longer* periods of psychological stress than ordinary hostages. But the undergoing of risk that does not eventuate in harm over a long period of time tends to reduce fear – we learn to live with the Bomb. Short, salient risks of death produce much greater psychic effects: Considering psychological distress alone, most of us would surely prefer to endure the strain of living under current nuclear dangers for decades rather than experience for days the terror of those held hostage by hijackers.

It is time to take stock of the implications of my argument to this point. Terrorists' hostages suffer two major apparent wrongs – risk of death and loss of liberty – whereas nuclear hostages suffer only the former. Furthermore, the psychological component of the former wrong is very probably much worse for terrorist hostages than for nuclear hostages. There are considerations on the other side which suggest that nuclear hostage holding may be worse. But these are basically consequentialist considerations – in particular, the risks could be (for all we know) more probable in the nuclear case, and they are imposed on a much greater number of people. This means that viewed strictly as a deontological argument focusing on the wrong done to its victims, the nuclear hostage argument is unpersuasive. The deontological case against nuclear hostage holding is considerably weaker than the corresponding deontological argument against terrorist hostage taking.

TWO WRONGS OF HOSTAGE TAKING

We have so far focused on the wrongs done to hostages. But deontological arguments against hostage taking might instead focus on the wrongs done *by* hostage takers. I will argue, however, that this way of viewing the matter merely reinforces our earlier conclusion that the deontological case against nuclear hostage holding is much weaker than the case against terrorist hostage taking.

The most fully developed deontological theory about uses of force is traditional just war theory. This theory sets out a number of criteria, all of which must be satisfied, if the use of force by an organized group is to be justified. Some of these criteria, by their very nature, cannot possibly be satisfied by terroristic uses of force. (For example, terrorist acts – as usually understood – are aimed at civilians and are not sanctioned by governments; thus they violate the principles of discrimination and rightful authority.) Let us therefore disregard such criteria and look instead at two just war criteria that terrorist acts of hostage taking could, in principle, satisfy: the requirement that the use of force in question have a *reasonable chance of success*, and the requirement that the act be *properly motivated*.[7]

These requirements are worth considering because each provides a plausible account of what may be wrong with the hostage taker and his action. They thus can ground deontological arguments against hostage taking that are agent-centered, rather than victim-centered. Violation of the (proper) motivation requirement directly implies a moral flaw in the agent, and violation of the (reasonable chance of) success requirement indicates a faulty willingness, on the hostage taker's part, to harm the innocent seriously with little prospect of providing compensating benefits to others.

In principle, an act of terrorist hostage taking could satisfy both requirements. It might be motivated solely by the desire to achieve just political results that could not otherwise be achieved, and it might be highly likely to succeed. But in reality, terrorist hostage taking is much less likely to satisfy either requirement than is nuclear hostage holding.

Consider first chances of success. Because political agents usually turn to terrorism only when other means of achieving their ends have failed, terrorist acts are often acts of desperation with little chance of success.[8] Put more bluntly, terrorism is notoriously a tool of the weak against the strong, and in such contests, the strong usually win.

Even more important, terrorists usually seize hostages in an attempt to change the status quo, to force other parties to take positive actions that will constitute gains for the terrorists and losses for their opponents.[9] Nuclear hostage holding, by contrast, is part of a policy of deterrence that seeks to prevent others from upsetting the status quo, from making gains at one's expense. Given the well-documented tendency of people to resist losses much more fiercely than they seek gains,[10] nuclear hostage holding is more likely to succeed than terrorist hostage taking simply because it seeks to deter acts the hostage taker dislikes rather than compel acts she likes.

For two reasons then, terrorist hostage taking is much more likely than nuclear hostage holding to exemplify the morally abhorrent category of "harming the innocent with little realistic hope of achieving positive outcomes." Those willing to perform such acts reveal a ruthlessness, a fanatical devotion to disputable political ends, that must be morally objectionable.

Let us now turn to the just war theory requirement of proper motivation. This says that groups using force must be motivated by the desire to achieve morally legitimate ends. To the extent that they are motivated by greed, revenge, arrogance, or lust for power, acts of force are morally dubious regardless of their effects. Here again, in principle, the requirement could be satisfied by acts of terroristic hostage taking. Terrorists could seize hostages with feelings of deep regret, rather than anger and triumph, and motivated solely by the apparent necessity of doing so to achieve what they perceive as greater moral goods. But the often cruel treatment of innocent hostages by their captors is strong evidence of the much-less-than-perfect motivations of actual terrorists.[11] By way of contrast, it is natural to think of the operations-level personnel who carry out a policy of nuclear deterrence (e.g., missile and bomber crews) as moved essentially by benign motives – professionalism, defense of country, obedience to legitimate authority, and so on. Put more bluntly, the facts of psychological distancing are such that a decent person can more easily become a potential nuclear button pusher than an airplane hijacker.[12]

At the leadership level, the issue of motivations becomes more murky. High officials of nuclear nations and leaders of terrorist groups or movements may have similar motivations – aggrandizement of personal political power, sincere devotion to what they perceive as a just political cause, a sense of responsibility to those under their leadership and protection, and so on. Perhaps, given the greater odds against the success of their ventures, terrorist leaders must be more willing to stake the well-being of innocents on a gamble. But nuclear leaders seem willing to stake the well-being of *more people* on a gamble, though almost surely a lesser one. So on this motivational issue, there may be little to choose between them.

The upshot of this section is that we have some agent-centered deontological reasons, as well as victim-centered reasons, for regarding terrorist hostage taking as substantially worse than the nuclear version. Terrorist hostage taking involves a willingness to harm innocent people with little chance of achieving compensating benefits. And it typically involves worse motives among the hostage takers, at least at the operational level. When we combine these points with our previous observation that terrorist hostage taking limits victims' liberty along with risking their lives (and is likely to have worse psychological effects on them), the following conclusion emerges. There are good reasons for regarding deontological objections based on hostage taking as having considerably less force in the case of nuclear deterrence than in the case of terrorism. These reasons may justify us in regarding nuclear deterrence (in some form) as morally permissible, while at the same time morally condemning the seizure of hostages by terrorists.

DEONTOLOGY AND CONSEQUENTIALISM

There are two distinct ways one might attempt to salvage the argument against nuclear deterrence that is based on the idea that it involves holding innocent people hostage. First, one might advocate an *absolute* moral prohibition on knowingly using innocent people, by imposing risks of death on them without obtaining their consent or providing them with compensating benefits.[13] On this view, it does not matter that the deontological moral case against nuclear hostage holding is weaker than the case against terrorist hostage taking. Both forms violate absolute moral prohibitions, and hence are wrong.

The problem with this approach is that any absolute prohibition against knowingly imposing risks of death on the innocent is implausible. Imagine, for example, that I discover a bomb about to explode in my classroom, and can protect myself and my students only by immediately heaving it out the window where I know it may kill innocent passersby. I thereby knowingly impose a risk of death on the other people on campus (who may be strolling by the window) without providing them with compensating benefits or obtaining their consent. Yet few would deny that it is permissible for me to toss the bomb to save myself and my students.[14]

Absolutists might attempt to get around this sort of counterexample by rephrasing their principle so it prohibits only *intentionally* imposing risks of harm on the innocent. In other words, they may retreat to reliance on some version of the doctrine of double effect. This is not the place to enter into the mysteries of that venerable doctrine. I will simply state that its defenders have not, to my knowledge, provided a precise criterion that adequately distinguishes intended effects from unintended side effects, nor have they given convincing reasons for supposing that intended effects (however defined) have greater intrinsic moral significance than nonintended ones.[15]

Whatever the ultimate fate of the doctrine of double effect and the absolutist defense of the hostage argument against nuclear deterrence, I here wish to focus on an alternative defense of that argument that seems to me of greater interest. This alternative is advanced by Steven Lee, who acknowledges that the deontological moral case against nuclear deterrence is weaker than the case against ordinary hostage taking because nuclear hostages are (as noted at the beginning of this essay) hostages in place.[16] Since nuclear hostage holding involves using the innocents held hostage, Lee claims that we still have a significant (though not necessarily conclusive) deontological moral reason for condemning the practice. And the existence of this deontological reason has an interesting methodological consequence, one that has also been endorsed by Jefferson McMahan: A slight consequentialist advantage will not suffice to justify the practice of nuclear deterrence. Since there are deontological reasons counting against deterrence, its consequentialist advantages (e.g., enhanced security) must be powerful and compelling enough to outweigh *both* its undesirable consequences (e.g., risks of nuclear war) *and* its deontological defects.[17]

This methodological claim of Lee's and McMahan's is extremely important for the following reason. Consequentialist assessments of nuclear deterrence vary in their conclusions depending upon the factual assumptions the assessors use and the principles of choice under uncertainty that they employ.[18] And even some of those who, as I do, endorse deterrence on essentially consequentialist grounds do not claim that the consequentialist case for deterrence is either clearcut or overwhelming.[19] Hence, if Lee and McMahan are right in their methodological claim, the consequentialist moral defense of nuclear deterrence is in serious danger of collapse.

But Lee and McMahan are not right *if there are deontological reasons in favor of nuclear deterrence*. For these reasons may suffice to counterbalance the deontological arguments against nuclear deterrence. If so, consequentialist considerations are left in play to determine the overall moral status of nuclear deterrence. And if these consequentialist considerations seem to favor deterrence overall, we may be justified in regarding that practice as morally justified, even if the balance in its favor is slight or uncertain.

As I have argued elsewhere, there are deontological arguments, based on the right to defend oneself and innocent others, that do serve to counterbalance deontological objections to nuclear deterrence.[20] If this argument is correct, despite Lee's and McMahan's claims, it may be sensible to decide the moral case for or against nuclear deterrence on straightforward and unmodified consequentialist grounds.[21]

THE RIGHT OF SELF-DEFENSE

The argument of the last section depends upon there being some valid principle of collective self-defense that provides a deontological justification for practicing nuclear deterrence. A *strong* principle, one that says a nation is justified in doing whatever its leaders and citizens reasonably believe is necessary for the nation's defense, would apparently suffice. Such a principle is a collective version of Thomas Hobbes's Right of Nature, "which . . . is the Liberty each man hath, to use his own power, as he will himselfe, for the preservation of his own Nature; that is to say, of his own Life; and consequently, of doing any thing, which in his own Judgement, and Reason, hee shall conceive to be the aptest means thereunto."[22]

It may be objected that such strong principles of self-defense, at both the individual and the collective levels, are much too permissive.[23] In particular, it may be claimed that there are moral limits on the means we may use to protect ourselves, and that these limits include prohibitions on harming (or imposing risks upon) the innocent – especially when death is the harm in question. At least two considerations support this claim. In law, coercion and duress are not allowed as defenses against a charge of murder.[24] And our intuitions about hypothetical cases, such as that of Thomson's violinist who hooks himself up to your kidneys (without permission) to save his life,[25] indicate that some possible acts of self-preservation are morally wrong.

Perhaps then, the only valid principles of self-defense take a *weak* form, such as: You may do whatever reasonably seems necessary to protect yourself, except when so doing involves significantly harming (or imposing risks upon) other innocent people. Such weak principles would not sustain a self-defense argument for nuclear deterrence, since such a practice imposes risks of death on enemy civilians. If weak principles of self-defense are the best we can do, my reply to Lee and McMahan will not succeed.

My own view is that any valid principle of self-defense would have to be a *moderate* one that falls between strong and weak principles of the sort indicated here. That is, such a principle would disallow some acts reasonably thought necessary for self-defense (e.g., murdering many innocents to save your own life), while allowing some self-defending acts that impose risks on the innocent (e.g., the dynamite tossing I proposed earlier). Later in this section I attempt to formulate such a principle, but it – like all principles concerning the limits of self-defense – will surely prove controversial.

There are straightforward reasons for this. Intuitions about when acts of self-defense are justified are various, murky, and difficult to systematize.[26] Actual cases in which the innocent must be harmed to save one's life are relatively rare, and usually involve controversial epistemic issues about what the self-defender knew or should have known about the various options available and risks involved. Nor is the law an unambiguous and reliable guide to moral correctness here. For it must answer to standards of public policy, practical applicability on the basis of publicly determinable evidence, and understandability by those whose conduct is to be regulated, as well as to strictly moral considerations. Further, what legal cases there are on the subject seem only to reexpress our intuitive ambivalences – with self-defensive killings of the innocent typically resulting in nonprosecution or in murder convictions followed by commuted sentences.[27] The whole matter is further complicated by disagreement about what sort of examples of individual self-defense are relevantly similar to the cases of collective self-defense in which we are interested.[28]

In the face of these difficulties, it seems to me that there are two ways in which we might proceed. We could plow ahead to try to find a relatively precise moderate principle that tells us when acts of self-defense are morally permissible, and when they are not. We might do this by noting various potentially relevant distinctions (e.g, between killing and letting die, between innocent threats and innocent shields,[29] between intentionally imposed risks and risks imposed as side effects), applying our intuitions to real and hypothetical cases of self-defense involving the distinguished features in various combinations, and seeing if we can formulate some general systematizing principle that both explains our intuitions about cases and fits into some generally acceptable (or at least recognizable) moral framework. In other words, we can try to reach something like a Rawlsian reflective equilibrium in our beliefs about the limits on the right of self-defense.[30]

Whether or not this project ultimately succeeds, what matters for present purposes is that it is not likely to succeed in a way that undermines my reply to Lee and McMahan. For any acceptable reflective-equilibrium principle of self-defense is going to be a moderate principle that allows nuclear deterrence, *if deterrence is justified on consequentialist grounds*. There are at least three reasons why.

First, nuclear deterrence involves *risk* imposition on the innocent rather than harm imposition. Risk, by its very nature, is a matter of degree and is governed by principles of proportion, rather than absolute prohibitions. Any plausible principle of self-defense is going to allow risk imposition that is proportionate to the harm avoided, where proportionality is largely determined by such consequentialist features as amount of harm, probability of harm, and number of people harmed.[31]

Second, it has been forcefully argued by Bernard Williams and others that morality allows one to give priority to interests, projects, and attachments of one's own (or of those with whom one closely identifies) over those of others.[32] If this is true, justifiable principles of individual or collective self-defense might even allow some "disproportionate" redistributions of risk onto other innocents. That is, we might sometimes be justified in avoiding somewhat smaller risks to ourselves, our loved ones, and our countrymen by shifting (part of) these risks onto other innocent parties *even when the overall magnitude of risk thereby increases*. Practicing nuclear deterrence might then be justified even if the balance of consequentialist reasons were somewhat against it.

Third, the idea of allowing "at least proportionate" redistribution of risks is strengthened, in the nuclear deterrence case, by the fact that we are talking about people defending *each other*, rather than simply themselves. Any worries we might have about the egoistic bias involved in redistributing risks onto others are lessened in cases in which the agent is not the prime (or only) beneficiary of such redistribution. Put crudely, group-egoistic redistribution of risk is less suspect than individual-egoistic redistribution, and utilitarian redistribution is even less suspect. The group-defense idea also makes clear that practicing nuclear deterrence might be something we are obligated to do, as well as something we have a right to do.

These considerations suggest that the following is an acceptable moderate principle of collective self-defense: It is permissible for a nation (and obligatory for its leaders) to do whatever it (and they) reasonably believe is necessary for national defense, provided such measures do not impose substantially disproportionate risks or harms on other parties. (It is understood that the appropriate measure of proportionality takes account of degrees of culpability for the danger at hand, as well as the standard utilitarian notions of degree, probability, and extent of harm or risk.)[33] This principle is admittedly vague on the key issue of how to integrate the various relevant components into an overall measure of proportionality. And even with this thorny issue set aside, there may be counterexamples to the principle lurking in the minds of clever deontologists. So although I find it reasonable to suppose that there is some acceptable moderate principle of self-defense of roughly this form, I would not claim that all reasonable people would necessarily agree on this point, even if situated behind a suitable "veil of ignorance."[34]

So it is important to consider briefly an alternative way of looking at the whole matter. Perhaps there is no way to systematically reconcile our deontological duty not to harm (or impose risks on) the innocent with the valid deontological permission (or obligation) to do what is necessary to defend ourselves. Perhaps there is no acceptable formula for determining when one of these deontic considerations cancels or overrides the others. Each stands as a deontological principle carrying independent weight, and if they conflict we may have to appeal to intuition, or other kinds of moral principles (e.g., straightforward consequentialist ones), to determine what we should do. Perhaps, in some such cases, we will even face genuine moral dilemmas or paradoxes.[35]

If this alternative view is correct, my reply to Lee and McMahan is again sustained. The right of self-defense does provide a deontological counterweight to objections to nuclear deterrence based on the idea that deterrence wrongfully imposes risks on innocent civilians by making them hostage to the good behavior of their governments. My final conclusion, then, is conditional but significant. Consequentialist arguments for nuclear deterrence may or may not succeed. But *if* they do succeed on their own terms, they may provide sufficient moral justification for the practice of deterrence.

NOTES

I am grateful to the American Council of Learned Societies and the Ford Foundation for fellowship support, and to Steven Lee, Jefferson McMahan, Christopher Morris, and Walter Sinnott-Armstrong for helpful comments on an earlier draft. I blame all remaining error on the distractions of parenthood.

1   I discuss what sort of nuclear deterrence policy might be permissible in the introduction to my *Moral Paradoxes of Nuclear Deterrence* (Cambridge: Cambridge University Press, 1987). However, recent international developments have rendered certain aspects of that discussion obsolete.
2   Thomas Schelling, *The Strategy of Conflict* (New York: Oxford University Press, 1963), p. 239.
3   Some versions of the nuclear hostages argument might involve

the claim that nuclear deterrence is itself a form of terrorism. I ignore this matter to focus on the underlying normative issue of whether nuclear deterrence (wherever it falls in the terrorist/nonterrorist classification scheme) shares the morally objectionable features present in paradigmatic cases of terrorist hostage taking.

4 See Michael Walzer, *Just and Unjust Wars* (New York: Basic, 1977), p. 271; and my "Nuclear Deterrence: Some Moral Perplexities," in *The Security Gamble*, ed. Douglas MacLean (Totowa, N.J.: Rowman and Allanheld, 1984), sec. 1, reprinted, with revisions, as chap. 4 of *Moral Paradoxes of Nuclear Deterrence*.

5 Steven Lee (private correspondence, December 1988) has pointed out that nuclear deterrers *use* people to influence third parties, whereas toxin dumpers do not. Though this is true, it does not undermine the force of the analogy. For terrorist hostage takers also use people to influence third parties, and do so in ways that limit their liberties as well as threaten their lives. Put in Lee's terms, my point is that, other things being equal, a "using" that harms someone in one way is not as bad as a "using" that harms that person in the same way *and* in an additional way.

6 It is interesting to note that Walzer's recent sophisticated attempt to provide theoretical grounding for traditional just war theory ends up endorsing nuclear deterrence, in principle, on the grounds that it is a necessary response to a "supreme emergency." See *Just and Unjust Wars*, chap. 17.

7 For a recent influential summary of the just war criteria, see National Conference of Catholic Bishops, *The Challenge of Peace: God's Promise and Our Response* (Washington, D.C.: United States Catholic Conference, 1983), pp. 28–30. The requirement of proper motivation is implied by the traditional criteria of just cause and right intention.

8 On terrorists' general lack of success, see Schelling, "What Purposes Can 'International Terrorism' Serve?" in this volume.

9 They pursue a policy of "compellence" rather than "deterrence," in the terminology of Schelling, *Arms and Influence* (New Haven, Conn.: Yale University Press, 1966), pp. 69–78.

10 I have noted this tendency previously, in *Moral Paradoxes of Nuclear Deterrence*, pp. 165–6. For theoretical backing, see Dan-

iel Kahnemann and Amos Tversky, "Prospect Theory," *Econometrica* 39 (March 1979): 263–92.

11 See also Alan Ryan, "State and Private; Red and White," in this volume.

12 This is not to say there is nothing morally problematic about the order-following button pusher. I am simply making a comparative claim about the characters of terrorists and (nuclear) soldiers, on average, given the truth of certain general psychological principles.

13 Absolutism is the view that certain kinds of acts (e.g., torture, murder) are always morally wrong, regardless of how good their consequences may be in a particular situation (or, more accurately, regardless of how horrible the consequences of not performing them are). Thus, for example, a typical absolutist will hold that it is wrong to torture one person even if it is known with certainty to be the only way to prevent the torture of very many people. Few contemporary moral theorists are absolutists. But see G. E. M. Anscombe, "War and Murder," in *Nuclear Weapons and Christian Conscience*, ed. Walter Stein (London: Merlin, 1961), pp. 45–62; Charles Fried, *Right and Wrong* (Cambridge, Mass.: Harvard University Press, 1978); and Alan Donagan, *The Theory of Morality* (Chicago: University of Chicago Press, 1977).

14 This conclusion is *not* a mere artifact of the statistical lives phenomenon, whereby we tend to value lives of particular identifiable people more than lives of unidentified victims. For it is still permissible to toss the bomb even if I know what particular individuals may be walking past the window at this hour. For the certain danger to me and to my students outweighs the possible danger to those particular individuals.

15 On the former problem see Philippa Foot, "The Problem of Abortion and the Doctrine of Double Effect," in *Moral Problems*, ed. James Rachels, 2d ed. (New York: Harper and Row, 1975); pp. 59–70. On the latter problem, see Jonathan Bennett, "Morality and Consequences," in *The Ethics of War and Nuclear Deterrence*, ed. James Sterba (Belmont, Calif.: Wadsworth, 1985); pp. 23–9. An interesting recent interpretation of double effect may be found in Warren Quinn, "Actions, Intentions, and Consequences: The Doctrine of Double Effect," *Philosophy and Public Affairs* 18 (Fall 1989): 334–58. As Quinn's article il-

lustrates, one need not be an absolutist to lend credence to the doctrine of double effect.

16 Steven Lee, *Morality, Prudence, and Nuclear Weapons* (Cambridge: Cambridge University Press, forthcoming), chap. 2. The relevant passage is in the section entitled "Nuclear Deterrence as Hostage Holding" in the draft manuscript of this chapter that Professor Lee kindly provided to me.

17 Ibid.; Jefferson McMahan, "Is Nuclear Deterrence Paradoxical?" *Ethics* 99 (January 1989): 410. The deontological defects of nuclear deterrence that McMahan emphasizes are the ones we have acknowledged: the risks imposed on, and suffered by, innocent civilians. George Draper has pointed out to me a passage that suggests that Douglas Lackey may share the view of Lee and McMahan on this point. See Lackey's "Immoral Risks: A Deontological Critique of Nuclear Deterrence," in *Nuclear Rights/Nuclear Wrongs*, ed. Ellen Frankel Paul et al. (Oxford: Blackwell, 1986), p. 171.

18 For contrasting factual assessments, compare my *Moral Paradoxes of Nuclear Deterrence*, chaps. 3 and 6; and Douglas Lackey, *Moral Principles and Nuclear Weapons* (Totowa, N.J.: Rowman and Allanheld, 1984), chap. 5. For contrasting principles of choice, compare my chap. 3 with Leslie Pickering Francis, "Nuclear Threats and the Imposition of Risks," in *Political Realism and International Morality*, ed. Kenneth Kipnis and Diana T. Meyers (Boulder, Colo.: Westview, 1987), pp. 153–7.

19 See my *Moral Paradoxes of Nuclear Deterrence*, chap. 3.

20 Kavka, *Moral Paradoxes of Nuclear Deterrence*, chap. 4. A number of other philosophers have also presented defenses of nuclear deterrence based on some version of a right of self-defense. See, e.g., Walzer, *Just and Unjust Wars*, chap. 17; and James Child, "Political Responsibility and Noncombatant Liability," in Kipnis and Meyers, eds., *Political Realism*; pp. 61–74. In a recent doctoral dissertation ("On Deontological Justifications of Nuclear Risks," University of California, Irvine, 1989), George Draper argues against Lee's and McMahan's claim on other grounds.

21 Indeed, if the deontological arguments for deterrence should turn out to be *stronger* than those against it, deterrence could be defended on the grounds that its consequences are *not much worse* than those of its alternatives. Here, Lee's and McMahan's claim would be turned on its head.

22 Thomas Hobbes, *Leviathan*, ed. C. B. Macpherson (Harmonds-worth: Penguin, 1968), chap. 14, p. 189.

23 I assume, for the purposes of this essay, that restrictions on individual and collective rights of self-defense are strictly parallel. For discussion of the relationship between individual and collective rights of self-defense, see Walzer, *Just and Unjust Wars*, chap. 4.

24 Alan Wertheimer, *Coercion* (Princeton; N.J.: Princeton University Press, 1987), pp. 155–6.

25 Judith J. Thomson, "A Defense of Abortion," *Philosophy and Public Affairs* 1 (Fall 1971): 47–66.

26 Here I disagree with Thomas Donaldson ("Nuclear Deterrence and Self-Defense," in *Nuclear Deterrence: Ethics and Strategy*, ed. Russell Hardin et al. [Chicago: University of Chicago Press, 1985], p. 168), who apparently holds that our intuitions about individual self-defense "unambiguously" favor weak principles over stronger ones. For views very different from Donaldson's, see Mack, "Three Ways to Kill Innocent Bystanders," in Paul et al., eds., *Nuclear Rights/Nuclear Wrongs*, pp. 1–26; and Child, "Political Responsibility and Noncombatant Liability."

27 See Wertheimer, *Coercion*, p. 145, including n. 6.

28 Note, for example, the differences between the "individual analogues" to nuclear deterrence offered in my *Moral Paradoxes of Nuclear Deterrence*, chap. 4, and Donaldson's "Nuclear Deterrence and Self-Defense." My own view is that the more accurate the analogy to nuclear deterrence, the less clear and definite are our moral intuitions about the corresponding cases involving individual self-defense.

29 Robert Nozick, *Anarchy, State and Utopia* (New York: Basic, 1974), pp. 34–5.

30 John Rawls, *A Theory of Justice* (Cambridge, Mass.: Harvard University Press, 1971), secs. 4 and 9.

31 Though I have my doubts about the validity of Lackey's principle of parallelism concerning risks and harms ("Immoral Risks," pp. 167–71), the claims about risk offered in this paragraph are entirely consistent with that principle.

32 Bernard Williams, "A Critique of Utilitarianism," in Williams and J. J. C. Smart, *Utilitarianism: For and Against* (Cambridge: Cambridge University Press, 1973), pp. 77–150; Samuel Schef-

fler, *The Rejection of Consequentialism* (Oxford: Oxford University Press, 1982).

33 Cf. my *Moral Paradoxes of Nuclear Deterrence*, p. 92.

34 The veil of ignorance is a hypothetical information constraint designed to facilitate consensus by depriving parties of information about themselves that is morally irrelevant to the issue at hand. See Rawls, *A Theory of Justice*, secs. 4, 24.

35 On moral dilemmas in general, see Christopher Gowans, ed., *Moral Dilemmas* (New York: Oxford University Press, 1987). On nuclear deterrence as paradoxical, see Kavka, *Moral Paradoxes of Nuclear Deterrence*, pt. 1.

Chapter 12

Rape as a terrorist institution

C L A U D I A   C A R D

HOW BAD IS RAPE?

A feminist critic in the United States argued recently that "while rape is very bad indeed, the work that most women employed outside the home are compelled to do is more seriously harmful insofar as doing such work damages the most fundamental interests of the victim, what Joel Feinberg calls 'welfare interests,' whereas rape typically does not."[1] This judgment takes rape as an individual act, ignoring its relationship to institutional rules and thereby its terrorist implications. Rape, *as an institution*, has severe consequences both for women raped and for women terrorized into compliance. It underlies women's willingness to do whatever work men find suitable for women to do. So understood, rape indeed damages women's fundamental interests, though information on it is less public than (other) information on working conditions in the paid labor force.

The term "terrorism" as used in public media suggests a kind of political activity, often with international significance, focused on the powers of states or other territorial governments.[2] The restriction to *territorial* politics, however, ignores the terrorism of *sexual* politics. Ethically, that exclusion is arbitrary and irresponsible. It maintains an invisibility of routine violence against women, underlying visible sexist stereotypes.

Rape and domestic violence are both forms of terrorism, a backdrop to the daily lives of women in sexist societies. In this essay I take up only the institution of rape.[3] The philosophical significance of treating rape as a form of terrorism is twofold. On the one hand, philosophical discussions of terrorism can be enlarged and our understanding of terrorism's workings deepened by including the data of terrorist sexual politics. For they exemplify profoundly *institutionalized* forms of terrorism that tend to be overlooked in media portrayals of the terrorist. At the same time, the meaning and significance of rape and domestic battery can be clarified in relation to women's oppression by an appreciation of their terrorist implications.

My aim is to elucidate what it means to call rape a *terrorist institution*. I do not attempt to support empirical claims about the facts of rape. What is philosophically interesting is that without disputing the facts many do not yet apply the concept of "terrorism" to rape. Recognizing that the concept applies is yet another step in clarifying what is wrong with rape and how bad it is in relation to other abuses.[4] It is also important to stopping rape that we learn to avoid its terroristic potentialities, which attach to the institution whether or not they also attach to individual acts of rape.

The claim that rape is a terrorist institution involves two views that some will find surprising. One is that rape is an *institution*. The other is that it is a form of *terrorism*. I take up these ideas in that order. For it is important to understand rape as an institution in order to show how it works as a form of terrorism.

RAPE AS AN INSTITUTION

Rape is an institution not in the sense that it names an organization, such as the SS, KGB, FBI, or CIA, but in the sense that war and punishment are institutions. It is a kind of practice, with many historical embodiments.[5] As the institution of war can include the practice of punishment, both can include that of rape. As others have done, I use the terms "practice" and "institution" more or less interchangeably here and mean by both a form of social activity structured by rules that define roles and positions, powers and opportunities, thereby distributing responsibility for consequences.[6] The more established a practice is, the more natural it seems to refer to it as an institution.

Many participants in the institution of rape appear not to think of themselves as participating in an institution or practice, a matter to which I shall return. They encourage each other to think of their behavior as natural, at least self-originating, or, at its most complicated, as a response to provocation by women.

A practice can take root, become institutionalized, so firmly that it is not necessary for anyone to supervise the operation as a whole. Individual participants find that they have their own good reasons or, failing that, excuses, for what they do. Such institutions form the core subject matter of what Kate Millett called "sexual politics."[7] "Sexual politics" does not refer simply to the politics of the state (or any other territorial political body) with respect to sexual activity, although it includes that. Nor is it concerned only with sexual behavior. "Sexual politics" refers to social norms that create and define a distribution of power among and between members of the sexes, considered as such. Historically, rape has been a major sexuo-political institution.

"Rape," like "punishment," is ambiguous. It can refer to a kind of act, abstracted from its institutional setting, often (not necessarily) violent and painful. The same term can refer to an institution governing that act, an institution defined by rules that establish roles and positions, distribute responsibilities and opportunities, and create or withdraw power.[8] In the institution of punishment, some rules prohibit behaviors and specify penalties for offenses. Others govern the processes of policing, arrest, detention, and trial. Only some participants actually administer penalties. One may be hard put to say *how much* responsibility a particular individual participant bears for the punishment, or release, of any accused person. Yet communities supporting and benefiting from such institutions can be held responsible and can take responsibility for the institution and its operations. The same is true for rape.

Although there is controversy over the goals of punishment, most grant that deterrence of would-be criminal offenders is a legitimate aim. Whatever the justifying goals, they need not be supposed to correspond with intentional aims of participants at every stage or in every role. In particular, they need not correspond with the aims of those who administer penalties. Ordinarily, one supposes, those who administer penalties do it for the money, although there is room also for sadism. Still, they participate *in the practice* to the extent that they guide and evaluate their behavior by its norms, even if they are not motivated by the goals served by the practice.

Analogous observations apply to the institution of rape. Just as deterrence from crime is a major task of punishment, a major task of rape is the subordination and subservience of women to men. Just as with punishment, the *threat* does most of the work.[9] Not all who support or follow the rules carry out or even witness particular acts of rape. Those who do commit rape may have private motives of their own, such as revenge on other men. As with those who abide by the law, not all who follow the rules of rape need have the aims or consequences of the practice "in mind" as they do. In the case of punishment, it may be primarily judges and juries, formal and informal, backing the rules in particular cases, who have such things "in mind." Similarly, in the case of rape, it may be primarily judging observers who have such things in mind as they judge. For the most part, however, the rules become "second nature," like the rules of grammar, and those guided need not be aware of the rules as learned norms. There is also room for controversy about how much female compliance with male desire is due to the threat of rape. Just as with the relationship between punishment and motives for obedience to law, there is more than one story to be told here.

An ostensible difference between punishment in modern

democratic states and rape is that punishment as defined (if not as practiced) by modern democratic states, as a temporary or permanent withdrawal of certain rights, is meant to be humane, not terrorist. This has not always been true of state punishments. In a democracy punishment is supposed to play the role of a stabilizer, to provide people with a mutual assurance of general obedience to their common laws, and thus to make it rational for individuals to do their part. It is to be the sort of thing people might justifiably propose be carried out against themselves, should they fail to live up to their commitments, as a gesture of good faith and in recognition of their common liability to temptation.[10] Rape is not this sort of thing. It is not a liability to which one might reasonably submit, fantasy notwithstanding.[11] Some rapes are less brutal than others. Yet rape is not meant to be humane, regardless of how it is done.

RAPE AS TERRORISM

Stereotypes of the terrorist as mad bomber or airplane hijacker present terrorism as *public*, often idiosyncratically motivated *rebellion*, and focused on the power of *state governments*. The terrorism of rape does not fit that model. It is not entirely public. It is not focused on the power of state governments. It is not ordinarily a form of rebellion. Much about rape is clandestine. Its concern is sexual politics, rather than territorial politics. Laws officially prohibit rape. Yet constant danger to women offers men a ready source of material services in exchange for "protection." Governments have been better at protecting men from accusations of rape than at protecting women from rape.

Critics of popular views of terrorism, such as Jonathan Glover and, earlier, Emma Goldman, have rightly challenged the idea that terrorism is perpetrated only by *enemies* of the state. Glover writes: " 'Our' cause is usually supported by the resistance, by the underground, or by freedom fighters, while 'their' cause is often supported by terrorists. The use of the word 'terrorism' is often so loose and so loaded that it is tempting to abandon it."[12] Recognizing state terrorism should make us realize that terrorism is not always *public*. State terrorism can be carried out by secret organizations and accompanied by public disavowals from government bodies.

When terrorism is thought of as public, it may be tempting to admire terrorists somewhat for courage and honesty or alternatively to deplore their manifest lack of shame. Thus Annette Baier has asked: "Does the fact that the killing is done openly, with an eye to publicity, make it better or worse than killings done quietly and with attempted secrecy? . . . The person we call a terrorist typically does her violence in the public eye."[13] It may be neither courage nor lack of shame, however, so much as necessity dictated by terrorists' goals that determines whether terrorism is public or private. Terrorists working in the public eye aim to terrorize a certain public. Showing that they do not fear punishment can be necessary to success in terrorizing a government or other powerful body. Terrorists already relatively powerful need not make that point. They may have more to fear from publicity. For publicity could reveal that those terrorized into compliance were not acting voluntarily.

Terrorism is distinguished less by its ends or by the character traits it manifests than by its process. It is a tactic used to gain control of situations, or to fix or shift a balance of power, public or private. Terrorism is a shortcut to power or authority, a resort of the relatively powerless *or of those unable to justify their uses of power to a public*.

If humane deterrence threatens penalties liability to which one might reasonably accept, terrorism often manipulates target populations into compliance with demands they should reject, if rational, under calmer conditions. Terror as a tactic is an alternative to persuasion and argument, which are slower and riskier, and to humane forms of deterrence, also riskier and often more expensive. The work of Emma Goldman and Jonathan Glover on "state terrorism" suggests that terrorism is distinguished from the formally defined public threat of legal punishment in modern states more by the nakedness of its appeal to the motive of terror than by the political status of its perpetrators.

Terrorism involves planned or systematic manipulation. Terror, panicky and heightened fear, makes us vulnerable to manipulation. We feel an urgent need to act before it is too late. Thus we are in a poor position to reflect, get things in perspective. We are in a poor position to be prudent or even just. Our attention is riveted by the threat of disaster and what we can do to prevent it. We are thus not so apt to pay attention to the terrorizer's situation, options, motivations, or aims, except as they define what we must do to avoid disaster. We feel our options narrowed to the point of almost no control.[14] There is a danger for the terrorist of going too far, of paralyzing instead of merely terrorizing, with the result that manipulation is impossible. Terrorists, like other torturers, develop sensitivities and skills to avoid this consequence.

Like other terrorisms, rape has two targets: "bad girls" and "good girls," those who are expendable ("throw-away women") and those to whom a message is sent by way of the treatment of the former.[15] Women to whom the message is sent may not directly confront men they perceive as rapists. Some may not often *feel* terrorized by rape. It does not follow that they are not victims of terrorism. When terrorism is successful, the second target population (the one to whom the message is sent) need not experience continual terror. Women successfully terrorized, and others socialized by them, comply with men's demands. As reward and inducement to continue, they are granted "protection" that they feel they have "earned." The feeling of "earned protection" gives a sense of control. Daughters of terrorized mothers may be shielded for a long time by being "properly brought up."

Women whose encounters with violence are most immediate and most traumatic, however, are not always most liable to manipulation by fear of violence. Survivor rage can overcome fear. Having faced the apparent worst, some women become dedicated to *non*compliance. Like their sisters who did not survive, such women and others who have been tortured or mutilated may be useless to men except to send a message to other women to try thereby to secure the services of those women: This is what will happen to you if you are not "good," if you fail to do as we say.

An allegedly obsolete meaning of "rape" is "to carry off forcibly," a kind of theft. Rape has historically been treated by men as a crime of theft against other men. That idea is not totally obsolete. Men still often regard the rape of a woman as an offense against her guardian – the theft of something (the woman's "honor") that has a monetary value, a prestige value, or both. From the guardian's point of view, rape is a source of anger, indignation, resentment, even bitterness, but not terror. It is only from the point of view of *women* (or of men treated as women) that rape is terrorist. Omnipresent fear of rape controls women's mobility. Rapes of prostitutes, lesbians, and other women with no male guardians – and so with no one to "steal" anything from – receive less legal uptake than rapes of women who have male guardians. Yet the terror of rape is a fact of daily life for prostitutes, lesbians, and others who have no male guardians. These are among the expendables ("throw-aways") liable to being used to send a message to women more likely to be compliant.

THE PROTECTION RACKET

Feminists aside, philosophers have said little about rape. This should be surprising, considering how much they have said about violence against men. Except for accusations invented by European Americans to "justify" lynchings of African Americans, rape has not been, until recent years, even an *issue* – that is, discussable.[16] Men have officially acknowledged it as wrong, but so obviously wrong that what was there to discuss? Feminists have had to make an issue of rape.

Since Susan Griffin's classic essay on rape as the "all-American crime," it has become commonplace among feminists to regard rape as the linchpin of a male protection racket in sexist societies. Griffin wrote: "In the system of chivalry, men protect women against men. This is not unlike the protection relationship which [organized crime] established with small businesses in the early part of this century. Indeed, chivalry is an age-old protection racket which depends for its existence on rape."[17] Rackets *create* danger to sell "protection." Historically, organized crime expanded its power base by securing service and payment through terrorist means, from bombings to individual torture and mutilation. Historically, also, rape and the threat of rape have secured women's services for men who have represented themselves as protectors while terrorizing other women or supporting other men who did.

In an essay with the memorable title "Coercion and Rape: The State as a Male Protection Racket," Susan Rae Peterson argued that rape is a state-sponsored institution.[18] Rape is a "Rawlsian kind of 'practice,' " she said, a "form of activity specified by a system of rules which define offices, rules, moves, penalties, defences, and so on, and which give the activity its structure."[19] If a state fails to protect women against rape but succeeds in protecting at least certain classes of men against rape *charges*, she argued, it supports a "racket." I would go further and say that a state supports a racket even when it penalizes rapists, if it can be shown to be responsible for the continued threat of rape and to benefit from that continued threat.

Offers of "protection" are offers women have dared not refuse. If we refuse the bargain – refuse to pay protection and insist upon moving about without a guardian – we are held responsible for dangers we meet in response to our self-assertion. When we are raped, we hear that we brought it on ourselves, as Hegel said of the punishment visited upon a criminal by the state.[20] For we could have stayed home or gone out only with a guardian. Our position is in some ways worse than that of the person who buys from the crime syndicate. For our success in eliciting offers of protection, the need for which we learn early, requires that we comport and decorate ourselves in ways said to bring on and intensify the dangers from which we are to be protected. We hear that not to so groom ourselves is not to care about our appearance. Belatedly, we find that a male guardian can often protect us from no one but himself, and we are at his mercy there. The protectorate tends not to recognize rape by guardians or by males to whom we have once been accessible. Because access is controlled by the protectorate, those who pay protection are unable to control the need for protection.[21]

RAPE MYTHOLOGY UNDERMINED BY AMIR'S RESEARCH

Important to rape as a terrorist institution is the myth that rapists are weirdos lurking in the bushes or stalking beautiful innocent (or naughty) women who walk alone. According to this myth, rape serves only the perverse desires of *madmen*, who are always mysterious strangers. Sociologist Menachem Amir, whose study of 646 rapes reported in Philadelphia for the years 1958 and 1960 was published in 1971, has done much to discredit this madman myth and the "irresistible impulse" theory of rape as well.[22] Amir found that the majority of the rapes he studied were planned, not spontaneous (in gang rapes, 90 percent were planned; in pair rapes, 83 percent; in single rapes, 58 percent), that nearly half the rapists were personally known to the women they targeted, that a high proportion of rapes occurred in the homes of either the perpetrators or the women targeted, and that 43 percent involved multiple rapists.[23] Defending his *situational* – as opposed to *psychological* – approach to studying rape, Amir reported that "studies indicate that sex offenders do not constitute a unique clinical or psychopathological type; nor are they as a group invariably more disturbed than the control groups to which they were compared."[24] It appears that men convicted of rape are no more crazy than other men. It does not follow, of course, that other men are not crazy, or even that they do not rape. On the contrary, such studies raise the question how common rape is among men who regard each other as respectable.

Amir's research is a turning point. Prior studies focused on the psychologies of rapists and the women they targeted, assuming that individual rapes had sufficient explanations in individual eccentricity. Patriarchal tradition blames, ultimately, the women in the case – women targeted for rape, rapists' mothers, rapists' wives – and reserves sympathy for rapists, who "have a problem." Amir focused on situational aspects, rather than individual psychologies: where the rape was done, when, how, and what were the prior relationships, if any, between the perpetrators and the women they targeted. His findings upset popular mythology about who rapists are, whom they target, and where and when they do it.

Imaginatively, it is a short step from searching for social *patterns*, understood as statistical generalizations (as Amir did), to formulating social *norms* defining an institution by which people *guide and evaluate* their behavior.[25] The alternative to individual separate explanations of rapes is not necessarily a conspiracy, although Amir's study certainly turned up enough conspiracies. A more interesting alternative is that of a sexuo-political institution, rules of which, learned by example and precept, are presented as though they were empirical generalizations about women and men, or even scientific claims about female and male nature.

Combining Amir's research with Griffin's protection racket theory yields the idea of rape as a terrorist institution. This is a relatively optimistic view. It demystifies rape; it does not rest upon conjectures about the mysteries of male biology but presents rape as learned behavior. It suggests that rape, like slavery, can be abolished, however inconceivable that may seem to those whose material well-being presently depends on its existence.

DOUBLETHINK AND ILLEGITIMATE INSTITUTIONS

Rackets are illegitimate institutions. Illegitimate institutions involve clandestine operations. The sense in which agents carrying out clandestine operations *participate* in institutions generating the operations can be problematic. Some are clear that they are committing, condoning, or supporting rape, but not that it is part of a political operation. Others seem unclear about whether what they did was rape. Many do not care.

The clandestine nature of the institution is part of the explanation why many do not imagine that they are taking part in an institution. Some, manipulated by others, may not be aware of roles they play. Secret terrorism authorized by institutions that have governing bodies can help us get a fix on how terrorist policing institutions work. Participants in secret state practices or crime syndicate operations act with varying degrees of awareness that they are participating in a large and complex institution. Institutions with clandestine operations launder evil deeds like dirty money, passing them through a series of agents with ever-decreasing information about what is being done and why. Agents administering violent deaths and torture are sometimes paid or coerced outright. But sometimes they are punished, instead of rewarded, by those whom they have served, as a public disavowal of responsibility by the latter. Unpunished rapists may be like hangmen doing the dirty work of others who, perhaps not loving them for it, nevertheless see that they are enabled to go on doing what they do.

What George Orwell called "doublethink" is a common institutional tool of manipulation.[26] Doublethink makes a thing seem its opposite. The rules of rape use doublethink to shield participants from having to recognize rape when doing so might be counterproductive. Consequently, women often find it impossible to convince officials that a rape was really a rape. The problem is *not* a slippery slope from polite refusal to teasing seduction on women's part. The problem is that women's wills in rape situations become *irrelevant*. Despite clear demonstration of undisputed, unwanted violence, rape rules can block official recognition, especially when the assailant is no stranger to the woman he targets.[27]

Consider the following case, known to me personally from

307

about a decade ago. I choose it because it is not unusual and so is helpful in making a point about rape generally. A female university student did not understand until a full week later that she had been raped by the male student with whom she went home to study, even though she was completely conscious that he forcibly detained her, threw her to the floor, pinned her in place by methods that I will spare you, and sexually penetrated both ends of her body, causing her physical injuries and loss of blood. How could she not know she was raped? She was in shock afterward. But that was not it. She said *she went voluntarily to his apartment,* in response to his invitation. Woman who do this hear that they have "asked for it."

In the city of this assault, police have been taught not to disregard a rape charge for that kind of reason. Hearing this, the student went to the district attorney. I watched the jury return a verdict of "not guilty." The defense attorney denied only that the woman withheld consent. He argued that because she was angry instead of ashamed, his client had probably made her feel *rejected* and that she probably invented the rape charge as revenge.

The thing to notice is what makes it standardly impossible to answer the question what really happened and how this impossibility functions in a terrorist practice. Doublethink turns rape into something the perpetrator and target did together or into an "event" that "happened between us," as the man in this case put it to the woman who later charged him with rape. This is achieved by rules defining "consent," defining it out of existence.

THE RULES

Many of the rules of rape are unwritten, although the first, pertaining to wives, is still found explicitly in jurisdictions not yet affected by recent feminist criticism.[28] The first rule, embedded in older legal definitions, is that husbands cannot rape their wives. Or, alternatively, husbands are permitted to rape their wives with impunity. The rule permits husbands carnal access regardless of their wives' wills. When rape is defined as forcible carnal knowledge by a man of a woman not his wife, nothing a man does to a woman married to him is allowed to count as "real" rape.[29] If we understand "forcible" in its ordinary sense, this is doublethink. Wives *can* be sexually forced, "accessed" against their wills. Only if wives are *normatively disabled* from withholding consent is it not rape.

This is an example of rules defining categories of women who are not allowed to count as rape targets, at least for certain men. No matter what the men do to them, it is not really rape, because *the rules give the women's status itself the value of consent.* Other examples are prostitutes, women who are not "virgins" (including women previously raped), a woman who has had past voluntary sexual relations with a particular man (nothing *he* does to her afterward counts as "real" rape).

Another kind of rule gives female appearance, rather than status, the value of consent. Consider the rule that women who dress or move "provocatively" are "asking for it." There are basically two ways for women to "provoke" male sexual aggression. First, there is the "sexy" way, where our clothes and manner accent femininity. Second, there is the "castrating bitch" way, where our clothes and manner manifest, rather, a refusal to make a feminine or "sexy" display of femaleness, and we consequently need to be "taught our place." The implication might seem to be that women should wear nothing. Yet we hear that this is the most "provocative" of all – except when it is disgusting.

Most interesting, perhaps, are the situational rules, such as the rule that a woman alone is "asking for it." There are three ways of being alone. First, a woman may be unaccompanied by anyone at all. Second, women who are accompanied by other women are represented as being "all alone," which sounds even more alone than before (although it can be the safest situation in fact).[30] Third, a woman may be *alone with* a man. "Alone with" sounds like a self-contradiction. Yet the description is apt. A woman alone with a man is physically present *with* someone – as the female student was physically present with the male student in his apartment – who is not, however, presumed to be *with* her in the sense of being *on her side*. The alternative to these three ways of being alone is to be accompanied by a guardian – who can, of course, do anything he pleases without it counting as rape.

These rules confer the value, or part of the value, of consent upon a woman's status, appearance, behavior, or situation. Still others confer that value simply upon the female body itself and upon its involuntary experience. Contemporary patriarchal society treats the female body itself as provocative. There are rules to the effect that a woman who is sexually aroused is willing and that one who experiences pleasure is likewise willing. As empirical generalizations, these claims are false. But they are not simply false empirical generalizations. They are political norms, redefining "consent" and thereby the meaning of "rape."

Yet another rule is that consent once given cannot be withdrawn.[31] We have already seen this implicitly in the cases of status, such as marriage, which may be acquired through consent. But it also comes into play on an ordinary date if a woman wishes to change her mind in the course of an evening. Contrast this with acceptance of an invitation to have lunch together. If I no longer feel like eating at the time, I may just keep you company and have something to drink while you eat. It is difficult to imagine wanting a woman to eat anyway, just because she agreed to earlier, if she no longer wants food when the time comes. Force-feeding as a way of handling such disappointment would be found neither natural or excusable. Yet the rules of rape legitimize its analogue regarding sex.

Related to the rule that consent once given cannot be withdrawn is the rule that men once sexually aroused are no longer responsible for their conduct. As an empirical claim, this is less plausible than corresponding claims about men who are hungry or thirsty. Self-gratification is readily obtainable in the case of sexual arousal. It makes sense, however, once we recognize it as not an empirical claim but a political norm. Men sexually aroused are, by the rules, *absolved* of responsibility for their behavior.

Considered one by one, most of the rules do not ask the impossible. They thus create the impression that failing to meet their requirements is doing something bad. Yet taken together they leave no alternatives by which women can be genuinely secure against sexual violation by men. Trying our best to live up to them still leaves us at the mercy of men (as men have long believed they were at the mercy of their God), who can always find a "violation" if they wish, but who may spare us if we are evidently trying to be "good," that is, if we are sufficiently deferential. Curiously, the result has not been to rob women of motives for trying to please. Inexperienced women may not appreciate the incoherence of the large picture. But experienced women often see no better alternative than trying to please those in power, accepting the humiliating position of being "wrong" no matter what, and trying by ingratiation to reduce the likelihood of abuse.

The most blatant rule, summing up the spirit of the institution of rape, is that when a woman says no she means yes. What must she say to mean no? Nothing she *says* counts for much. Historically, she was expected to resist physically to her utmost, a process that was also a turn-on for the rapist. If both no and yes mean yes, neither means anything. The net result is that women are politically disabled from withholding consent to male sexual access.

Whereas most rules make it impossible for women to withhold consent, a few do just the opposite: Girls *cannot give* consent – clearly, a political norm, not an empirical claim. Likewise, the unofficial racist rule that white women cannot consent to black men is a transparently political norm. Like the others, these rules also divorce consent from the will. However, their functions are different. Rules that disable women from giving consent enable some men to control other men by marking certain females as off limits to them. Such rules may seem to offer women real protection. However, white racist rules have been designed to protect the "purity of the (white) race." In this area they control white women as well as men of color. Jailbait rules, which might also seem to offer young women some real protection, are designed to protect female marriageability, a commodity of value to guardians and potential guardians, by controlling men who are not (yet) a woman's guardian. Such rules have not protected girls from abuse by adult men in their homes.

Rules that disable women from withholding consent help to make sense of myths about rape that are otherwise puzzling, even mutually contradictory although simultaneously believed. For example, rape is popularly considered both normal and impossible. The myth that it is impossible to rape a woman means that no man could physically succeed with a woman who really did not consent. Taken empirically, this claim appears to deny that women are forced at gunpoint or knifepoint or by gangs to submit to acts to which they would otherwise not submit. However, guns, knives, muscles, and so on are irrelevant to the consent. It is sufficient that the woman either is or is not wearing clothes that highlight her femaleness, that she is alone either with or without other men or women, that she says either yes or no, and so on. If it is impossible to rape a woman, that is because the rules of rape discredit her refusals. They thereby make a certain sense of the myth that only a crazy man would rape, that the act is not normal. A man would have to be crazy not to fit his behavior into rules under which nothing he did would *count* as rape. Because of those rules, however, rape also appears normal, because it is very ordinary. For women unable to withhold consent are also unable to give it.

The rules also make sense of male paranoia regarding women falsely crying "rape." Offhand, this paranoia is puzzling, considering how much rape goes unreported. However, since the rules do not meaningfully distinguish between women who really do consent and women who do not, it should not be surprising that men wonder whether women have any way to make that distinction in reporting what men did to them.

A CONCLUDING NOTE ON STOPPING RAPE TERRORISM AND ON THE LIBERALISM OF JOHN STUART MILL

It is commonplace among feminists that *preventing* rape should not be women's responsibility. Preventing rape should be the responsibility of those who commit it, support it, are served and empowered by it. Women's energies are needed for healing, mutual support, and getting on with our lives. Yet women have an interest in *avoiding* rape and rape terrorism.[32] Exposing the rules of the institution is helpful toward this end, suggesting strategies of avoidance – such as self-fulfilling prophecies that women who say no mean no, and that women together are not alone. Women's transit organizations, rape crisis centers, and battered women's shelters, heavily dependent on volunteer work, confront the protection racket directly by offering alternative sources of protection so that women need not seek protection from those who create or benefit from the existence of the danger. The critic who found women's working conditions more harmful than "typical acts of rape" could still make this point: If women cease to *value* the "sexual purity" that has historically caused rape to reduce women's value to men, there is one thing less to *fear* from rape. Reevaluating the significance of rape is one strategy for avoiding rape terrorism.

Despite the belief that preventing rape should not be women's responsibility, many are taking aggressive steps to combat it, in addition to learning to avoid it. The most popularly controversial strategy of combating rape may be feminist attacks on media propaganda that set up women for rape by conveying to men the message that women like to be manhandled and by encouraging women to develop rape fantasies. Pornography is the vehicle of this propaganda, not only dirty books and magazines but also pornographic scenes sprinkled commonly throughout modern theater entertainment and commodity advertising. A little more than a decade ago a low-budget documentary film entitled *Rape Culture* showed scenes glorifying rape from popular movies in the United States, including *Gone with the Wind*, *Straw Dogs*, and *Butch Cassidy and the Sundance Kid*.[33] In each, rape is presented as thrilling and fulfilling for a woman. Scarlett O'Hara is never more radiant than the morning after Rhett Butler rapes her. In *Straw Dogs* the rapist beats up a woman and drags her about by the hair before he finally rapes her, and at the moment of penetration, her agonized face melts into ecstatic pleasure. These scenes remind us how women learn to develop the kinds of "rape fantasies" that facilitate real rape.

One may wonder whether rape fantasies fit the idea of rape as a *terrorist* institution. Some, of course, clearly do. Not all rape fantasies are of being raped; many are of killing the rapist or getting various sorts of revenge. Yet even the kinds of rape fantasies encouraged by pornography fit the idea of rape as terrorism. The word "rape" is not used in the film scenes just mentioned. Rather, they present the rapist as a woman's protector. The fantasy that pornography teaches women to enjoy is of rape by a "prince" who then protects her from other men, who are sources of terror. The "prince" is the "good rapist," although even he *was* a source of terror prior to the act.

In recent years pornography has been defended by appeal to the liberty principle of John Stuart Mill, a use of that principle which Mill seems not to have foreseen.[34] His principle is that interference in someone's conduct (other than by persuasion and argument), whether by the state or by an individual, is not justified except to prevent the agent interfered with from harming others. He interprets "harm" as injury inflicted without the informed consent of those on whom it is inflicted. Mill applied his principle to religious and political censorship as well as to undefined "experiments in living," but did not explicitly apply it to such things as pornography or prostitution. Those who make the latter applications tend to assume that viewers, users, and those participating in production and exchange are not "harmed" in the relevant sense, as long as they are *consenting adults*, and that no one else need be harmed because no one else need be involved. However, Mill himself was not content to rest his evaluations of women's choices at this level. In *The Subjection of Women*, he argued that the fact that adult women seem to consent to certain arrangements, such as marriage without the possibility of divorce or lack of the political franchise, is not a sufficient basis for the conclusion that they are not harmed by those arrangements.[35] He gave several reasons why not: One is that what is interpreted as consent (frequently only the absence of protest) is often motivated by realistic fear that protest will bring reprisals. Another is that "consent" often is no more than a ranking of alternatives in the construction of which the chooser had no part, none of which are tolerable but one of which must be chosen and is chosen as least intolerable. Still another is that many desires and ambitions underlying the "consent" are socially constructed by practices that stifle rather than foster women's development. In pursuing such questions as "Why are there no great women artists?" and "What if women don't *want* to vote?" Mill was led to inquire into the foundations of women's apparent consent to exclusionary practices and into the social processes by which ill-founded views of women's nature are constructed. His liberalism is, in principle and in practice, significantly qualified by these inquiries. Studies of the clandestine and domestic terrorism to which women have been subjected for centuries would be more in keeping with Mill's social ethics than defenses, in the name of his liberty principle, of the sale and inhumane portrayal of women who consent, or appear to consent, to such things.

NOTES

This essay has benefited from discussions at the Wisconsin Philosophers' Association Conference, Madison, in April 1983; at Northern Michigan State University, Marquette, in November 1987; and at the II Encuentro Internacional de Feminismo Filosofico, Buenos Aires, in November 1989; and from many helpful papers presented at the conference "Violence, Terrorism, and Justice" at Bowling Green State University, Ohio, in November 1988. I also thank Marcia Baron, Victoria Davion, Lynn McFall, and Richard Mohr for helpful comments, and the editors of the present volume for encouraging me to focus this material around the concept of terrorism.

1   Harriet Baber, "How Bad Is Rape?" *Hypatia: A Journal of Feminist Philosophy* 2, no. 2 (Summer 1987): 125.
2   Representative of current literature that understands terrorism in this way are Walter Laqueur, *The Age of Terrorism*, rev. and expanded ed. (Boston: Little, Brown, 1987); Benjamin Netanyahu's anthology, *Terrorism: How the West Can Win* (New York: Farrar, Straus and Giroux, 1986); and Gayle Rivers's *War Against the Terrorists: How to Win It* (New York: Stein and Day, 1986).
3   I focus on men's rape of women. Analogous observations can be made about men's rape of men within male prisons. See Jean Genet, *Our Lady of the Flowers*, trans. Bernard Frechtman (New York: Grove, 1963); and various prison biographies of men. (Interestingly, women's prisons exhibit an entirely different phenomenon with respect to same-sex intimacies, a friendly phenomenon that sociologists have called "familying," whereby women who fall in love with other women adopt each other's friends as "mother," "father," "sister," etc., complete with "incest" prohibitions. See Rose Giallombardo, *Society of Women: A Study of a Women's Prison* [New York: Wiley, 1966], chap. 9.)
4   For silence-breaking philosophical inquiries into what is wrong with rape, see the four essays in the "Rape" section of *Feminism and Philosophy*, ed. Mary Vetterling-Braggin, Frederick A. Elliston, and Jane English (Totowa, N.J.: Littlefield, Adams, 1977), by Susan Griffin, Pamela Foa, Carolyn Shafer and Marilyn Frye, and Susan Rae Peterson. The earliest theorists I know to connect rape with terrorism are Susan Griffin (see, also, n. 17 below) and Barbara Mehrhof and Pamela Kearon in their essay "Rape: An Act of Terror," in *Radical Feminism*, ed. Anne Koedt, Ellen Levine, and Anita Rapone (New York: Quadrangle, 1973), pp. 228–33.
5   A memorable chapter of Susan Brownmiller's *Against Our Will* (New York: Simon & Schuster, 1975) documents the routineness of rape by the victors in war.
6   Compare John Rawls's definition of "practice" or "institution"

in *A Theory of Justice* (Cambridge, Mass.: Harvard University Press, 1971), p. 55.

7   Kate Millett, *Sexual Politics* (New York: Random House, 1970).
8   Philosophical essays of the late 1950s and early 1960s discuss this ambiguity of "punishment," e.g., H. L. A. Hart's "Prolegomenon to the Principles of Punishment," reprinted in his *Punishment and Responsibility: Essays in the Philosophy of Law* (Oxford: Clarendon, 1968), pp. 1–27.
9   See J. D. Mabbott, "Punishment," *Mind* 48 (1939): 152–67.
10 See Rawls, *A Theory of Justice*, pp. 241, 314, 575, for sketches of such an understanding.
11 I take up issues raised by rape fantasies in the last two sections of this essay.
12 Jonathan Glover, "State Terrorism," in this volume. Emma Goldman made similar points in her essays. "The Psychology of Political Violence" and "Anarchism: What It Really Stands For," reprinted in Goldman, *Anarchism and Other Essays* (New York: Dover, 1969), pp. 79–108, 47–67.
13 Annette C. Baier, "Violent Demonstrations," in this volume.
14 See, e.g., Marilyn Frye's discussion of pimps' seasoning of new prostitutes, "In and Out of Harm's Way: Arrogance and Love," in Frye, *The Politics of Reality* (Trumansburg, N.Y.: Crossing Press, 1983), pp. 52–83; and accounts in Kathleen Barry's *Female Sexual Slavery* (Englewood Cliffs, N.J.: Prentice-Hall, 1979), including the terrorizing of Patty Hearst (chap. 7).
15 I am indebted to Onora O'Neill, "Which Are the Offers *You* Can't Refuse?" in this volume, for the point about the two targets in relation to terrorism in general and for noting the different skills called upon to reach each target.
16 On rape and lynching, see Ida B. Wells-Barnett, *On Lynchings* (New York: Arno, 1969), reprinting pamphlets from her antilynching campaigns of the 1890s and the turn of the century.
17 Susan Griffin, "Rape: The All-American Crime," in Vetterling-Braggin et al., eds., *Feminism and Philosophy*, p. 320. This essay, from *Ramparts* magazine in 1971 (shortly after the publication of Menachem Amir's *Patterns in Forcible Rape* [Chicago: University or Chicago Press, 1971], which it discusses), is a classic used in rape crisis center training programs across the United States. It appears as the first chapter of Griffin's book, *Rape: The Power of Consciousness* (New York: Harper and Row, 1979).
18 Susan Rae Peterson, "Coercion and Rape: The State as a Male

Protection Racket," in Vetterling-Braggin et al., eds., *Feminism and Philosophy*, pp. 360–61.

19 Ibid. The idea is not that rape meets Rawlsian principles of justice, of course, but only that it fits Rawls's understanding of the concept of a practice.

20 G. W. F. Hegel, *Hegel's Philosophy of Right*, trans. T. M. Knox (Oxford: Oxford University Press, 1942), pars. 99–104 and Additions, pp. 246–7.

21 See Marilyn Frye's discussion of access as a face of power in "Some Reflections on Separatism and Power," in her *Politics of Reality*, pp. 95–109.

22 Amir, *Patterns in Forcible Rape*.

23 Ibid., p. 143.

24 Ibid., p. 314.

25 Amir seems to move somewhat in that direction in the theoretical discussion at the end of the book.

26 George Orwell, *Nineteen Eighty-Four* (London: Secker and Warburg, 1949; New York: Harcourt, Brace, 1949).

27 See Susan Estrich, *Real Rape* (Cambridge, Mass.: Harvard University Press, 1987), on "simple rape" as nearly impossible to establish in court as *real rape*. "Simple rape" contrasts with "aggravated rape," i.e., aggravated by such conditions as the assailant's being a stranger to the victim or using a weapon.

28 As a result of liberal feminist criticism, some jurisdictions now use the language of "sexual assault," breaking down the possibilities into degrees of seriousness, and have abandoned the term "rape." Many radical feminists retain the concept of rape because it conveys, in a way that "sexual assault" does not, who, historically, has assaulted whom.

29 In the sense meant by Estrich, *Real Rape*, i.e., actionable rape.

30 Lily Tomlin says she actually saw a man walk up to four women in a bar and ask, "What are you doing here sitting all alone?" in *Lily Tomlin: On Stage* (New York: Arista Records, 1977), act 1 (side 1), end of band 4.

31 This rule is discussed in Carolyn Shafer and Marilyn Frye, "Rape and Respect," in Vetterling-Braggin et al., eds., *Feminism and Philosophy*, p. 335.

32 For practical strategies that have worked, see Pauline Bart and Patricia H. O'Brien, *Stopping Rape: Successful Survival Strategies* (New York: Pergamon, 1985).

33 I was shown the film more than ten years ago but have been

unable to find documentation on it. Critics soon pointed out that all the imprisoned rapists interviewed in it appeared to be black (one white rapist's face was in shadow), so that it contributed to a racist stereotype. The film seems to have disappeared from circulation shortly thereafter.

34 J. S. Mill, *On Liberty* (1859, many editions), chap. 1.
35 J. S. Mill, *The Subjection of Women* (1869, many editions); see, especially, chaps. 1 and 3.

Printed in the United States
1264100004B/107